Organizations Behaving Badly

Destructive Behavior and Corrective Responses

A Volume in Research in Organizational Science

Series Editor

Daniel J. Svyantek
Auburn University

Research in Organizational Science

Daniel J. Svyantek, Series Editor

Organizations Behaving Badly: Destructive Behavior and Corrective Responses (2021)
edited by Daniel J. Svyantek

Sports and Understanding Organizations (2017)
edited by Daniel J. Svyantek

Organizational Processes and Received Wisdom (2014)
edited by Daniel J. Svyantek and Kevin T. Mahoney

Received Wisdom, Kernels of Truth, and Boundary: Conditions in Organizational Studies (2013)
edited by Daniel J. Svyantek and Kevin T. Mahoney

Emerging Themes in International Management of Human Resources (2010)
edited by Philip Benson

Refining Familiar Constructs: Alternative Views in OB, HR, and I/O (2007)
edited by Daniel J. Svyantek and Elizabeth McChrystal

A Closer Examination of Applicant Faking Behavior (2006)
edited by Mitchell H. Peterson and Richard L. Griffith

Organizations Behaving Badly

Destructive Behavior and Corrective Responses

Edited by

Daniel J. Svyantek
Auburn University

IAP

INFORMATION AGE PUBLISHING, INC.
Charlotte, NC • www.infoagepub.com

Library of Congress Cataloging-in-Publication Data

CIP record for this book is available from the Library of Congress
http://www.loc.gov

ISBNs: 978-1-64802-354-5 (Paperback)

978-1-64802-355-2 (Hardcover)

978-1-64802-356-9 (ebook)

Printed in the United States of America

CONTENTS

CHAPTER 1

INTRODUCTION

Organizations Behaving Badly: Using Destructive Organization Behaviors to Inform Corrective

Daniel J. Svyantek
Auburn University

This volume of *Research in Organizational Sciences* is titled, *Organizations Behaving Badly: Destructive Behavior and Corrective Responses*. This volume's history has been interesting. It is the interesting outcome of calls for papers for *Research in Organizational Sciences*. These calls asked for contributions to understanding organizational behavior and organizational theory through the use of historical and/or military examples. As the reader will see, the scope of this volume expanded based on the manuscripts received from these calls. This expansion of scope, however, has a common theme exhibited in all the chapters in this volume.

The common theme in the chapters in this volume is the interaction of person and organizational context. Each chapter in this volume deals with the issue of destructive behaviors that occur within organizations

Organizations Behaving Badly:
Destructive Behavior and Corrective Responses, pp. 1–8

(e.g., unethical behavior directed internally or externally). Each chapter examines this behavior through the lens of a deceptively simple perspective on behavior proposed by Funder (2001, 2006). Funder proposed a model of behavior in which three factors are considered for understanding behavior: predicting behavior and drawing inferences about actors in situations. These three factors are (1) the actual behavior that a person may or may not perform in a situation; (2) the individual differences of actors within a situation; and (3) the context in which the behavior is occurring. For example, suppose you see an individual hitting another person. You need to consider the actual behavior—was the hit violent and aggressive or done for protection? You need to consider the individual differences of the actors—are the actors of similar build and gender or are there physical differences among the actors? You need to consider the context of the behavior—are you watching a barroom brawl or are you watching a boxing match?

We draw different inferences about the nature of behavior and the nature of people based on these three factors. This simple model has two related constructs in the study of organizational behavior. These are the concepts of person-environment fit (Kristof, 1996) and the attraction-selection-fit model (Schneider, 1987a, 1987b).

Kristof (1996) describes two forms of fit with relevance for understanding organizational behavior. First, *person-job (PJ) fit* is concerned with the degree to which there is a match between an employee's skills and abilities and the requirements of the job the employee holds. This form of fit is concerned with the ability of the individual in a job to perform the tasks necessary for the job. Second, *person-organization (PO) fit* is concerned with the degree to which there is a match between employee characteristics and the characteristics of the organization (e.g., organizational culture) in which the employee works. Here fit refers to the relationship between the individual actor's values and characteristics and the organization's values and characteristics. For example, we will see some organizational contexts support particular behaviors (e.g., unethical behavior or self-serving behavior). Better fit implies the actor is more likely to perform the behavior supported by the organization than someone with less fit.

The attraction-selection-attrition model (Schneider, 1987a, 1987b) provides an important means of understanding of how organizational actors and organizational contexts come to parallel each other. According to Schneider (1987a) this is due to three main processes. First, it occurs because people are attracted to places that they prefer (attraction). People will seek out organizational environments in which they are comfortable being a member. Individuals who enjoy working in groups, for example, are drawn to organizations emphasizing teamwork. Second, organizations base hiring and selection practices, at least partially, on whether an individual being evaluated acts like successful organizational members. This is a decision of compatibility (selection). Third, if people are hired because of person-job fit and enter an environment that is not a fit for them in terms of person-organization fit they will tend to leave it (attrition).

Each of the chapters in this volume draw, at least in part, on these social and organizational concepts to describe the actions of organizational members in differing situations. The eight chapters in this volume all, in some way, strive to use these concepts to understand basic processes leading to potentially negative and destructive organizational behavior. In addition, each paper tries to provide organizational practitioners with new ideas for improving human resource practices in organizations that make these behaviors less likely.

Doerr's chapter outlines processes through which organizational newcomers learn what behaviors and perspectives are expected and desirable (versus those which are undesirable) within their work context. This chapter proposes that *who* newcomers learn their information from plays a chief role in *what* the newcomers learn. The aims of this chapter are to examine the means through which organizational culture and values perpetuate via socialization processes. This chapter demonstrates how and from whom newcomers may learn information, what techniques newcomers may use to seek information, and how assimilation encourages the continuance of preexisting norms and corporate culture across generations of organizational members.

Brown and January's chapter looks at the impact of military sexual trauma on commitment in the United States Military. This chapter describes how the sexual harassment and assault continues in the military despite the punishments and policies derived from the 1991 Tailhook incident. The authors' note that since the Tailhook incident researchers and policy-makers have extensively studied and scrutinized the antecedents and consequences of military sexual harassment and assault. This chapter focuses on how sexual harassment and assault impacts organizational commitment in the United States military—an environment where a strong commitment to the military is sought. Their chapter is particularly concerned with how the psychological contract established between the military and service members can be breached by events like military sexual trauma. Workplace sexual harassment and assault are major violations of a psychological contract, both in employer-employee and employee-employee relationships. There is often a written expectation that the workplace will remain free from harassment and assault. When sexual harassment or assault occurs, it constitutes a psychological contract breach in that what actually occurs does not meet the expectations understood by all parties. The result is a perceived lack of fit with the organization and potential workplace deviance or attrition of organizational members. The author's provide ways for organizations to both manage the organizational commitment of individuals to buffer them against such sexual harassment trauma along with ways for organizations to improve human resource practices to combat such sexual harassment behavior.

Svyantek's chapter uses the U.S. Navy's response to the USS Stark and USS Vincennes incidents of the 1980s to explore how punishment is used to change specific behaviors of individuals within a particular job classification. During the 1980s in the Persian Gulf, there were several incidents threatening, or damaging, US naval ships (Arkin, 1989). First, the USS Stark was struck by two cruise missiles fired by an Iraqi jet on May 17, 1987. Second, the USS Samuel Roberts struck a mine. Third, the USS Vincennes shot down an Iran Air flight, killing 290 civilians, on July 3, 1988. These incidents have an underlying similarity. Each involves the captain of a U.S. naval ship making a decision to protect or not protect his vessel from incoming airplanes. Each captain faced uncertainty based on information being received and processed about approaching airplanes. These airplanes may or may not constitute a threat to each ship. The final decision in each situation required the captain to decide whether to fire missiles at the incoming airplanes and destroy the potential threat to each vessel. The chapter uses Funder's three factors to explore how a specific behavior can be changed with punishment of an individual as a signal that past behaviors are no longer tolerated to others in the same job classification. This change is based on the effects' of such punishment signals on an actor's perception of what the context both no longer supports and what new behavior is supported. Moreover, the analysis of this situation shows that the negative behavior exhibited by the punished actor might be chosen by other organizational members' in the same situation. The context must change to change the behavior. While not discussed in this chapter (the finished manuscript was received in February 2020), Svyantek's chapter helps understand some of the issues faced by police organization directly involved in the recent George Floyd and Rayshard Brooks' killings by police in Minneapolis, MN and Atlanta, GA. Punishment of the police acting in these situations must be publicly sought by the justice system to signal to other individuals in the same jobs that these behaviors will not be tolerated. This punishment serves as a signal to not just the two police organizations involved: This message is being sent to all members of the police in the United States. However, the behavior(s) replacing such intolerable acts must be well defined and understood by the individuals in this job classification. Then proper training can be provided so that these behaviors do not occur again.

Whitman's chapter uses military examples to explore the ideas of technological determinism. The chapter uses examples derived from military history to make its points. World War II provides these examples. The role of drugs in the initial successes of the German military during World War II shows the effects of new pharmacological technology on the human part of a sociotechnical system. Amphetamines were used to raise military capability in Nazi Germany. These amphetamines may have fueled the success of blitzkrieg. The actual drug, Pervitin, was classified as decisive for the war effort by the Nazi government. The chapter describes how such stories become part of the organizational narratives used to communicate organizational culture and inform employees of expected behaviors in an organization. A second example, the merger of U.S. West and Qwest, explores the unique risks posed by the ideas of technological determinism in today's closely and tightly linked world. Narratives of technological determinism possess implications that may leave the organization vulnerable in another fashion entirely as new technologies such as cloud computing are faced with security breaches. This is because the human element, in the face of technological deterministic ideas, is discounted. This is associated with reductions in the human responsibility for the behavior of the organization. Another example of this discounting of the human element is present in the computer algorithms that function in the world's stock markets. These algorithms lead to fluctuations in prices that often are greater than human observers' perceive warranted. This chapter provides some questions to consider when designing systems that emphasize the role of computer technology as a decision-making system.

Wilmore's chapter looks at how deviant behaviors in financial institutions occur and impact the larger social environment. Deviant behaviors in organizations not only cost organizations billions of dollars each year, but also harm both organizations' internal and external stakeholders. With the increase in globalization and the use of technology in organizations, properly deterring deviant behaviors in organizations may pose an even greater challenge. The behavior of members of Wells Fargo is used as a case to provide insight into how such deviant behavior occurs. The chapter focuses on how three perceptions of an organization's values impact deviant behavior of that organization's members. These three individual processes are (1) perceptions of unfairness, (2) perceived norms for behavior, and (3) a bottom-line mentality being supported by the organization. This chapter provides potential solutions to prevent unethical behavior from occurring in organizations by (1) including increasing empathy in communication; (2) using measures of emotional stability and empathy in selection decisions for supervisors; (3) providing supervisors with training in justice rules; (4) giving employees greater voice in decisional processes; (5) utilizing descriptive and injunctive norms; and (6) changing incentive systems.

The final three chapters are empirical studies of the issues raised in the first five chapters. Two chapters are field studies and one chapter describes laboratory research.

Gaskin and Borry's chapter looks at workplace bullying, and its effects on organizational members. This chapter looks at the tone established by workplace bullying within an organization. This tone helps define the organizational context in which employees exist. This chapter sought to understand the prevalence of and attitudes toward bullying in local government organizations using survey methodology. Four primary research questions were asked. These were (1) does workplace bullying occur in local governments in the United States?; (2) which workplace bullying behaviors are prevalent? (3) do local government employees perceive their organizations as having a policy against workplace bullying?; and (4) what are the perceived outcomes of workplace bullying? The survey respondents were familiar with "workplace bullying." While a smaller number of participants indicated being a victim, perpetrator, or witness to bullying, it is clear that employees are familiar with it as an issue. The most common bullying behaviors witnessed were nonviolent behaviors, such as malicious gossiping/spreading rumors, verbal abuse, threats/intimidation, cruel comments, and harsh criticism. Respondents also indicated that their organization has policies in place to address workplace bullying, but results are mixed on how those policies are communicated. The authors' note that currently there is no Federal, mandated anti-workplace bullying policy in the United States. The authors' provide guidance for developing such policies using model state policies against workplace bullying.

Ritterbush et al.'s chapter provides insight into the relationship between behavior, actor, and context through two laboratory studies. This chapter explicitly tests the three factors proposed by Funder in these two studies. The chapter explores the influence of all three factors on ethical behavior. The first study explores the way in which personality traits affect ethical behaviors within different decision contexts. There is no direct manipulation of the situation itself. Building on the results of this study, the second study assesses the effects of personality and the situation together on different ethical behaviors. Findings indicated support for theories presented by Funder. Personality and context interact to predict behavior. The prediction of ethical behavior within organizations is of particular importance to understand because of the nature of organizations and organizational stakeholders. Poor fit is not necessarily a deficit of either the person or the organization. Rather, *misfit* occurs when there is a mismatch between employee value systems and organizational culture. However, for ethical behavior in organizations, organizations may create unethical climates vis-à-vis outsiders and external stakeholders. Here fit will lead to improved career success for organizational members at the expense of these outsiders. This may explain why patterns of unethical behavior may exist among organizations and organizational members when these members do not possess supposed personality traits linked to unethical behaviors. The situation may determine the behavior. These studies show a need to consider contextual differences when developing human resource methods for jobs requiring heightened levels of integrity.

Bond and Svyantek's chapter looks at the role of emotional intelligence (EI) and the organizational context in which military officers find themselves. The chapter looks at differences in *trait emotional intelligence* between pre-career and mid-career military officers. This study was designed to investigate the way in which the context and EI work together to highlight differences between leaders in the military. This chapter also seeks to identify critical experiences of officers that might contribute increases in EI so that recommendations for training emphasis and leader development may be made. The results of this study reinforce the building body of evidence in the private sector, and indicate that emotional intelligence could be a useful construct to identify successful leaders. The study looked at cohort differences. However, the authors' note that the context effects should be more broadly studied. In addition, samples of leaders who are currently or recently served in key and developmental positions, such as command or high-profile staff positions (to include operations officers and executive officers) might be studied. These positions are the professional gates that successful officers must navigate through in order to be viable candidates for promotions and selective assignments. By studying the role of EI and its influences on successful careers, better training and development opportunities may be provided junior officers.

These chapters in this volume all, in some way, provide insight into the value of investigating all aspects of a Funder's behavioral triangle. The actor, context, and the act itself, are all factors that must be assessed to successfully understand and change potentially destructive behaviors in organizations It is this volume's hope that these chapters will provide insight into the important role the interaction between these three factors plays in understanding organizations across the world. This deceptively simple approach provides researchers and practitioners with a model for improving the effectiveness of organizations.

REFERENCES

Arkin, W. (1989). Troubled waters: The Navy's aggressive war strategy. *Technology Review*, *92*(1), 54.

Funder, D. C. (2001). Accuracy in personality judgment: Research and theory concerning an obvious question. In B. W. Roberts & R. Hogan (Eds.), *Personality psychology in the workplace* (pp. 121–140). Washington, DC: American Psychological Association.

Funder, D. C. (2006). Towards a resolution of the personality triad: Persons, situations, and behaviors. *Journal of Research in Personality, 40,* 21–34.

Kristof, A. L. (1996). Person-organization fit: An integrative review of its conceptualization, measurement, and implications. *Personnel Psychology, 49*, 1–49.
Schneider, B. (1987a). E=f(P,B): The road to a radical approach to person-environment fit. *Journal of Vocational Behavior, 31*, 353–361.
Schneider, B. (1987b). The people make the place. *Personnel Psychology, 40*, 437–453.

CHAPTER 2

FORMATION AND MAINTENANCE OF CORPORATE CULTURE VIA SOCIALIZATION

Alexa Doerr
Towson University

Organizational socialization is concerned with the transmission of organizational and role information from more experienced organizational members to newcomers (Van Maanen & Schein, 1979). A newcomer must obtain the social knowledge and skills necessary to take on the responsibilities of their new role. In doing so, new organizational members must learn what behaviors and perspectives are expected and desirable within their work context in addition to what ones are not (Van Maanen & Schein, 1979).

Socialization experts have deliberated how certain patterns of thought and action are "passed from one generation of organizational members to the next" (Van Maanen & Schein, 1979, p. 210). Van Maanen and Schein (1979) imply that *what* people learn about their work is typically influenced by *how* they learn it. So as not to disrupt the traditions and culture of the organization, new members must be taught to see the organization as do

Organizations Behaving Badly: Destructive Behavior and Corrective Responses, pp. 9–29

their more experienced coworkers (Van Maanen & Schein, 1979). Thus, patterns of behavior are passed on via the transmission of information and values to newcomers. As this teaching and learning process takes place, newcomers become integrated into an organization's patter of activities (Anderson et al., 1999). Adding to Van Maanen and Schein's (1979) work, this chapter will posit that *who* newcomers learn their information from should also play a chief role in *what* the newcomers learn. In this chapter, I will further explore how the transmission of information from tenured organizational members to newcomers contributes to the persistence of company values and culture.

Newcomers are tasked with learning various aspects of their position including both context and role information.Chao and colleagues (1994) identified six categories of information, or socialization dimensions, to be transmitted during the newcomers' onboarding with the organization. First, *performance proficiency* refers to the extent to which a newcomer has learned the tasks involved in their organizational position. Second, *organizational politics* concerns a newcomer's success in acquiring knowledge of formal and informal work relationships. This also includes gaining a heightened awareness of which individuals are more knowledgeable and powerful than others (Pfeffer, 1981). Third, newcomers gather information about *language*. This dimension involves whether a newcomer has learned the profession's technical language including acronyms, slang, and jargon that are unique to the organization. Fourth, *information about people*, or who makes up the organization, is vital to a newcomer's success. Socialization ideally involves the establishment of fruitful and fulfilling work relationships with coworkers. Fifth, *organizational values or shared goals* should be learned by the newcomer. A chief goal of socialization is for the newcomer to gain an understanding of the rules or principles that maintain the integrity of an organization (Schein, 1968). The sixth and final dimension outlined by Chao and colleagues is *organizational history*. Through an organization's traditions, customs, myths, and rituals, information is transmitted to newcomers about the organization's culture (Ritti & Funkhouser, 1987). Accurate transmission and acceptance of this information by newcomers should aid in the perseverance of the existing culture.

The aims of this chapter are to examine the means through which organizational culture and values perpetuate via socialization processes. In doing so, organizational culture will be defined and explored. Then information sources and organizational tactics will be presented and deliberated. Next, I will discuss the newcomer's role in socialization processes and the information-seeking tactics commonly employed by newcomers to gain knowledge about their organizational role and setting. Lastly, normative organizational behavior and the persistence of corporate culture will be examined.

ORGANIZATIONAL CULTURE

Just as individuals have traits, knowledge, and abilities that make them unique from one another, organizations can be conceived as unique entities comprised of characteristics that set them apart from other organizations. In early stages of new organizations, the organizational members interact and make decisions that provide a basis for establishing common values, mission statements, and normative patterns of behavior. As defined by Schein (1990, 2004) organizational culture refers to a pattern of shared fundamental assumptions that a group has externally adapted and internally integrated. Employees esteem organizations that use recruitment and socialization practices guided by overt, consistent, and well-imposed norms, and find socialization more challenging when norms are ambivalent, inconsistent, and poorly imposed (Deal & Kennedy, 1982). Additionally, Orpen (1993) found that the effect of personnel practices on newcomer commitment was more positive among organizations with strong as opposed to weak cultural norms regardless of how the personnel practices themselves were perceived.

Schneider (1987) has suggested that organizations will likely become more homogeneous through the process of recruiting and socializing like-minded people to the organization. He proposed the attraction-selection-attrition model (ASA) as a means to describe how this process might occur. Attraction involves mutual liking between the applicant and the organization. Selection refers to when the selected applicant is extended an offer and when the applicant accepts the offer. Finally, attrition occurs when an employee is fired or when the employee elects to terminate his or her employment. If both the employee and the organization remain happy with their work arrangement, attrition is less likely to occur. Things that may be deemed attractive from an employee's standpoint are competitive salary, a good location, career advancement opportunities, or perceived organizational support. Conversely, organizations may look for employees with a high level of education, motivation, experience, and/or team orientation. Depending on what an organization looks for in job candidates, organizations may attract, select, and retain an increasingly homogenous group of employees. Schneider has eluded that a high degree of homogeneity within organizations could lead the organization into a period of stagnation according to his homogeneity hypothesis. Consequently, the organization may become less capable of responding to changes, threats, and opportunities in the external environment.

In addition to efforts to recruit and hire employees with shared backgrounds, characteristics, and orientations, organizations sometimes seem to encourage assimilation and conformity to preexisting standards set forth by the institution. New employees observe and absorb much information within their first few months of employment. Desire to be socially accepted and to be positively evaluated by their peers, workgroups, and supervisors will likely motivate new hires to adopt norms and integrate organizational values with their own (Ashforth et al., 2007). Socialization is particularly effective in strong, well-defined situations and strong organizational cultures. According to the Meyer et al. (2014), the defining features of strong situations include (1) information about work-related responsibilities or requirements are available (i.e., *clarity*), (2) cues regarding work-related responsibilities are compatible with each other (i.e., *consistency*), (3) individuals' freedom of decision and behavior is limited by forces outside of his or control (i.e., *constraints*), and (4) individuals' decisions or behaviors have significant positive and negative consequences (i.e., *consequences*). When clarity, consistency, constraints, and consequences are well-defined, there will likely be less variance in individual employees' work-related decisions and actions (Meyer et al., 2014). As an extension, when newcomers join an organization with a strong organizational culture, it is easier to access information about the behaviors that the organization expects and finds desirable (Deal & Kennedy, 1982). Moreover, information presented to newcomers about expected and desirable behaviors, regardless of the source, is likely more consistent when organizational culture is strong.

INFORMATION SOURCES

According to stage models outlining the socialization process (see Feldman, 1981; Louis, 1980; Van Maanen, 1976), in the first months in their new positions, new hires typically focus on gathering information, learning about job-specific tasks, and clarifying their role in the organization. To do so, newcomers use available sources including interpersonal sources such as supervisors, colleagues, and mentors, in addition to non-interpersonal sources such as written materials, vicarious observation, and experimentation (Ostroff & Kozlowski, 1992). Socialization is often described as an ongoing process and as such, various sources of information and many learning processes may contribute to an employee's understanding of the organization around them (Ostroff & Kozlowski, 1992).

Previous research has demonstrated the instrumental role of supervisors, colleagues, and mentors in the learning process (Ashford & Cummings, 1985; Louis et al., 1983; Posner & Powell, 1985). Supervisors are crucial to the new employee's ultimate success or failure, and are key figures in establishing a shared system of understanding suggestive of assimilation (Ostroff & Kozlowski, 1992). Other organizational members may help new employees to piece information together (Van Maanen, 1984), and may convey elusive values, norms, or expectations (Schein, 1988). Mentors assist by providing support, guidance, and insider information (Kram, 1985). Supervisors, coworkers, and mentors not only formally advise newcomers, but also impart a great extent in narrative form including event-driven stories, myths, and folklore that ostensibly express both positive and negative cultural cues at play (Bauer et al., 1998; Kitchell et al., 2000; Swap et al., 2001).

Written literature can be a helpful source for a newcomer to learn about organizational policies, procedures, and task-related duties (Ostroff & Kozlowski, 1992). Schein (1988) implicates that new employees can also learn through the rewards or punishments associated with new behaviors and/or through experimentation aimed at problem-solving. Additionally, new employees may observe behaviors of others to glean information regarding how to perform a task, expected behaviors, and organizational values (Miller & Jablin, 1991). This vicarious observation can provide newcomers with models to follow when performing new behaviors and skills (Bandura, 1977).

There are three primary ways in which newcomers obtain information, (a) monitoring, (b) direct inquiry, and (c) indirect inquiry (Ashford et al., 2003). There are also ways in which organizations strive to impart information to newcomers. By providing orientation, training, and other socialization resources, organizations aim to reduce the uncertainty and anxiety that newcomers often face upon joining a new organization (Allen & Shanock, 2013). Information or resources that are provided may pertain to organizational or relational aspects. Both organizational and newcomer tactics used to facilitate the socialization process will be discussed.

THE ORGANIZATION'S ROLE IN SOCIALIZATION

It is beneficial to the organization if systems are put in place to support the socialization process of new hires to the organization. Organizations employ six bipolar tactics to guide newcomers from outsiders to insiders (Van Maanen & Schein, 1979). These six tactics are outlined below.

1. The *collective* rather than *individual* socialization tactic refers to when newcomers are grouped together and put through common learning experiences.
2. *Formal* socialization denotes separating the newcomers from organizational insiders to conduct training and orientation activities whereas *informal* socialization involves less structured training activities and integration of newcomers with other organizational members.

3. The *sequential* tactic progresses newcomers through a fixed series of adjustment practices whereas the *random* tactic is comprised of varying activities that do not occur in a particular order.
4. *Fixed* socialization involves the newcomer being put through set schedule for moving from one adjustment step to another whereas *variable* socialization refers to a more flexible progression that does not take the newcomer from one step to the next.
5. The *serial* as opposed to *disjunctive* socialization tactic involves learning from a role model such as a supervisor, mentor, or more tenured peer.
6. Lastly, the *investiture* instead of *divestiture* tactic highlights the new hire's incoming identity, aptitudes, and qualities.

Jones (1986) classified collective, formal, sequential, fixed, serial, and investiture as institutionalized socialization tactics by which organizations guide newcomer integration using standard methods or procedures. In contrast, Jones grouped individual, informal, random, variable, disjunctive, and divestiture tactics into what he called individualized socialization. In individualized socialization, the newcomer is left to undergo the socialization process quite independently with little hand-holding or spoon-feeding. According to a review conducted by Saks and Ashforth (1997), institutionalized socialization appears to be negatively associated with role ambiguity, role conflict, and intentions to quit yet positively associated with task mastery, job satisfaction, and organizational commitment. Others have found institutionalized tactics to be predictive of person-organization fit (Cable & Parsons, 2001; Cooper-Thomas et al., 2004; Gruman, Saks, & Zeig, 2006; Kim, Cable, & Kim, 2004), person-job fit (Gruman et al., 2006; Riordan et al., 2001), social integration (Anakwe & Greenhaus, 1999; Gruman et al., 2006), organizational embeddedness (Allen, 2006), and fewer perceived violations of psychological contracts (Robinson & Morrison, 2000). Some studies indicate that organizations may utilize the institutionalized tactics to promote role conformity, but this is not to say that these tactics cannot be used to encourage innovation (Ashforth & Saks, 1996). Institutionalized tactics generally come off as more deliberate and structured, and can give the impression that the newcomer is valued (Riordan et al., 2001).

Formal Versus Informal Socialization

Of the six bipolar tactics, this chapter is most concerned with the differences between formal and informal tactics. Formal socialization processes are commonly found in organizations where it is important for the newcomer to learn the "right" attitudes, values, and procedures of their role

(Van Maanen & Schein, 1979). This may be especially relevant when the work to be performed involves high levels of potential risk. Alternatively, informal tactics involve more trial and error, and in most cases such tactics put the newcomers in a position where they must select their own socialization agents. The value of the information obtained by that agent is largely dependent upon the relevant knowledge possessed by the agent, and the agent's ability to transfer that knowledge (Van Maanen & Schein, 1979). Thus, when newcomers are left to select their own informal leader they may choose inadequately and consequently, learn the "wrong" attitudes, values, and procedures. By selecting a poor mentor, a newcomer may diminish their ability to thrive in the organization. The next sections will outline the methods by which newcomers attempt to become organizational insiders.

Van Maanen and Schein (1979) mention that formal socialization tactics potentially represent the "first wave" of socialization, which is then followed by a "second wave" of informal socialization when the newcomer begins to discover the actual practices that go on in the organization (Inkeles, 1966). During the second wave recruits may "unlearn" much of what they learned in the formal processes and begin to replace proper and accepted ways of accomplishing tasks with practical or smart methods. When the discrepancy between what is learned during formal socialization and informal socialization is large, the newcomer often comes to disregard nearly everything learned in the formal socialization processes. Furthermore, formal processes are often under the control of agents or instructors whose credibility is lacking rather than people who are actually doing the work (Van Maanen & Schein, 1979). Therefore, informal socialization does have the potential to shape work behavior, and often has a more lasting effect.

THE NEWCOMER'S ROLE IN ORGANIZATIONAL SOCIALIZATION

When new members join organizations, much of their focus is on figuring out their role as a contributing organizational member. Organizations make efforts to provide new employees with information that is relevant to their new roles. Yet, insufficiencies may be present in the nature and scope of the information offered. In a previous study, newcomers admitted to feeling as though they received less information from those around them than they believe is required (Jablin, 1984). Many factors may contribute to the perception of "information deprivation" (Jablin, 1984, p. 622). For example, more tenured colleagues may forget what it was like to enter the organization, and consequently they may unintentionally omit communicating some key information to recruits (Miller & Jablin, 1991). In other cases, management may deliberately send vague messages to encourage new employees to develop their role ((Schieffelin & Eisenberg, 1984). Inadequacies may also result from a newcomer's inability to interpret or decode information provided by incumbents (Miller & Jablin, 1991). Incumbents often aim to be helpful, yet newcomers may instead feel overwhelmed by all the new information. Thus, newcomers may need to seek assistance to recall, clarify, amplify, or discount received messages. The focus of the next section will be on the newcomer's predicament and the socialization tactics used by newcomers to overcome characteristic challenges faced during the encounter stage.

Uncertainty Avoidance

During the encounter stage, newcomers are described as actually entering the organization and confronting its realities while coping with the discrepancies between expectation and experience (Ashforth et al., 2007). Notably, during the encounter, or entry, phase of organizational assimilation, newcomers rely upon information from others to establish role clarity. Because the information new hires receive is frequently interpreted by the newcomer as inadequate, new hires typically experience fairly high levels of uncertainty (Jablin, 1982; Louis, 1980; Salancik & Pfeffer, 1978). Uncertainty takes form in the role ambiguity and role conflict that newcomers often experience and these may then have an impact on employees' job satisfaction, productivity, and, ultimately, job tenure (Ashford & Cummings, 1985; Jackson & Schuler, 1985). To reduce uncertainty, and thus prevent adverse outcomes, newcomers are advised to seek out the assistance and information they need to conduct their work effectively rather than waiting for it to be provided. Due to higher levels of anxiety, newcomers will be more attuned to the values and behaviors to be learned than are their more tenured colleagues, and will be more focused on how to obtain the information they need (Miller & Jablin, 1991).

Newcomer Socialization Tactics

Naturally, some queries may be apparent to targets, whereas in other circumstances, targets may be oblivious to the fact that newcomers have been eliciting information from them (Miller & Jablin, 1991). Likewise, newcomers may, at times, pursue specific information whereas at other times they may search for more generalized information such as a coworker's perception of the company's mission or values. A repertoire has been established by Miller and Jablin (1991) of seven information-seeking tactics utilized by newcomers that vary in the level of overtness and specificity associated with information sought.

Overt Questions. Use of overt questions implies that newcomers are comfortable gathering information from a source as overt questioning requires direct interaction with information targets (Miller & Jablin, 1991). Advantages of this tactic are that it is an efficient means to get specific information, it can be employed to clarify ambiguities in messages received, and it can promote further relational development allowing for easier access to the source in the future. Newcomers have also admitted to using direct questioning as a means to convey to their supervisors that they are putting effort into doing a good job (Miller & Jablin, 1991).

However, some hesitation with using overt questioning may occur when newcomers are concerned that it could harm their self-image or when something they have a question about seems trivial or simple (Berger & Bradac, 1982). Additionally, colleagues and supervisors may get visibly irritated by repetitive questioning and this may discourage direct questioning on the part of the newcomer (Berger & Bradac, 1982; Goody, 1978). Furthermore, findings of a study conducted by Walther (1978) revealed that children felt comfortable asking questions of their peers, but were less comfortable asking questions of their teachers, who in this case represented those of higher status. Therefore, individuals will likely only use overt questions to the degree that they feel at ease in making such information requests to a given target. Along these lines, Brown and Levinson (1978) have suggested that, in general, individuals may employ overt information requests when they assess that there is little to no chance of being embarrassed, or "losing face," by requesting the information. In the short-term, using a direct manner for requesting information is efficient, yet such an approach may be injurious to the newcomers' relationships with others in the long run. For example, Ashford (1986) found significant negative correlation between employees' frequent use of direct inquiry and organizational tenure implying potential long-term social costs resulting from relying on others for information. If these costs are realized, employees may develop alternative approaches to information seeking that are more covert in nature.

Indirect Questions. When newcomers are uncomfortable in seeking information from a target, they may attempt to obtain information through indirect questions. Indirect questions may be substituted for direct questioning as a means to ask questions in a manner that can spare embarrassment or discomfort for the newcomer (Miller & Jablin, 1991). This tactic may involve non-interrogative questions or hinting, which may be used to bring topics to targets' attention. Research shows that indirect questions are generally used as "face saving" tactics (Brown & Levinson, 1978; Goody, 1978), which newcomers are especially likely to use when they are apprehensive about seeking information directly from a source or if the topic they wish to discuss is deemed awkward or obvious.

Indirect questions act as "face saving" options in that information sources can avoid replying to questions and newcomers can conceal the information-seeking intent of a communication (Brown & Levinson, 1978). On the contrary, potential drawbacks of this method include information sources that are unaware of or unresponsive to indirect questions and sources who respond adversely toward roundabout information-seeking attempts. Because hinting and indirect methods rely on targets' reacting to cues and masked references, it may be beneficial for newcomers to use this strategy when they seek information of which they are fairly confident and when the newcomers can decode a correspondingly masked response (Miller & Jablin, 1991).

Third Parties. Third party information tactic refers to when a primary source of information, such as a supervisor, is substituted with a secondary source, such as another incumbent. This tactic is commonly utilized when the primary source is seemingly unavailable and/or when newcomer feels apprehensive about seeking information from a primary information target. Rather than primary sources, secondary sources may appear to be a more accessible and safe option. Third party information tactics also make available to newcomers a mode for verifying the meanings of a primary source's communications. To evade possible costs, newcomers should assess the secondary target's credibility as an information source and the likelihood that the secondary target will tell the primary source of the information-seeking occurrence (Berger & Bradac, 1982).

Although little is known about organizational newcomers' use of third-party information, research suggests that students often use third parties as sources of information in efforts to alleviate uncertainty about their romantic partners' feelings (Baxter & Wilmot, 1984). Research also indicates that third party tactics are frequently used to "second guess" information from primary sources (Hewes et al., 1985). Newcomers have admitted to pursuing information from secondary sources because their supervisors' descriptions were unclear and/or because their supervisors did not have the technical expertise to respond to these inquiries (Miller & Jablin, 1991). However, researchers have cautioned that exclusive use of this tactic could result in receiving inaccurate or misleading information that may conflict with the organization's and/or supervisor's wishes (Lodahl & Mitchell, 1980; Miller & Jablin, 1991).

Testing Limits. Newcomers may also seek information by testing limits or generating circumstances that require information targets to respond in some way. Information seekers observe the targets' responses as a means to figure out targets' perceptions toward specific behaviors or topics (Miller & Jablin, 1991). Using this approach could be potentially costly to the information seeker if the target develops unfavorable opinions and evaluations about the information seeker. Moreover, the information obtained using these tactics may be inconsequential and/or ambiguous.

Testing limits may include deliberate breaking of explicit rules to learn how prominent the rules are in the organization and when these rules will be imposed (Garfinkel, 1967). This approach allows the information seeker to advance their knowledge about the organization through experience instead of through speculation. Another mode of testing limits involves deviating from rules to assess how much the target will tolerate (Baxter & Wilmot, 1984). In the organizational context, newcomers stated that they perceived testing limits to be a useful tool in obtaining role clarity (Miller & Jablin, 1991). While testing tactics may reveal useful information about work procedures and relationships, those who deviate will likely be treated as rate-busters and as such will be promptly brought back into conformity (Roethlisberger & Dickson, 1939). The potentially high cost of testing tactics coupled with newcomers' desire for social acceptance lend support that these tactics may be best reserved as a last resort.

Disguising Conversations. In a fifth information-seeking tactic, one may disguise their attempts to acquire information as a natural element of conversations (Miller & Jablin, 1991). Disguising conversations both puts the information sources at ease and delicately encourages discussion of particular topics. A possible disadvantage of this tactic is that although targets may be encouraged to address a certain topic, there is no assurance that information sources will stay on topic or reveal the specifics that are sought.

Specifically, this tactic may comprise of joking, the use of items in the environment, and self-disclosure. Through demonstration of common experience or values, information seekers may attenuate the target's defensiveness (Brown & Levinson, 1978). Meanwhile, the target's reactions to jokes may provide evidence of the target's attitudes on certain topics. Another form of disguising conversations involves verbal prompts that encourage targets to remain on the same line of reasoning or clarification (Berger & Kellerman, 1983). On the other hand, by means of self-disclosure the information seeker reveals information about their lives in hopes that the target will reveal information in return. According to the "norm of reciprocity," others are inclined to reciprocate information comparable in scope and type that one is willing to disclose about him- or herself (Berger & Bradac, 1982; Knapp, 1984). If used in moderation, initiators of self-disclosure tend to be viewed positively by targets (Gilbert & Hornstein, 1975; Knapp, 1984; Worthy et al., 1969).

Individuals have proven rather sophisticated in their ability to solicit information without bringing attention to their intent. Disguising conversations may be ideal in situations where anticipated social costs are high and/or when the information that one seeks is potentially embarrassing (Miller & Jablin, 1991). Compared with overt questions, this tactic is not quite as efficient, but it occurs as a natural part of conversation and can assist in the development of relationships.

Observing. When individuals want to acquire information inconspicuously and unobtrusively, they may observe behaviors of target others under certain circumstances. Newcomers may use this information seeking tactic to gain insight as to a target's attitude or information on how to perform a task (Berger & Bradac, 1982). Newcomers may observe behaviors enacted by their work group that result in reward or punishments and use this information to identify their supervisor's values and expectations. When learning novel skills, new employees can observe others performing those tasks and this can provide individuals with a model to emulate when they go to perform that same task (Bandura, 1977; Weiss, 1977). Because coworkers are more likely to perform similar tasks to what will be expected of the newcomer and because coworkers are usually more available, it is more likely that this tactic would be used for a newcomer to obtain information from coworkers than from a supervisor. New employees are also able to assess the quality of their output and performance by comparing their work to that of other more tenured organizational members. Social comparison theory posits that evaluating our own abilities and beliefs relative to those of others offers a means to acquire information regarding where we stand and motivates us to improve our current standing (Festinger, 1954). While more objective indicators of one's standing for purposes of accurate self-assessment may be preferred, in certain contexts our position may only have meaning in a comparative respect (Swencionis & Fiske, 2014).

Limitations of this tactic rest in the extent of accurate information that can be acquired regarding the targets' attitudes and behavioral motivations. Attempts to construe rationale for another's behavior frequently leads to false attributions (Tversky & Kahneman, 1974). Previous research shows that observers prefer to watch targets interacting informally with others rather than observe targets executing tasks in formal or solitary capacities (Berger & Douglas, 1981; Berger & Perkins, 1978). Advantages of this tactic are that there are meager, if any, negative consequences, it can be used in conjunction with other tactics, and it encourages sense making of one's role through comparison of past knowledge with current stimuli (Miller & Jablin, 1991).

Surveillance. The final tactic included in Miller and Jablin's (1991) repertoire of newcomer socialization tactics is surveillance. Surveillance also involves the use of inconspicuous attempts to acquire information, but primarily focuses on retrospective sense making. Whereas observation is concerned with learning information about specific attitudes or specific behaviors, surveillance focuses on cues given through comprehensive messages or experiences (Jablin, 1987). Information acquired via surveillance, or monitoring, is typically serendipitous and made sense of through reflective evaluations. Work conducted by Salancik and Pfeffer (1978) supports the concept that new employees may monitor the conversations of their coworkers, and may be specifically attuned to the aspects of work that incumbents most regularly talk about. In another study, newcomers have reported that they commonly listen in on their coworkers' conversations to ensure that they are not missing any vital information (Miller & Jablin, 1991). Ashforth (1985) concluded that newcomers may also make note of coworkers' social constructions of events (i.e., ceremonies, parties, and rituals) to gain insight regarding attitudes and assumptions indicative of the organization's culture.

Surveillance requires reflection that integrates new stimuli with past experiences to assist newcomers in making sense of their new environments. Cumulatively these retrospective accounts may facilitate in attributing meaning to current circumstances and allow formation of a mental framework for interpreting new information (Weick, 1979). Due to heightened awareness, newcomers tend to be more sensitive to new stimuli early on and therefore, may utilize surveillance techniques more frequently during the entry stage than at any other time during their organizational term (Miller & Jablin, 1991).

Social Costs

All interactions with others consist of costs or social exchange (Berger & Bradac, 1982; Huston & Burgess, 1979; Nord, 1980; Parks, 1977; Roloff, 1981), and the anticipated costs of information-seeking may deter a newcomer from asking for assistance or information. Social exchange has been defined as voluntary transmission of some item or activity from one individual to another to receive alternative items or activities (Roloff, 1981). Resources involved in these exchanges may be cognitive, affective, or material in nature. Individuals are typically aware of the rewards and costs of the transaction. Rewards may include obtaining information as a means to reduce uncertainty, or experiencing positive affect resulting from feelings of social acceptance or approval (Blau, 1964). Costs may include social rejection rather than social approval and/or the absence of rewards (Roloff, 1981).

Distress may lead a newcomer to proceed with greater caution when there is a high level of anticipated costs involved in seeking resources from others (Nord, 1980; Walster et al., 1978). Newcomers are particularly apprehensive about the negative costs and consequences associated with their relationships. Feeling as though they are irritating their colleagues with their inquiries and fearful that they will be cut off from future information, newcomers have reported becoming increasingly hesitant to ask questions (Jablin & Miller, 1991). Jablin and Miller (1991) also found that newcomers were anxious about approaching their supervisors for information that they thought they should already possess because they did not want to seem stupid. In hopes of minimizing what they consider to be high social costs connected to seeking information from specific sources, newcomers may choose more covert information-seeking tactics that are less easily detectable by the source or target of that information (Miller & Jablin, 1991).

Newcomer Proactivity

As has been shown, newcomers need not be passive actors in the socialization process. Challenging the notion that organizations have control during organizational entry, ample research has demonstrated that employees can also play a substantial role in the organizational entry process (Ashford & Black, 1996; Bauer & Green, 1998; Griffin et al., 2000; Morrison, 1993; Wanberg & Kammeyer-Mueller, 2000). Moreover, research has demonstrated that some employees exercise greater proactivity during socialization than others do (Ashford & Black, 1996; Crant, 2000). Proactive individuals may take initiative in seeking information and may network with insiders with intent to learn and adopt the norms and culture of their organization. Proactivity can take various forms including positive framing, sense making, and relationship building (Kim et al., 2005). Recently, newcomer proactive efforts were found to relate to supportive manager behaviors, and the researchers posited that this was at least partially attributable to managers' evaluations of newcomers' commitment to their own socialization process (Ellis et al., 2017).

TRANSMISSION OF NORMS AND CULTURE TO NEW ORGANIZATIONAL MEMBERS

Social information processing theory posits that people "as adaptive organisms, adapt attitudes, behavior, and beliefs to their social context and to the reality of their own past and present behavior and situation" (Salancik & Pfeffer, 1978, p. 226). As such, a new employee should adapt their attitudes, behavior, and beliefs to be appropriate given their new context. A person's immediate social environment delivers an indispensable source of information conveying cues which may be used to construct and interpret events and that allude what a person's attitudes and opinions should be.

Miller and Jablin (1991) identified interaction with peers as most helpful to newcomer's acquisition of information. In a literature review, Jablin

(2001) stated that newcomers use overt and observing tactics most abundantly and that colleagues and supervisors are the most common targets of information. This review also concluded that as the perceived social cost of information requests increases, newcomers rely more heavily on covert rather than overt/direct tactics.

Stohl (1986) posited that messages from more tenured and respected organizational members regarding particular events can become internalized as memorable maxims that shape a newcomer's perspective of the organization's normative structure. Other researchers have advocated that newcomers may learn about their organization's culture and their place within it as a byproduct of decoding critical incidents (Gundry & Rousseau, 1994; Teboul, 1997). Notably, evidence also suggests that organizational members have a tendency to identify more strongly with and feel more commitment toward their occupations and subunits rather than the organization at large (Ashforth & Johnson, 2001; Moreland & Levine, 2001; Riketta & Van Dick, 2005).

The influence of norms ultimately rests with the extent of general acceptance of those norms within the culture (Bennett et al., 2005). Organizational members may be influenced by norms that are broadly recognized within their environment but that are not necessarily acceptable in other organizations or settings (Bennett et al., 2005). This may become an issue if the norms that persist within a given organization are unethical or have negative implications. Culture and norms are maintained by the established reinforcement or punishment systems within an organization, and the culture may or may not be consistent with societal or conventionally moral standards. However, when there is a discrepancy between what newcomers believe is morally acceptable and valid organizational conduct and the way work is actually carried out at an organization, this can have negative implications on newcomer adjustment. Smith and colleagues found that when a newcomer's pre-entry beliefs were at odds with how work was truly done at an organization, organizational identification and perceived organizational trustworthiness was diminished over time and subsequently so was self-efficacy (Smith et al., 2016). This may also play into the attraction-selection-attrition model that was presented earlier in this chapter. Individuals may be more inclined to leave an organization if there is a large enough discrepancy between what the newcomer deems as legitimate organizational conduct compared to how an organization actually conducts business.

CONCLUSION

As a new organizational member, desire for social acceptance and role clarity encourage efforts to learn the ropes and to acquire the expected patterns of behavior. The organization also seeks to assimilate the newcomer into their role and the patterns of daily processes. Various tactics exist to accomplish these ends. Moreover, stronger organizational culture has positive implications regarding the success and satisfaction of the newcomer with the socialization process. This chapter demonstrates how and from whom newcomers may learn information, what techniques newcomers may use to seek information, and how assimilation encourages the continuance of preexisting norms and corporate culture. Areas for future research in this field could include how normative patterns of behavior are most frequently learned, how organizational tactics differentially affect degree of assimilation, and how much control organizations have on the types of information newcomers are receiving from their social environments. Future research could also examine the development of deviant behavior within newcomers resulting from observation of poorly selected role models (i.e., informal leaders) or through adoption of subunit norms. Overall, this chapter aims to provide an overview of how culture is transmitted to and acquired by newcomers through the socialization process. These processes contribute to the maintenance and perpetuation of an organization's culture when organizational knowledge and attitudes are shared from one generation of employees to the next.

REFERENCES

Allen, D. G. (2006). Do organizational socialization tactics influence newcomer embeddedness and turnover? *Journal of Management, 32*, 237–256.

Allen, D. G., & Shanock, L. R. (2013). Perceived organizational support and embeddedness as key mechanisms connecting socialization tactics to commitment and turnover among new employees. *Journal of Organizational Behavior, 34*, 350–369.

Anakwe, U. P., & Greenhaus, J. H. (1999). Effective socialization of employees: Socialization content perspective. *Journal of Managerial Issues, 11*, 315–329.

Anderson, C. M., Riddle, B. L., & Martin, M. M. (1999). Socialization processes in groups. In L.R Frey, D. S. Gouran, & M. S. Poole (Eds.), *The handbook of group communication theory and research* (pp. 139–163). SAGE.

Ashforth, B. E. (1985). Climate formation: Issues and extensions. *Academy of Management Review, 10*, 837–847.

Ashforth, B. E., & Johnson, S. A. (2001) Which hat to wear? The relative salience of multiple identities in organizational contexts. In M. A. Hogg & D. J. Terry (Eds.), *Social identity processes in organizational contexts* (pp. 31–48). Psychology Press.

Ashforth, B. E., & Saks, A. M. (1996). Socialization tactics: Longitudinal effects on newcomer adjustment. *Academy of Management Journal, 39*, 149–178.

Ashforth, B. E., Sluss, D. M., & Harrison, S. H. (2007). Socialization in organizational contexts. In G. P. Hodgkinson & J. K. Ford (Eds.), *International Review of Industrial and Organizational Psychology* (Vol. 22, pp. 1–70). John Wiley & Sons.

Ashford, S. J. (1986). The role of feedback seeking in individual adaptation: A resource perspective. *Academy of Management Journal, 29*, 465–487.

Ashford, S. J., & Black, J. S. (1996). Proactivity during organizational entry: The role of desire for control. *Journal of Applied Psychology, 81*, 199–214.

Ashford, S. J., Blatt, R., & VandeWalle, D. (2003). Reflections on the looking glass: A review of research on feedback-seeking behavior in organizations. *Journal of Management, 29*, 773–799.

Ashford, S. J., & Cummings, L. L. (1985). Proactive feedback seeking: the instrumental use of the information environment. *Journal of Occupational Psychology, 58*, 67–79.

Bandura, A. (1977). *Social learning theory*. Prentice Hall.

Bauer, T. N., & Green, S. G. (1998). Testing the combined effects of newcomer information seeking and manager behavior on socialization. *Journal of Applied Psychology, 83*, 72–83.

Bauer, T. N., Morrison, E. W., & Callister, R. R. (1998). Organizational socialization: A review and directions for future research. In G. R. Ferris (Ed.), *Research in personnel and human resources management* (Vol. 16, pp. 149–214). JAI Press.

Baxter, L. A., & Wilmot, W. W. (1984). "Secret tests": Social strategies for acquiring information about the state of the relationship. *Human Communication Research, 11*, 171–202.

Bennett, R. J., Aquino, K., Reed, A. I., & Thau, S. (2005). The Normative Nature of Employee Deviance and the Impact of Moral Identity. In S. Fox & P. E. Spector (Eds.), *Counterproductive work behavior: Investigations of actors and targets* (pp. 107–125). American Psychological Association.

Berger C. R., & Bradac, J. I. (1982). *Language and social knowledge: Uncertainty in interpersonal relations.* Edward Arnold.

Berger, C. R., & Douglas, W. (1981). Studies in interpersonal epistemology, III: Anticipated interaction, self-monitoring, and observing context selection. *Communication Monograph, 48*, 183–196.

Berger, C. R., & Kellerman, K. A. (1983). To ask or not to ask: Is that a question? In R. N. Bostrom (Ed.), *Communication yearbook* (Vol. 7, pp. 342–368). SAGE.

Berger, C. R., & Perkins, I. W. (1978). Studies in interpersonal epistemology I: Situational attributes in observational context selection. In B. Ruben (Ed.), *Communication yearbook* (Vol. 2, pp. 171–184). Transaction.

Blau, P. M. (1964). *Exchange and power in social life*. Wiley.

Brown, M. H. (1985). That reminds me of a story: Speech action in organizational socialization. *Western Journal of Speech Communication, 49*, 27–42.

Brown, P., & Levinson, S. (1978) Universals in language usage: Politeness phenomena. In E. N. Goody (Ed.), *Questions and politeness: Strategies in social interaction* (pp. 260–289). Cambridge University Press.

Cable, D. M., & Parsons, C. (2001). Socialization tactics and person-organization fit. *Personnel Psychology, 54*, 1–22.

Chao, G. T., O'Leary-Kelly, A. M., Wolf, S., Klein, H. J., & Gardner, P. D. (1994). Organizational socialization: Its content and consequences. *Journal of Applied Psychology, 79*, 730–743.

Cooper-Thomas, H. D., van Vianen, A., & Anderson, N. (2004). Changes in person-organization fit: The impact of socialization tactics on perceived and actual P-O fit. *European Journal of Work and Organizational Psychology, 13*, 52–78.

Crant, J. M. (2000). Proactive behavior in organizations. *Journal of Management, 26*, 435–462.

Deal, T., & Kennedy, A. (1982) *Corporate cultures*. Addison-Wesley.

Ellis, A. M., Nifadkar, S. S., Bauer, T. N., & Erdogan, B. (2017). Newcomer adjustment: Examining the role of managers' perception of newcomer proactive behavior during organizational socialization. *Journal of Applied Psychology, 102*, 993–1001.

Feldman. D. C. (1981). The multiple socialization of organization members. *Academy of Management Review, 6*, 309–318.

Festinger, L. (1954). A theory of social comparison processes. *Human Relations, 7*, 117–140.

Garfinkel. H. (1967). *Studies in ethnomethodology*. Prentice-Hall.

Gilbert, S. I., & Hornstein, D. (1975). The communication of self-disclosure: Level versus valence. *Human Communication Research, 1*, 316–322.

Goody, E, N. (1978). Toward a theory of questions. In E. N. Goody (Ed.), *Questions and politeness: Strategies in social interaction* (pp. 17–43). Cambridge University Press.

Griffin, A., Colella, A., & Goparaju, S. (2000). Newcomer and organizational socialization tactics: An interactionist perspective. *Human Resources Management Review, 10*, 453–474.

Gruman, J. A., Saks, A. M., & Zweig, D. I. (2006). Organizational socialization tactics and newcomer proactive behaviors: An integrative study. *Journal of Vocational Behavior, 69*, 90–104.

Gundry, L. K., & Rousseau, D. M. (1994). Critical incidents in communicating culture to newcomers: The meaning is the message. *Human relations, 47*, 1063–1088.

Hewes, D. E., Graham, M. L., Doelger, I. L., & Pavitt, C. (1985). "Second guessing": Message interpretation in social networks. *Human Communication Research, 11*, 299–334.

Huston, T. L. & Burgess. R. (1979). Social exchange and developing relationships: An overview. In R. Burgess & T. L. Huston (Eds.), *Social exchange and developing relationships* (pp. 3–28). Academic Press.

Inkeles, A. (1966). Social structure and the socialization of competence. *Harvard Educational Review, 36*(3), 265–283.

Jablin, F. M. (1982). Organizational communication: An assimilation approach. In M. E. Roloff & C. R. Berger (Eds.), *Social cognition and communication* (pp. 255–286). SAGE.

Jablin, F. M. (1984). Assimilating new members into organizations. In R. Bostrom (Ed.), *Communication yearbook* (Vol. 8, pp. 594–626). SAGE.

Jablin, F. M. (1987). Organizational entry, assimilation, and exit. In F. M. Jablin, L. L. Putnam, K. H. Roberts, & L. W. Porter (Eds.), *Handbook of organizational communication* (pp. 679–740). SAGE.

Jablin, F. M. (2001). Organizational entry, assimilation, and disengagement/exit. In F. M. Jablin & L. L. Putnam (Eds.), *The new handbook of organizational communication: Advances in theory, research, and methods* (pp. 732–818). SAGE.

Jackson. S. E., & Schuler. R. S. (1985). A meta-analysis and conceptual critique of research on role ambiguity and role conflict in work settings. *Organizational Behavior and Human Performance, 36*, 16–78.

Jones, G. R. (1986). Socialization tactics, self-efficacy, and newcomers' adjustments to organizations. *Academy of Management Journal, 29*, 262–279.

Kim, T., Cable, D. M., & Kim, S. (2005). Socialization tactics, employee proactivity, and person-organization fit. *Journal of Applied Psychology, 90*, 232–241.

Kitchell, A., Hannan, E., & Kempton, W. (2000). Identity through stories: Story structure and function in two environmental groups. *Human Organization, 59*, 96–105.

Knapp, M. L. (1984). *Interpersonal communication and human relationships.* Allyn & Bacon.

Kram, K. E. (1985). *Mentoring at work: Developmental relationships in organizational life*. Scott, Foresman and Company.

Lodahl, T. M., & Mitchell, S. M. (1980). Drift in the development of innovative organizations. In J. R. Kimberly & R. H. Miles (Eds.), *The organizational life cycle* (pp. 184–207). Jossey-Bass.

Louis, M. R. (1980). Surprise and sense-making: What newcomers experience in entering unfamiliar organizational settings. *Administrative* Science *Quarterly, 25*, 226–251.

Louis, M. R., Posner, B. Z., & Powell, G. N. (1983). The availability and helpfulness of socialization practices. *Personnel Psychology, 35*, 857–866.

Meyer, R. D., Dalal, R. S., José, I. J., Hermida, R., Chen, T. R., Vega, R. P., Brooks, C. K., & Khare, V. P. (2014). Measuring job-related situational strength and assessing its interactive effects with personality on voluntary work behavior. *Journal of Management, 40*, 1010–1041.

Miller, V. D., & Jablin, F. M. (1991). Information seeking during organizational entry: Influences, tactics, and a model of the process. *The Academy of Management Review, 16*, 92.

Moreland, R. L., & Levine, J. M. (2006). Socialization in organizations and work groups. In J. M. Levine & R. L. Moreland (Eds.), *Small groups* (pp. 469–498). Psychology Press.

Morrison, E. W. (1993). Longitudinal study of the effects of information seeking on newcomer socialization. *Journal of Applied Psychology, 78*, 173–183.

Nord. W. E. (1980). The study of organizations through a resource-exchange paradigm. In K. I. Gergen, M. S. Greenberg, & R. H. Willis (Eds.), *Social exchange: Advances in theory and practice* (pp. 119–140). Plenum Press.

Orpen, C. (1993). The effect of organizational cultural norms on the relationships between personnel practices and employee commitment. *The Journal of Psychology: Interdisciplinary and Applied, 127*, 577–579.

Ostroff, C., & Kozlowski, S. W. (1992). Organizational socialization as a learning process: The role of information acquisition. *Personnel Psychology, 45*, 849–874

Parks. M. R. (1977). Relational communication: Theory and research. *Human Communication Research, 3*, 372–381.

Pentland, B. T. (1999). Building process theory with narrative: From description to explanation. *The Academy Of Management Review*, *24*, 711–724.

Pfeffer, J. (1981) Management as symbolic action: The creation and maintenance of organizational paradigms. In L. L. Cummings & B. M. Staw (Eds.), *Research in organizational behavior* (Vol. 3, pp. 1–52). JAI Press.

Posner, B. Z., & Powell, G. N. (1985). Female and male socialization experiences: An initial investigation. *Journal of Occupational Psychology*, *58*, 81–85.

Riketta M., & Van Dick, R. (2005). Foci of attachment in organizations: A meta-analytic comparison of the strength and correlates of workgroup versus organizational identification and commitment. *Journal of Vocational Behavior*, *67*, 490–510.

Riordan, C. M., Weatherly, E. W., Vandenberg, R. J., & Self, R. M. (2001). The effects of pre-entry experiences and socialization tactics on newcomer attitudes and turnover. *Journal of Managerial Issues*, *13*, 159–176.

Ritti, R. R., & Funkhouser, G. R. (1987). *The ropes to skip and the ropes to know* (3rd ed.). Wiley.

Robinson, S. L., & Morrison, E. W. (2000). The development of psychological contract breach and violation: A longitudinal study. *Journal of Organizational Behavior*, *21*, 525–546.

Roethlisberger. F. J., & Dickson, W. J. 1939. *Management and the worker*. Harvard University Press.

Roloff, M. E. (1981). *Interpersonal communication: The social exchange approach*. SAGE.

Saks, A. M., & Ashforth, B. E. (1997). Socialization tactics and newcomer information acquisition. *International Journal of Selection and Assessment*, *5*, 48–61.

Salancik, G. R., & Pfeffer, J. (1978). A social information processing approach to job attitudes and task design. *Administrative Science Quarterly*, *23*(2), 224–253.

Schein, E.H. (1968). Organizational socialization and the profession of management. *Industrial Management Review*, *9*, 1–16.

Schein, E. H. (1988). *Process consultation* (Revised ed.). Addison-Wesley.

Schein, E. H. (1990). Organizational culture. *American Psychologist*, *45*, 109–119.

Schein, E. H. (2004). *Organizational culture and leadership* (3rd ed.). Jossey-Bass.

Schieffelin, B. B., & Eisenberg, A. R. (1984). Cultural variations in children's conversation. In R. L. Schieffelbusch & J. Pickar (Eds.), *The acquisition of communicative competence* (pp. 378–420). University Park Press.

Schneider, B. (1987). The people make the place. *Personnel Psychology*, *40*, 437–453.

Smith, L. G., Gillespie, N., Callan, V. J., Fitzsimmons, T. W., & Paulsen, N. (2017). Injunctive and descriptive logics during newcomer socialization: The impact on organizational identification, trustworthiness, and self-efficacy. *Journal of Organizational Behavior*, *38*, 487–511.

Stohl, C. (1986). The role of memorable messages in the process of organizational socialization. *Communication Quarterly*, *34*, 231–249.

Swap, W., Leonard, D., & Mimi Shields, L. A. (2001). Using mentoring and storytelling to transfer knowledge in the workplace. *Journal of Management Information Systems*, *18*, 95–114.

Swencionis, J. K., & Fiske, S. T. (2014). How social neuroscience can inform theories of social comparison. *Neuropsychologia*, *56*, 140–146.

Teboul, J. B. (1997). 'Scripting" the organization: New hire learning during organizational encounter. *Communication Research Reports, 14*, 33–47.

Tversky, A., & Kahneman, D. (1974). Judgment under uncertainty: Heuristics and biases. *Science, 185*, 1124–1131.

Van Maanen, J. (1976). Breaking-in: Socialization to work. In R. Dubin (Ed.), *Handbook of work, organization, and society* (pp. 67–130). Rand McNally.

Van Maanen, J. (1984). Doing new things in old ways: Chains of socialization. In J. Bess (Ed.), *Education and organization theory* (pp. 211–246). New York University Press.

Van Maanen, J., & Schein, E. H. (1979). Towards a theory of organizational socialization. In B. M. Staw (Ed.), *Research in organizational behavior* (Vol. 1, pp. 209–264). JAI.

Walster, E., Berscheid, E., & Walster, G. (1978). *Equity: Theory and research*. Allyn & Bacon.

Walther, K. E. P. (1978). *Effects of naturalistic settings on spontaneous verbal information-seeking behavior of 6th grade girls* (Unpublished doctoral dissertation). University of Texas Austin.

Wanberg, C. R., & Kammeyer-Mueller, J. D. (2000). Predictors and outcomes of proactivity in the socialization process. *Journal of Applied Psychology, 85*, 373–385.

Weick, K. E. (1979). *The social psychology of organizing* (2nd ed.). Addison Wesley.

Weiss, H. M. (1977). Subordinate imitation of supervisor behavior: The role of modeling in organizational socialization. *Organizational Behavior and Human Performance, 19*, 89–105.

Worthy, M., Gary, A. L., & Kahn, G. M. (1969). Self-disclosure as an exchange process. *Journal of Personality and Social Psychology, 13*, 59–63.

CHAPTER 3

WE BUILD THEN WE BREAK

The Impact of Military Sexual Trauma on Organizational Commitment in the United States Military

Stephanie E. V. Brown and Samantha C. January
Texas A&M University

In 1991, a female naval aviation officer revealed that she had been a victim of sexual assault at the 35th Annual Tailhook Symposium, a yearly convention for U.S. naval aviators. Upon further investigation, 83 women and 7 men were found to have been assaulted over the course of that weekend. To make matters worse, the assaults happened while senior officers were present, and several aviators donned shirts stating, "Women are Property" (Department of Defense, 1993). The ensuing congressional hearings detailed the extent to which aviators were forced to endure harassment and assault at the hands of their peers and superior officers. As a result, Secretary of the Navy Henry L. Garrett, III was forced to resign, multiple admirals were given official reprimands, and the U.S. Navy and Department of Defense adopted a zero tolerance harassment policy (Winerip, 2013).

Organizations Behaving Badly:
Destructive Behavior and Corrective Responses, pp. 31–57

Nearly 30 years later, however, sexual harassment and assault in the military remain pervasive. In 2014, the military publication *Task and Purpose* brought to light the existence of a variety of junior enlisted, combat-oriented Facebook pages run by Marines and dedicated to the sexual objectification of their female peers (Jones, 2014). The pictures consisted of sexual selfies sent to romantic interests and surreptitiously taken photos of women which were then posted without their consent to the group. "Smash or pass?" the captions often read, inviting those on the page to comment on her appearance and whether or not they would have sex with the woman in question (Jones, 2014). Some commenters joked about raping or drugging the women in the pictures. Several active duty military members actively participated in these groups using their real names, posting overtly racist and sexist messages for all to see. Those who posted to these groups often claimed their postings were all in good fun or were reflective of true combat Marine culture, eschewing political correctness and reflecting a battle-hardened sense of humor. At the time, the Commandant of the Marine Corps stated that the military had few resources to deal with cyber-harassment of female Marines, but noted that the situation would be monitored.

In 2017, a joint expose by *War Horse* and the Center for Investigative Reporting revealed a revenge porn Facebook group titled "Marines United" (Brennan, 2017). Similar to the aforementioned Facebook groups, this site featured pictures of female service members and veterans in various states of undress that were posted without the target's consent, some by former romantic partners. At least one woman was stalked by the individual who took photos of her. Members of this private Facebook group were then encouraged to investigate and report the women's personally identifying information (PII), including their rank, duty location, unit information, social media handles, and home addresses. A year later, Naval Criminal Investigative Service (NCIS) investigators identified 119 individuals who were active participants on the Facebook page. To date, 55 of these individuals have faced punishments ranging from court martials, confinement, and bad conduct discharges to "adverse administrative actions" (Snow, 2018).

Since Tailhook, researchers and policy-makers have extensively studied and scrutinized the antecedents and consequences of military sexual harassment and assault. Thanks to the efforts of various investigators and researchers, we are better able to understand the extent of this problem, as well as the impact sexual harassment and assault has had on the U.S. armed forces and service members individually. However, as made clear by the aforementioned high-profile cases, the military continues to grapple with these challenges. To find a solution, we must turn to the literature to better understand the link between military sexual harassment and assault and organizational commitment.

Traditionally, much of the research on commitment in the workplace references organizations in which a victim holds the right (though maybe not the means) to leave at-will (Allen, 2003). This is not usually the case with the military, in which service members must serve to the completion of their contracted service commitment. Additionally, most research on the impact of harassment and assault focuses on individuals whose identities are not as interwoven into their self-concept as military service members.

Throughout the course of this chapter, we will focus on how sexual harassment and assault impacts organizational commitment in the United States military—an environment where a strong commitment to the force is purposefully built and maintained. We begin by providing a broad overview of the antecedents and outcomes of organizational commitment, including an examination of the different commitment profiles. Then we describe how the military builds and maintains high levels of organizational commitment, and how the psychological contract established between the military and service members can be breached by events like military sexual trauma. Finally, we talk about how the ways in which the military deals with military sexual trauma can lead to very different organizational commitment outcomes.

ORGANIZATIONAL COMMITMENT

When first conceptualized, organizational commitment sought to explain why employees decide to leave an organization, aside from job dissatisfaction (Porter et al., 1974). Broadly speaking, organizational commitment is defined as both identification with and active involvement in an organization (Porter et al., 1974). Other common themes include commitment as a psychological state, bond, or attachment that binds the employee to the organization (Allen & Meyer, 1990; Mathieu & Zajac, 1990). Furthermore, individuals can commit to various entities, including (but not limited to) their organization, career, occupation, team, and supervisor (Becker, 2016).

Today, most scholars subscribe to the three component model of commitment (TCM; Meyer & Allen, 1991, 1997), which outlines the three components of organizational commitment: affective, normative, and continuance commitment. Affective commitment is generally defined as "the employee's emotional attachment to, identification with, and involvement in the organization" (Meyer & Allen, 1991, p. 67). Continuance commitment is characterized by a mindset of having to stay employed in an organization because the perceived costs of leaving are too high or there are a lack of perceived job alternatives (Meyer & Allen, 1991). Lastly, normative commitment is a mindset characterized by feelings of obligation and is theorized to have a dual nature (Meyer & Allen, 1991). When experienced in combination with strong affective commitment, normative commitment is said to reflect a moral imperative to do what is right (Gellatly et al., 2006). In contrast, when combined with strong continuance commitment, normative commitment is said to reflect feelings of indebted obligation to the organization (Gellatly et al., 2006).

In general, affective commitment is negatively correlated with turnover intention and turnover (Meyer et al., 2002). That is, high levels of affective commitment are associated with lower levels of turnover intention and actual turnover. Affective commitment is also positively correlated with on the job behaviors such as organizational citizenship behaviors (OCBs) and job performance, such that individuals with higher levels of affective commitment tend to be less absent from work, exhibit higher levels of OCBs, and have higher job performance (Meyer et al., 2002). Similar to affective commitment, normative commitment is negatively correlated with turnover intention, turnover, attendance, OCBs, and job performance, although the relationships are strongest for affective commitment (Meyer et al., 2002). Continuance commitment has also been shown to be negatively associated with turnover intentions and turnover but unlike normative and affective commitment, is shown to have zero to negative relationships with on the job behavior such as attendance, OCBs and job performance (Meyer et al., 2002).

Conceptually, the three mindsets of commitment are not mutually exclusive. At any point in time, individuals hold varying levels of affective, normative, and continuance commitment. Recently, scholars focused on modeling organizational commitment in this way through the use of person-centered approaches (Kabins et al., 2016; Kam et al., 2016; Meyer et al., 2013). The growing interest in the person-centered view of organizational commitment was sparked by Meyer and Herscovitch (2001). Their model described how the three components of commitment can combine within individuals to form commitment profiles, with implications for the occurrence of discretionary and non-discretionary behavior (Meyer & Herscovitch, 2001). The overarching goal of person-centered approaches is to identify and classify individuals into different subpopulations, which vary qualitatively or quantitatively in the configuration of commitment mindsets (Meyer & Morin, 2016). Person-centered analyses of commitment mindsets have found up to seven commitment profiles, which vary in both their level and shape of commitment configurations (Kabins et al., 2016; Meyer et al., 2013). At the broadest level, variable-centered views focus on examining relationships between variables, whereas person-centered approaches focus on identifying subgroups or classes of individuals who have similar characteristics or configurations of different variables (Meyer et al., 2013). More specifically, the person-centered approach takes a more interactionist view, and seeks to understand how all three mindsets of commitment interact with each other within individuals. On the other hand, the variable-centered view seeks to understand the antecedents, correlates, and consequences of the three mindsets of commitment separately.

Individual commitment mindsets and commitment profiles can be categorized as value-based, exchange-based, or weak. Kabins et al. (2016, p. 884) describe commitments best when they say "[v]alue-based commitments are characterized by shared ideologies, beliefs, and deep identification between the person and the organization." Value-based mindsets include affective and moral imperative commitments. Value-based profiles include invested, emotionally committed, morally committed, and fully committed profiles (Kabins et al., 2016). Value-based profiles include any profile that has high levels of affective commitment (Kabins et al., 2016; Meyer et al., 2006).

Exchange-based profiles, on the other hand, are "typified by a transactional mindset, whereby the person's sense of membership is based upon fulfillment of a contract and/or performance is contingent on an exchange of goods or services" (Kabins et al., 2016, p. 884). Several researchers agree that in order to be classified as an exchange-based profile, there should be low levels of affective commitment and high levels of either/both normative and continuance commitment (Kabins et al., 2016; Meyer et al., 2006). Exchange-based commitment mindsets include continuance and indebted obligation commitments (Meyer et al., 2006). Unlike value or exchange-based profiles, weak commitment profiles are not dominated by any one specific mindset, with relatively equal levels of all three components of commitment (Kabins et al., 2016). Weak profiles include weakly and moderately committed profiles (Kabins et al., 2016).

Organizational Commitment in the Military

There are a variety of ways and levels at which an employee commits to the organization. There are differences in how commitment unfolds over time, including how commitment is initially formed, how organizational commitment is maintained and strengthened over time, and how certain events can impact commitment. While organizational commitment is an important construct measured in every type of organization, it can be argued that there are few career fields which work as fervently to bind an individual to the organization as the military. Gal (1985) wrote, "For most military professionals, belonging to the armed forces is not merely a question of a place to work, a job, or an occupation. It is a way of life and frequently a lifetime commitment" (p. 553). Gal also recognized that commitment extended past the organization to include other service members, their assigned team, and their assigned task.

Scholars have theorized about the differences between commitment in civilian and military contexts, including differences in how the three commitment mindsets are experienced and the different foci of service members' commitment (Allan, 2003). Affective commitment is said to be experienced by individuals who describe their commitment to the military as stemming from duty and service to the country as well as gaining a sense of fulfillment and accomplishment (Griffith, 2009). Normative commitment is reflected in service members who feel camaraderie with their fellow service members and feel a sense of loyalty and moral obligation to remain in the military (Griffith, 2009). Lastly, continuance commitment is exhibited in service members who feel committed to the military based on the benefits received from their commitment, such as educational benefits, pay, retirement, and job skill training (Griffith, 2009).

Furthermore, individuals' views of their military service can impact the types and extent of organizational commitment that they hold. Some view their service as a calling, and others view military service as no more than a task or job to perform. The former describes individuals with an institutional view and the latter describes those with an occupational view. When individuals hold an institutional view, they have been socialized effectively into the military and feel a personal sense of obligation, duty, and loyalty to the organization (Griffith, 2009; Moskos, 1977). As such, it can be expected that these individuals hold high levels of affective and normative commitment, which allow them to remain committed to the organization in the face of adversity. These individuals are also more likely to go above and beyond the established tasks and duties of their role, engaging in OCBs like volunteering for nonmandatory events or helping newcomers to the unit. Finally, individuals with institutional views are intrinsically motivated to stay through rewards that hold symbolic meaning in the organization, such as nonmonetary awards and medals for their achievements and recognition at meetings (Griffith, 2009; Moskos, 1977). These rewards intrinsically help fulfill institutionally oriented individuals desire to serve their country.

In contrast, individuals with an occupational view of their service see the work as nothing more than a way to make a living, wherein individuals have a set number of working hours in a day, with a set amount of tasks and duties to complete. Therefore, when individuals exert extra effort by working overtime or completing extra training regimens, they expect to be compensated for those efforts (Griffith, 2009; Moskos, 1977). Thus, it is likely that individuals with an occupational view of their service will be high in continuance commitment. It is also likely that these individuals will not exhibit high levels of OCB's. Unlike those with an institutional view, those with an occupational view are motivated by extrinsic factors, such as bonuses, increased salaries, promotions, and time off (Griffith, 2009; Moskos, 1977).

BUILDING AND MAINTAINING ORGANIZATIONAL COMMITMENT

Organizations spend significant amounts of time and money training and developing employees, and the military is no different. The typical accession cost of an Army soldier from basic military training through advanced individual training (in which the soldier is trained for his or her specific job) is nearly 73,000 dollars per recruit (United States Army, 2013). The Air Force spends anywhere from three to 11 million dollars to train a single fighter pilot to be fully mission ready (Government Accountability Office, 2018). With investments like these, the military is motivated to get its money's worth. Not only do they want military members to successfully fulfill the terms of their contracts, but ideally they would like service members to remain for a full career. To do so, the military must establish organizational commitment from day one.

The most common way commitment is developed is through periods of organizational socialization. Organizational socialization is the process by which employees learn the necessary knowledge, skills, behaviors, and culture of the organization to become an effective employee of that organization (Bauer & Erdogan, 2011). This process occurs throughout the employee's tenure. Because of the clear importance of commitment to military organizations, it is crucial to understand how commitment is built and maintained over time.

Onboarding

While socialization occurs throughout the employee's time in an organization, the initial training or onboarding period can be conceptualized as the main socialization period for recently hired employees (Feldman, 1989). Unlike civilian organizations, the military seeks to build commitment through the formation of an entirely new identity. Social identity theory outlines three stages of becoming in-group members of a particular social group (Tajfel & Turner, 1979). First, individuals must define themselves as members of a group. Subsequently individuals seek out and learn the stereotypical norms of the group, often through socialization processes. Lastly, when their group membership becomes salient, individuals will use previous knowledge gained regarding the norms, values, and role expectations of group members to decide which behavior is appropriate to employ in the current situation (Tajfel & Turner, 1979).

The first two steps of this theory are best exemplified during the onboarding processes for all military members. Before their training, individuals complete the first step of gaining group membership by signing up for their service under some sort of contract. By doing so, individuals have now defined themselves as members of their respective service. Enlisted personnel in all military branches are sent to basic training. While enduring physical training, new recruits are taught the intricacies of what makes their branch of the military unique. For instance, Marine recruits learn that "Every Marine is, first and foremost, a rifleman" regardless of career field (Keane, 2012). They learn the insignia for various ranks, how to execute certain "customs and courtesies" (including how to salute, march, and address senior personnel), and many of the various traditions that constitute life in the military. Over the course of basic training, enlisted personnel will learn the values and expectations of life in the military as well.

The socialization process is different for military officers, but is still a way to integrate college educated civilians into the military lifestyle. Officers commonly commission through one of three sources: military academies, Reserve Officer Training Corps (ROTC) programs, or Officer Training/ Officer Candidate Schools (OTS/OCS). Officers are taught all of the same traditions and customs and courtesies as enlisted personnel, but while enlisted onboarding processes focus more on developing followership, officer onboarding programs focus more on developing leadership skills. All commissioning and military basic training programs serve to build a sense of camaraderie and esprit de corps, as well as to teach dependence and teamwork (Morral et al., 2015).

Continuous Socialization

After completing either basic training or a commissioning program, military members are often sent to follow-on training to learn their specific job. This is often an intensive course lasting anywhere from a few weeks to a year or more that focuses on the intricacies of the specific career field. However, these training programs or subsequent deployments are also a time where military members are introduced to more specific traditions and rituals that create a sense of belongingness within a person's career field (Akerlof & Kranton, 2005). For instance, military aviators going through flight school may be granted a "call sign," or nickname given to those in the flying community. Other traditions include the Navy's 2-day line-crossing ceremony, in which sailors who have never before crossed the equator ("pollywogs") are transformed into "shellbacks" upon their first equatorial crossing and inducted into the Order of Neptune (Richardson, 1977). Some traditions have been phased out under the label of hazing, including the tradition of "blood pinning," where an aviator has their newly earned wings punched into his or her chest hard enough to draw blood (McIntyre, 1997).

The military also reinforces commitment to the organization by including family members in certain military functions. Squadrons or battalions will often hold cookouts or potlucks on base where families are invited to socialize, network, and learn more about the duties of their military family member. Military spouse culture also serves to encourage military spouses to commit to the organization as well, with many spouses serving as "key spouses," or liaisons between military spouses and military base leadership. Even children are encouraged to participate in military life. The Air Force has a program named KUDOS (Kids Understanding Deployment Operations), which teaches military children about the deployment processes that their parents undergo (Araos, 2016). Programs aimed at helping family members better understand the demands of military life while simultaneously integrating those family members have been shown to increase organizational commitment (Bourg & Segal, 1999).

Promotion is another method of socialization. Assigning someone more responsibility, including responsibility for training and socializing subordinates, requires that employees to invest themselves and model the organizational goals for their subordinates, which in turn reinforces the knowledge and expectations laid out by the military. Similarly, additional job training or professional military education (PME) is another socialization technique used by the military. PME occurs right before big promotion periods in a service member's career timeline. Those in the Air Force colloquially refer to this process as "rebluing," which is a play on a gunsmithing technique to refurbish a weapon and the color blue (one of the Air Force colors) to describe a period when PME attendees become overly remotivated and reinspired about their roles in the military (Felch, 2013).

Organizational Identity Salience in Commitment Growth

Griffith (2009) notes that the military fosters an institutional focus, which embraces feelings of duty, loyalty, and obligation to something larger than oneself. A key aspect of both initial and continuous periods of socialization is to increase and maintain organizational identity salience. One of the main purposes of enlisted basic training and officer commissioning programs is to create a highly salient group identity by diminishing the individual's identity. In this way, a person thinks of his or herself as not only an employee of the federal government, but also a member of an elite group of Americans who chose military service in their specific branch. Many military members feel that their service gives them a sense of importance, purpose, and strengthened self-esteem (Smith & True, 2014). In other words, their identity is highly intertwined with their employer and encourages members to remain in the organization with others whom they consider to be part of their in group (Cole & Bruch, 2006).

This is especially key in government organizations like the military. Fewer than half of one percent of Americans currently serve on active duty in the U.S. Armed Forces (Chalabi, 2015), and those serving are often subjected to long work hours, extended deployments, temporary assignments away from family and friends, and (depending on the career field and rank of the individual) may not be paid as well as civilian counterparts in equivalent jobs. The purpose of many of the customs established in the military is to encourage people to strongly identify with fellow service members and remain in the armed forces despite the challenges inherent to life in the military (Akerlof & Kranton, 2005).

This has clear benefits to the military, especially as it has remained an all-volunteer force since the end of the Vietnam War. As any organizational leaders know, it is costly to train people, and once they are trained it is preferable to keep them in the organization and not working for other organizations. In recent years, for instance, pilots have been leaving the Air Force after their initial active duty service commitment (ADSC), in part because of the more flexible hours and higher pay the civilian sector can provide. If the Air Force cannot activate organizational commitment and pride as a means to retain pilots, they will have to provide additional incentives as a way to show the individual they are committed to them and their well-being. For instance, the Air Force uses Aviation Incentive Pay and the Aviation Bonus Program to help increase air crew salaries in an effort to stem the flow of aviators to commercial airlines and government contracting positions (Losey, 2017). Even still, the recommended additional monetary incentives necessary to break even with commercial civilian airlines is not something the Air Force is willing or able to meet, which has had negative impact on force retention (Mattock et al., 2016).

BREAKING ORGANIZATIONAL COMMITMENT

Just as organizational commitment can be built, so can it be broken. There are multiple ways that organizational commitment may change over time, and one such way is via psychological contract breach. A psychological contract is defined as

> an individual's beliefs regarding the terms and conditions of a reciprocal exchange agreement between that focal person and another party. Key issues, here, include the belief that a promise has been made and a consideration offered in exchange, binding the parties to a set of reciprocal obligations. (Rousseau, 1989, p. 123)

Psychological contracts are important because they help the employee decide how much they wish to contribute and invest in their organization in the future as well as how much they can expect from their organization in return (Rousseau, 1989).

Psychological contracts are most often categorized as relational or transactional. Relational psychological contracts are relationship-oriented and thus require a large emotional investment from the employee (Morrison & Robinson, 1997). Relational psychological contracts are also intangible, subjective, flexible, and long-lasting (Morrison & Robinson, 1997). On the other hand, transactional psychological contracts are more economic and require less emotional investment than relational psychological contracts (Morrison & Robinson, 1997). Transactional psychological contracts are also characterized as tangible, specific, static, and short-term (Morrison & Robinson, 1997).

PSYCHOLOGICAL CONTRACT BREACH

Social exchange theory places emphasis on organizational commitment as a primary exchange variable that embodies employees' socioemotional attachment to the organization and its members (Cropanzano & Mitchell, 2005). Researchers have gone further to show that high levels of organizational commitment lead individuals to feel obligated to behave in a manner that is beneficial for the organization and its members, known as positive reciprocity behaviors (O'Reilly & Chatman, 1986; Randall et al., 1990; Rhoades et al., 2001; Shore & Wayne, 1993). As a result, individuals feel that they are a valued and respected member of the organization and tend to reciprocate with high levels of emotional engagement and commitment to the organization (Hansen & Griep, 2016; Robinson, 1996). Furthermore, researchers have found that when employees display these positive reciprocity behaviors, they tend to refrain from engaging in workplace deviance (Liao et al., 2004; Tepper et al., 2008). Thus, if individuals have high levels of organizational commitment, they are less likely to engage in behaviors that may harm the organization or its members.

On the other hand, when employees sense that the organization has not fulfilled their end of the contract, they feel undervalued and disrespected by the organization and no longer have trust that the organization will uphold their end of the contract in the future (Hansen & Griep, 2016; Robinson, 1996). These shocks are known as psychological contract breaches, which can have detrimental effects for both the individual and their employer (Tomprou et al., 2015; Zhao et al., 2007).

Feelings of violation are described as the emotional response to psychological contract breach, which are often negative and can include feelings of anger and distress (Morrison & Robinson, 1997; Robinson & Morrison, 2000; Robinson & Rousseau, 1994). Feelings of violation can be triggered by a single event or a series of events. Because the organization is not living up to their end of the perceived contract, the individual adjusts their contributions and investments accordingly (Robinson, 1996; Solinger et al., 2016). The resulting feelings of violation often lead to lower levels of organizational commitment (Bal et al., 2008; Ng et al., 2010; Zhao et al., 2007).

The type of psychological contract that the individual holds has implications for how individuals view psychological contract breaches. Past research has found that relational psychological contracts are positively associated with important job attitudes such as organizational commitment to the job, overall organizational commitment, intent to remain, and job satisfaction (Raja et al., 2004; Shore et al., 2006). Put differently, individuals who hold relational psychological contracts tend to be more satisfied with their jobs and intend to stay in their current organization. Transactional psychological contracts have been found to be either negatively related or unrelated to the above job attitudes and have been found to relate positively with continuance commitment (Hughes & Palmer, 2007).

Military Sexual Trauma as a Contract Breach

Workplace sexual harassment and assault are major violations of a psychological contract, both in employer-employee and employee-employee relationships. There is often a written expectation that the workplace will remain free from harassment and assault. When sexual harassment or assault occurs, it constitutes a psychological contract breach in that what actually occurs does not meet the expectations understood by all parties (Tannenbaum et al., 1991). Prior research indicates that traumatic workplace events like military sexual trauma lead to feelings of violation, which can dissolve employees' emotional bond with the organization (Hansen & Griep, 2016; Morrison & Robinson, 1997; Robinson, 1996; Street et al., 2007).

Sexual harassment and assault occur in both military and civilian workplaces. In the civilian sector, the EEOC (n.d.) reports over 12,000 allegations of harassment each year between 2010 and 2017. Most often, women are the targets of such harassment and men are the perpetrators (O'Leary-Kelly et al., 2009). This mirrors the sexual harassment and assault situation in the military. However, those in the military are more likely to be harassed than their civilian counterparts: 22 to 31% of women and 5 to 7% of men are targets of unwanted sexual attention; 8 to 9% of women and 1 to 2% of men are targets of quid pro quo harassment; and 4 to 7% of women and 1 to 2% of males are sexually assaulted each year (Ilies et al., 2003; Stander & Thomsen, 2016). While, on average, women are most likely to be targeted, there have been certain years where more men than women have been targets of harassment and assault due to the very unequal numbers of men and women in the forces (approximately 85% to 15% percent, respectively).

In fact, sexual harassment and assault have become so prevalent in the military that the Department of Veteran Affairs (VA) has created a specific category for people who are treated in VA medical centers for issues stemming from their harassment or assaults. The term *military sexual trauma* is defined as repeated periods of sexual harassment or experiences of sexual assault experienced during one's military service (VA, 2018). This definition combines the traditional EEOC and Department of Justice categories of hostile workplace harassment, quid pro quo harassment, sexual assault, domestic violence, and rape under one large umbrella. Approximately one in four women and one in 100 men have indicated to VA providers that they have experienced military sexual trauma (VA, 2018). Sexual harassment and assault impacts job satisfaction more for military individuals than civilian individuals due to both the strong link between interpersonal and work-focused aspects of life in the military and the sometimes "life or death" importance of teamwork and trust between all team members (Willness et al., 2007). This is especially pertinent in light of the fact that approximately 90% of all past-year sexual assaults against military members on active duty were perpetrated by other military members, often in a military setting (Morral et al., 2015).

CONSEQUENCES OF MILITARY SEXUAL TRAUMA

There are various consequences of workplace sexual harassment and assault that impact the targeted employee, bystanders, and the organization as a whole. Without the proper care and attention, both the individual and the organization as a whole will greatly suffer.

Impact on the Individual

Sexual harassment and assault are linked to several negative outcomes including increased stress, decreased job satisfaction, increased turnover intentions, and increased absenteeism (Fitzgerald et al., 1997; Schneider et al., 1997; O'Connell & Korabik, 2000; Ilies et al., 2003; Willness et al., 2007). Targets of military sexual trauma can also suffer from posttraumatic stress disorder, anxiety, poor health, suicidal ideation, and self-harm (Harned et al., 2002; Martin et al., 2000).

Because sexual assault is often perpetrated by someone known to the target, and because the majority of sexual assault in in the military is perpetrated by other military members, targets often experience feelings of institutional betrayal. Institutional betrayal is defined as feelings of betrayal specifically when an organization in which a person places their trust (in this case, the military) fails to prevent or respond supportively to an individual's trauma (Smith & Freyd, 2013). This idea stems from betrayal trauma theory, or the notion that abuse within close interpersonal relationships is more harmful to the victim than abuse perpetrated by strangers because of the violation of trust (Freyd, 1994). These feelings of betrayal can lead to perceptions of a psychological contract breach and decreased organizational commitment. Research on trauma in the workplace has previously indicated that traumatic events in the workplace impact organizational commitment (Street et al., 2007). Sexual assault and harassment, clearly qualifying as traumatic events, makes individuals less likely to remain committed to organizational goals or continue employment at a given organization.

Individuals experiencing military sexual trauma, either as the target or as a bystander, may change from one type of psychological contract to another. More specifically, individuals may switch from a more desirable relational psychological contract to a less desirable transactional psychological contract. For example, an individual holding a relational psychological contract who previously intended to spend their career with the military may transition to a transactional psychological contract after experiencing sexual harassment or assault. Thus, the military lost a member who was highly committed and loyal to the organization and gained a member who just wishes to fulfill their contract terms and receive their allocated benefits from the organization. This new transactional psychological contract means that the individual will have weaker affective and normative commitment, but higher continuance commitment, than before.

Impact to the Organization

When individuals perceive psychological contract breaches, it can have rippling effects not only for the individual, but for the employing organization. For example, perceived psychological contract breaches have been associated with increases in cynicism and decreases in organizational trust and loyalty (Andersson, 1996; Andersson & Bateman, 1997; Robinson & Rousseau, 1994; Robinson & Morrison, 1995). Individuals are often less committed to their teams and experience increased team conflict (Faley et al., 1999). Prior research has also indicated that operational readiness is impacted as overall physical fitness after traumatic events decreases (Faley et al., 1999). Furthermore, when individuals lose organizational trust and loyalty, they are less willing to perform tasks above and beyond their job duties (Turnley & Feldman, 2000).

Traditionally, when employees feel that they have not been treated fairly or that their psychological contract with their organization has been breached, they tend to engage in retaliatory behavior such as workplace deviance. Workplace deviance includes any behavior by employees that harms either the interests of the employing organization or its members (Robinson & Bennett, 1995). Workplace deviance falls under the broader category of counterproductive work behaviors (CWBs). Counterproductive work behaviors include interpersonal retaliatory behaviors directed at individual members of the organization (CWB-I) as well as retaliatory behavior directed at the organization itself (CWB-O; Robinson & Bennett, 1995).

In contexts such as the military, individuals may not have the opportunity to engage in traditional retaliatory behaviors due to the high stakes nature of their jobs and the serious consequences that could ensue for the individual, team members, and organization as a whole. A key example is the case of Army Sergeant Bowe Bergdahl. Bergdahl abandoned his post in Afghanistan in 2009, in part because he felt the Army was not living up to his expectations and that he was seeing leadership failure that was likely to end in the death of his comrades (Koenig, 2015). Essentially, he felt the organization was breaching its psychological contract with him and the soldiers with whom he served. After deserting his post, he was kidnapped by the Taliban and held for five years. The military spent considerable amounts of money and manpower attempting to secure his release. This case highlights the importance of understanding how perceptions of psychological contract breach impact subsequent organizational attitudes and actions.

REBUILDING COMMITMENT

We know that military sexual trauma may be even more psychologically damaging than trauma experienced in other contexts, as military sexual trauma has been associated with higher levels of PTSD than other military or civilian traumas to include combat action (Fontana & Rosenheck, 1998; Himmelfarb et al., 2006). We also know that a single negative, traumatic workplace incident can completely destroy organizational commitment in mere weeks (Solinger et al., 2016). However, there are many lessons on rebuilding commitment which can be gleaned from previous encounters with military sexual trauma and its subsequent impact on organizational commitment. Prior research has indicated four different commitment trajectories occurring after a psychological contract breach: thriving, reactivation, impairment, and dissolution (Solinger et al., 2016). Whether or not an individual follows a given trajectory is based on many factors, including how distressing the psychological contract breach was to the target and the organizational response to the breach.

In the thriving and reactivated trajectories, organizational commitment either returns to baseline or is heightened after a contract breach, while those in the impaired and dissolved trajectories see a sharp decrease in organization commitment which could lead to turnover (Solinger et al., 2016). From an organizational standpoint, it is crucial to understand which actions lead to renewed and/or elevated commitment. From a military standpoint, specifically, it is especially important to understand which actions to take to rebuild commitment, as the military already spends exorbitant amounts of time and resources to build and maintain commitment in the first place.

Impairment and Dissolution

Those in impaired commitment trajectories remain in the organization, yet have lower levels of organizational commitment post-breach. This is likely the most common trajectory for victims of military sexual trauma, specifically because the Department of Defense has consistently failed to take actions that inspire trust and rebuild commitment. In impaired commitment trajectories, employees are often forced to accept less-than-ideal situations (Solinger et al., 2016). They may feel as though no one is watching out for them, and that the military is not fulfilling their end of the contract. Because many in the military are unable to quit due to contract obligations (typically ranging anywhere from four to ten years depending on their job), they invest the minimum amount of energy possible to remain in the position. This often results in declining commitment that stabilizes at lower levels than before.

In this trajectory, an employee may withdraw from the workplace, perform fewer OCBs, and engage in low-levels of workplace deviance. For instance, retaliation is a common CWB performed by those who have experienced a psychological contract breach (Skarlicki & Folger, 1997). This often happens because an employee is trying to take or regain what they believe is owed to them. Retaliation covers a wide array of behaviors from petty theft (e.g., taking office supplies) to time theft (e.g., leaving early, wasting time) to destruction of organizational property. In an environment where everyone is supposed to be performing at their peak, underperforming can have severe consequences.

A dissolved commitment trajectory occurs when commitment lowers to the point that the employee leaves the organization. This is somewhat less likely in the military, as many individuals are required to remain for the duration of their contracts and face penalties (up to imprisonment) for attempting to leave without permission. When a military member does have the option to leave, the process is lengthy and anything but straightforward. While a civilian can leave with little to no notice to the employer, a military member must coordinate separation with their commanding officer, who may or may not approve the separation depending on the needs of the service at the time. A 7-day option or declination of continued service on behalf of the military member is often the most expedited option, but requires that the service member notify their chain of command that they are refusing reassignment or the option to reenlist. At minimum, outprocessing takes 7 days, during which the military requires attendance at mandatory medical, financial, and transition assistance meetings.

To prevent impairment or dissolution, the military needs to invest more time and effort in combating military sexual trauma. Historically, the military has been indifferent at best or hostile at worst to targets of military sexual trauma. Change is often forced by congressional mandate after periods of whistleblowing and intense media and public scrutiny. Inaction or the inability to take swift, decisive actions have left many service members with the impression that the military is not committed to them or their well-being.

Many of these issues stem from military leadership failing to set strong cultural norms and enforce behavioral standards both before and after military sexual trauma occurs. Fitzgerald et al. (1997) state that organizational context strongly relates to the prevalence of sexual harassment and assault in the workplace. In this instance, organizational context refers to the organization's tolerance of sexual harassment in both word and deed. For instance, many organizations (to include all branches of the U.S. military) have zero tolerance policies in place for workplace harassment. Ideally, this would mean that those who are found to have harassed or assaulted other employees would face some sort of tangible punishment. However, in many instances such behaviors are not fully investigated or taken seriously, leaving the target and bystanders to wonder what zero-tolerance truly means.

A contentious portion of military regulations leaves commanders with the ability to determine, according to their discretion, whether or not a case will be referred to a court martial (SAPR, 2015). Commanders also have the opportunity to punish the targets of military sexual trauma for the situations surrounding their assault, like underage drinking, fraternization with military members of different ranks, or adultery (Chu, 2004). This system has left military members fearful of retaliation, and has ensured that many do not report harassment or assault. This fear is not unfounded. For many years, targeted military members have been diagnosed with bogus personality disorders after reporting their sexual assaults (Dao, 2012). In doing so, the military forces the target of military sexual trauma to separate from the military while the perpetrator often walks free. In response, many individuals and veterans' organizations have worked to remove commander discretion from the military justice system. Senator Kirsten Gillibrand introduced legislation to add civilian oversight and separate the military justice system from the military hierarchy altogether (Kheel, 2017). This is no different than a civilian organization using the civilian justice system (over which they have no control) to prosecute sexual assault or egregious workplace harassment. Removing the process from inside the military would also help safeguard against biased investigations and ensure that people would not feel forced to accept investigation results because a higher-ranking individual told them to.

Prior research indicates that a perpetrator's proclivity towards harassment and assault is often facilitated by factors within an organization (Pryor et al., 1993; Pryor et al., 1995). For instance, Holland et al. (2014) evaluated sexual assault training efforts in the military and found that both training and perceptions of training efficacy varied by military branch. A large portion of trainees indicated that they did not learn about critical topics, and some had forgotten what they had learned (Holland et al., 2014). The lack of consistency is concerning, considering that all military members are required to undergo sexual harassment and assault training, and such training is the cornerstone of military sexual assault prevention programs.

Job-gender context is yet another component impacting the prevalence of military sexual trauma (Fitzgerald et al., 1997). The job-gender context refers to the ratio of men to women in the workplace. As women have continued to enter the workforce, there are many career fields in which the job-gender context is almost equal: it is neither dominated by men nor women. However, there are many fields in which men still constitute the majority of the workforce, to include military professions. When men greatly outnumber women, as in the military, the prevalence of workplace sexual harassment and assault increases (Fitzgerald et al., 1997). Ensuring that women in the armed forces are treated equitably is crucial to promoting them to leadership positions where they can make real change. Working to balance the sex ratios and ensuring women have access to lead from the front by placing women in visible leadership positions can help reduce incidence of sexual harassment (Cortina & Berdahl, 2008).

Thriving and Reactivation

The thriving commitment trajectory is probably the most difficult to achieve, yet is the most beneficial for the organization. In a thriving trajectory, organizational commitment lessens after a psychological contract breach but increases beyond pre-breach levels, resulting in even higher levels of commitment than before. Solinger et al. (2016) note that in this scenario the employee's relationship with the employer will have actually improved, to the benefit of both parties involved. A reactivated commitment trajectory is one in which an individual experiences significantly lower organizational commitment immediately following a shock event or psychological contract breach, but rebounds to pre-breach levels of commitment after a period of time. In a sense, reactivation is the renewal of the initial psychological contract and requires that the offending party work to fulfill the original terms of the agreement.

In order to achieve either of these outcomes after a contract breach of sexual harassment or assault, an organization needs to re-assert their commitment to the employee. The contents of the psychological contract between the organization and employee would need to be either the same or better than the previous contract. Civilian organizations may have more leeway in this respect: the ability to renegotiate the terms of a psychological contract would be severely hindered by the bureaucratic red-tape present in the military. Switching jobs, promotions, and pay increases or bonuses that could be used as an incentive to stay in a civilian corporation are rarely, if ever, present in the military.

The best way for the military to reaffirm their commitment to the employee is by fully investigating the incident in a careful and considerate manner, ensuring that justice is swiftly served to the perpetrator. This also means that the military member should be taken care of, and reminded that they are an important part of the military community. Because of the high levels of commitment fostered in military organizations, the loss of a military career is more than the loss of a profession: it is the loss of close camaraderie and a unique lifestyle, and to be denied that can be utterly devastating. When the military has taken action against perpetrators of military sexual trauma, the effects are certain to be positive for the targeted individual and the bystanders both inside and outside of the military workforce. Those in the military are more likely to feel comfortable reporting, feel as though their concerns are heard and taken seriously, and are more likely to believe that justice will be served in their cases (Buchanan et al., 2014; Hulin et al., 1996).

Organizational climate surveys are another crucial tool to achieve thriving and reactivated commitment. Willness et al. (2007) found that organizational climate was the most important antecedent of workplace sexual harassment. If an organization has a negative climate where sexual harassment and assault is not taken seriously and where those who report are retaliated against, sexual harassment rates will rise alongside the other negative psychological and workplace outcomes related to sexual harassment (Bergman et al., 2002; Buchanan et al., 2014). The military has adopted the use of annual climate surveys in response to several high profile, systemic military sexual trauma incidents. These surveys, administered through the Defense Equal Opportunity Management Institute (DEOMI), can be used to measure organizational effectiveness and equal opportunity issues that may negatively impact unit climate. They can also be used to track the efficacy of current sexual harassment training initiatives and measure military sexual trauma incident rates. These confidential surveys can be crucial in analyzing and revamping organizational climate (DEOMI, 2018).

CONCLUSION

The development of strong commitment in the early stages of a service member's tenure with their branch of service helps them weather the storm of military sexual trauma from an organizational standpoint. When the organizational identity is most salient, targets of workplace harassment and assault are often willing to remain with and identify with the military if those in charge do their due diligence in investigating the case, prosecuting the perpetrator, and caring for the target. Building and maintaining high levels of organizational, unit, and/or team commitment over the course of a military career buffers the organization and individual from the negative impacts of low commitment after a psychological contract breach. While the examples and literature presented above have mainly focused on a military context, the lessons learned are applicable across a wide range of contexts, including public and private sector organizations.

REFERENCES

Akerlof, G. A., & Kranton, R. E. (2005). Identity and the economics of organizations. *Journal of Economic Perspectives, 19*(1), 9–32. https://doi.org/10.1257/0895330053147930

Allen, N. J. (2003). Organizational commitment in the military: A discussion of theory and practice. *Military Psychology, 15*(3), 237. https://doi.org/10.1207/S15327876MP1503_06

Allen, N. J., & Meyer, J. P. (1990). The measurement and antecedents of affective, continuance and normative commitment to the organization. *Journal of Occupational Psychology, 63*, 1–18. https://doi.org/10.1111/j.2044-8325.1990.tb00506.x

Andersson, L. M. (1996). Employee cynicism: An examination using a contract violation framework. *Human Relations, 49*, 1395–1418. https://doi.org/10.1177/001872679604901102

Andersson, L. M., & Bateman, T. S. (1997). Cynicism in the workplace: Some causes and effects. *Journal of Organizational Behavior, 18*(5), 449–469. https://doi.org/10.1002/(SICI)1099-1379(199709)18:5<449::AID-JOB808>3.0.CO;2-O

Araos, J. (2016, April 5). KUDOS educates military children. *Vandenberg Air Force Base News.* https://www.vandenberg.af.mil/News/Article-Display/Article/911973/kudos-educates-military-children/

Bal, P. M., De Lange, A. H., Jansen, P. G., & Van Der Velde, M. E. (2008). Psychological contract breach and job attitudes: A meta-analysis of age as a moderator. *Journal of Vocational Behavior, 72*(1), 143–158. https://doi.org/10.1016/j.jvb.2007.10.005

Bauer, T. N., & Erdogan, B. (2011). Organizational socialization: The effective onboarding of new employees. In S. Zedeck (Ed.), *APA handbook of industrial and organizational psychology* (Vol. 3, pp. 51–64). American Psychological Association.

Becker, T. E. (2016). Multiple foci of workplace commitments. In J. P. Meyer (Ed.), *Handbook of employee commitment* (pp. 43–55). Edward Elgar Publishing

Bergman, M. E., Langhout, R. D., Palmieri, P. A., Cortina, L. M., & Fitzgerald, L. F. (2002). The (un)reasonableness of reporting: Antecedents and consequences of reporting sexual harassment. *Journal of Applied Psychology, 87*(2), 230–242. https://doi.org/10.1037//0021-9010.87.2.230

Bourg, C., & Segal, M. W. (1999). The impact of family supportive policies and practices on organizational commitment to the Army. *Armed Forces & Society, 25*(4), 633–652. https://doi.org/10.1177/0095327X9902500406

Brennan, T. J. (2017, March 4). Hundreds of marines investigated for sharing photos of naked colleagues. *Reveal News.* https://www.revealnews.org/blog/hundreds-of-marines-investigated-for-sharing-photos-of-naked-colleagues/

Buchanan, N. T., Settles, I. H., Hall, A. T., & O'Connor, R. C. (2014). A review of organizational strategies for reducing sexual harassment: Insights from the US military. *Journal of Social Issues, 70*(4), 687–702. https://doi.org/10.1111/josi.12086

Chalabi, M. (2015, March 19). *What percentage of Americans have served in the military?* FiveThirtyEight. https://fivethirtyeight.com/features/what-percentage-of-americans-have-served-in-the-military/

Chu, D.S.C. (2004) *Collateral misconduct in sexual assault cases.* http://www.ncdsv.org/images/COLLATERALMISCONDUCT.pdf

Cole, M. S., & Bruch, H. (2006). Organizational identity strength, identification, and commitment and their relationships to turnover intention: Does organizational hierarchy matter? *Journal of Organizational Behavior, 27*(5), 585–605. https://doi.org/10.1002/job.378

Cortina, L. M., & Berdahl, J. L. (2008). Sexual harassment in organizations: A decade of research in review. In J. Barling & C. L. Cooper (Eds.) *Handbook of organizational behavior* (pp. 469-497). SAGE.

Cropanzano, R., & Mitchell, M. S. (2005). Social exchange theory: An interdisciplinary review. *Journal of Management, 31*(6), 874–900. https://doi.org/10.1177/0149206305279602

Dao, J. (2012, February 24). Branding a soldier with a 'personality disorder.' *The New York Times*. https://www.nytimes.com/2012/02/25/us/a-military-diagnosis-personality-disorder-is-challenged.html

Defense Equal Opportunity Management Institute. (2018, May 30). *Talking Paper on DEOCS 4.1*. https://www.deocs.net/DocDownloads/Talking-Paper-on-DEOCS-4_1-RMY.pdf

Department of Defense, Inspector General. (1993). *The Tailhook Report: The official inquiry into the events of Tailhook '91*. Tom Doherty Associates.

EEOC. (n.d.) Charges alleging sex-based harassment (charges filed with EEOC) FY 2010–FY 2017. https://www.eeoc.gov/eeoc/statistics/enforcement/sexual_harassment_new.cfm

Faley, R. H., Knapp, D. E., Kustis, G. A., & Dubois, C. L. (1999). Estimating the organizational costs of sexual harassment: The case of the US Army. *Journal of Business and Psychology, 13*(4), 461–484. https://doi.org/10.1023/A:1022987119277

Felch, D. (2013, May 31). *'Rebluing': Why do we say this?* http://www.af.mil/News/Commentaries/Display/Article/141239/rebluing-why-do-we-say-that/

Feldman, D. C. (1989). Socialization, resocialization, and training: Reframing the research agenda. In I. L. Goldstein, (Eds.), *Frontiers of industrial and organizational psychology:, The Jossey-Bass management series and The Jossey-Bass social and behavioral science series. Training and development in organizations* (pp. 376–416). Jossey-Bass.

Fitzgerald, L. F., Drasgow, F., Hulin, C. L., Gelfand, M. J., & Magley, V. J. (1997). Antecedents and consequences of sexual harassment in organizations: a test of an integrated model. *Journal of Applied Psychology, 82*(4), 578–589. https://doi.org/10.1037/0021-9010.82.4.578

Fontana, A., & Rosenheck, R. (1998). Focus on women: Duty-related and sexual stress in the etiology of PTSD among women veterans who seek treatment. *Psychiatric Services, 49*, 658–662. https://doi.org/10.1176/ps.49.5.658

Freyd, J. J. (1994). Betrayal trauma: Traumatic amnesia as an adaptive response to childhood abuse. *Ethics & Behavior, 4*(4), 307–329. https://doi.org/10.1207/s15327019eb0404_1

Gal, R. (1985). Commitment and obedience in the military: An Israeli case study. *Armed Forces & Society, 11*(4), 553–564. https://doi.org/10.1177/0095327X8501100405

Gellatly, I. R., Meyer, J. P., & Luchak, A. A. (2006). Combined effects of the three commitment components on focal and discretionary behaviors: A test of Meyer and Herscovitch's propositions. *Journal of Vocational Behavior, 69*(2), 331–345. https://doi.org/10.1016/j.jvb.2005.12.005

Government Accountability Office. (2018). *Military personnel: DOD needs to reevaluate fighter pilot workforce requirements* (GAO Report to the Committee on Armed Services, U.S. Senate, GAO-18-113). https://www.gao.gov/assets/700/691192.pdf

Griffith, J. (2009). After 9/11, what kind of reserve soldier? Considerations given to emerging demands, organizational orientation, and individual commitment. *Armed Forces & Society, 35*(2), 214–240. https://doi.org/10.1177/0095327X07312490

Hansen, S. D., & Griep, Y. (2016). Psychological contracts. In J. P. Meyer (Ed.), *Handbook of employee commitment* (pp. 119–134). Edward Elgar Publishing.

Harned, M. S., Ormerod, A. J., Palmieri, P. A., Collinsworth, L. L., & Reed, M. (2002). Sexual assault and other types of sexual harassment by workplace personnel: A comparison of antecedents and consequences. *Journal of Occupational Health Psychology*, 7(2), 174–188. http://dx.doi.org/10.1037/1076-8998.7.2.174

Himmelfarb, N., Yaeger, D., & Mintz, J. (2006). Posttraumatic stress disorder in female veterans with military and civilian sexual trauma. *Journal of Traumatic Stress, 19*(6), 837–846. https://doi.org/10.1002/jts.20163

Holland, K. J., Rabelo, V. C., & Cortina, L. M. (2014). Sexual assault training in the military: Evaluating efforts to end the "invisible war." *American Journal of Community Psychology, 54*(3–4), 289–303. https://doi.org/10.1007/s10464-014-9672-0

Hughes, L. W., & Palmer, D. K. (2007). An investigation of the effects of psychological contract and organization-based self-esteem on organizational commitment in a sample of permanent and contingent workers. *Journal of Leadership & Organizational Studies, 14*(2), 143–156. https://doi.org/10.1177/1071791907308052

Hulin, C. L., Fitzgerald, L. F., & Drasgow, F. (1996). Organizational influences on sexual harassment. In M. S. Stockdale (Ed.), *Women and work: A research and policy series, Vol. 5. Sexual harassment in the workplace: Perspectives, frontiers, and response strategies* (pp. 127–150). SAGE.

Ilies, R., Hauserman, N., Schwochau, S., & Stibal, J. (2003). Reported incidence rates of work-related sexual harassment in the United States: Using meta-analysis to explain reported rate disparities. *Personnel Psychology, 56*(3), 607–631. https://doi.org/10.1111/j.1744-6570.2003.tb00752.x

Jones, B. A. (2014, August 20). *The sexist Facebook movement the Marine Corps can't stop.* Task & Purpose. https://taskandpurpose.com/sexist-facebook-movement-marine-corps-cant-stop/

Kabins, A. H., Xu, X., Bergman, M. E., Berry, C. M., & Willson, V. L. (2016). A profile of profiles: A meta-analysis of the nomological net of commitment profiles. *Journal of Applied Psychology, 101*(6), 881. http://dx.doi.org/10.1037/apl0000091

Kam, C., Morin, A. J., Meyer, J. P., & Topolnytsky, L. (2016). Are commitment profiles stable and predictable? A latent transition analysis. *Journal of Management, 42*(6), 1462–1490. http://journals.sagepub.com/doi/abs/10.1177/0149206313503010

Keane, B. M. (2012). *'Every Marine is a rifleman' begins at recruit training.* http://www.tecom.marines.mil/News/NewsArticleDisplay/tabid/5055/Article/92579/every-marine-arifleman-begins-at-recruit-training.aspx.

Kheel, R. (2017, September 7). *Gillibrand: Military sexual assault 'as pervasive as ever.'* http://thehill.com/policy/defense/349672-dem-senator-military-sexual-assault-as-pervasive-as-ever

Koenig, S. (2015). DUSTWUN. *Serial* (Audio podcast). https://serialpodcast.org/season-two/1/dustwun/transcript

Liao, H., Joshi, A., & Chuang, A. (2004). Sticking out like a sore thumb: Employee dissimilarity and deviance at work. *Personnel Psychology*, *57*(4), 969–1000. https://doi.org/10.1111/j.1744-6570.2004.00012.x

Losey, S. (2017, August 25). Air Force ups monthly flight pay for officers, enlisted air crew. *Air Force Times*. https://www.airforcetimes.com/news/your-air-force/2017/08/25/air-force-ups-monthly-flight-pay-for-officers-enlisted-air-crew/

Martin, L., Rosen, L. N., Durand, D. B., Knudson, K. H., & Stretch, R. H. (2000). Psychological and physical health effects of sexual assaults and nonsexual traumas among male and female United States Army soldiers. *Behavioral Medicine*, *26*(1), 23–33.

Mathieu, J. E., & Zajac, D. M. (1990). A review and meta-analysis of the antecedents, correlates, and consequences of organizational commitment. *Psychological Bulletin*, *108*, 171–194. https://doi.org/10.1080/08964280009595750

Mattock, M.G., Hosek, J., Asch, B.J., & Karam, R. (2016). *Retaining U.S. Air Force pilots when the civilian demand for pilots is growing*. RAND Corporation. https://www.rand.org/content/dam/rand/pubs/research_reports/RR1400/RR1455/RAND_RR1455.pdf

McIntyre, J. (1997, January 31). *Pentagon brass 'disgusted' by Marine hazing ceremony*. CNN. http://www.cnn.com/US/9701/31/hazing/index.html

Meyer, J. P., & Allen, N. J. (1991). A three-component conceptualization of organizational commitment. *Human Resource Management Review*, *1*, 61–89. https://doi.org/10.1016/1053-4822(91)90011-Z

Meyer, J. P., & Allen, N. J. (1997). *Commitment in the workplace*. SAGE.

Meyer, J. P., Becker, T. E., & Van Dick, R. (2006). Social identities and commitments at work: Toward an integrative model. *Journal of Organizational Behavior*, *27*(5), 665–683. https://doi.org/10.1002/job.383

Meyer, J. P., & Herscovitch, L. (2001). Commitment in the workplace: Toward a general model. *Human Resource Management Review*, *11*(3), 299–326. https://doi.org/10.1016/S1053-4822(00)00053-X

Meyer, J. P., & Morin, A. J. (2016). A person-centered approach to commitment research: Theory, research, and methodology. *Journal of Organizational Behavior*, *37*(4), 584–612. https://doi.org/10.1002/job.2085

Meyer, J. P., Stanley, D. J., Herscovitch, L., & Topolnytsky, L. (2002). Affective, continuance, and normative commitment to the organization: A meta-analysis of antecedents, correlates, and consequences. *Journal of Vocational Behavior*, *61*(1), 20–52. https://doi.org/10.1006/jvbe.2001.1842

Meyer, J. P., Stanley, L. J., & Vandenberg, R. J. (2013). A person-centered approach to the study of commitment. *Human Resource Management Review*, *23*(2), 190–202. https://doi.org/10.1016/j.hrmr.2012.07.007

Morral, A. R., Gore, K. L., & Schell, T. L. (2015). *Sexual assault and sexual harassment in the US Military: Estimates for Department of Defense Service Members from the 2014 RAND Military Workplace Study* (Vol. 2). RAND National Defense Research Institute: https://www.rand.org/pubs/research_reports/RR870z2-1.html

Morrison, E. W., & Robinson, S. L. (1997). When employees feel betrayed: A model of how psychological contract violation develops. *Academy of Management Review, 22*, 226–256. https://doi.org/10.5465/amr.1997.9707180265

Moskos, C. C., Jr. (1977). From institution to occupation: Trends in military organization. *Armed Forces & Society, 4*(1), 41–50. https://doi.org/10.1177/0095327X7700400103

Ng, T. W. H., Feldman, D. C., & Lam, S. K. (2010). Psychological contract breaches, organizational commitment, and innovation-related behaviors: A latent growth modeling approach. *Journal of Applied Psychology, 95*(4), 744–751. doi:10.1037/a0018804

O'Connell, C. E., & Korabik, K. (2000). Sexual harassment: The relationship of personal vulnerability, work context, perpetrator status, and type of harassment to outcomes. *Journal of Vocational Behavior, 56*(3), 299–329. https://doi.org/10.1006/jvbe.1999.1717

O'Leary-Kelly, A. M., Bowes-Sperry, L., Bates, C. A., & Lean, E. R. (2009). Sexual harassment at work: A decade (plus) of progress. *Journal of Management, 35*(3), 503–536. https://doi.org/10.1177/0149206308330555

O'Reilly, C. A., & Chatman, J. (1986). Organizational commitment and psychological attachment: The effects of compliance, identification, and internalization on prosocial behavior. *Journal of Applied Psychology, 71*(3), 492–499.

Porter, L. W., Steers, R. M., Mowday, R. T., & Boulian, P. V. (1974). Organizational commitment, job satisfaction, and turnover among psychiatric technicians. *Journal of Applied Psychology, 59*, 603–609. http://dx.doi.org/10.1037/h0037335

Pryor, J. B., Giedd, J. L., & Williams, K. B. (1995). A social psychological model for predicting sexual harassment. *Journal of Social Issues, 51*(1), 69–84. https://doi.org/10.1111/j.1540-4560.1995.tb01309.x

Pryor, J. B., LaVite, C. M., & Stoller, L. M. (1993). A social psychological analysis of sexual harassment: The person/situation interaction. *Journal of Vocational Behavior, 42*(1), 68–83. http://dx.doi.org/10.1006/jvbe.1993.1005

Raja, U., Johns, G., & Ntalianis, F. (2004). The impact of personality on psychological contracts. *Academy of Management Journal, 47*(3), 350–367. https://doi.org/10.5465/20159586

Randall, D. M., Fedor, D. B., & Longenecker, C. O. (1990). The behavioral expression of organizational commitment. *Journal of Vocational Behavior, 36*(2), 210–224. https://doi.org/10.1016/0001-8791(90)90028-Z

Richardson, K. P. (1977). Polliwogs and shellbacks: An analysis of the equator crossing ritual. *Western Folklore, 36*(2), 154–159. doi:10.2307/1498967

Robinson, S. L. (1996). Trust and breach of the psychological contract. *Administrative Science Quarterly, 41*, 574–599. doi:10.2307/2393868

Robinson, S. L., & Bennett, R. J. (1995). A typology of deviant workplace behaviors: A multidimensional scaling study. *Academy of Management Journal, 38*(2), 555–572. https://doi.org/10.5465/256693

Robinson, S. L., & Morrison, E. W. (1995). Psychological contracts and OCB: The effect of unfulfilled obligations on civic virtue behavior. *Journal of Organizational Behavior, 16*(3), 289–298. https://doi.org/10.1002/job.4030160309

Robinson, S. L., & Morrison, E. W. (2000). The development of psychological contract breach and violation: A longitudinal study. *Journal of Organizational Behavior,*

21(5), 525–546. https://doi.org/10.1002/1099-1379(200008)21:5<525::AID-JOB40>3.0.CO;2-T

Robinson, S. L., & Rousseau, D. M. (1994). Violating the psychological contract: Not the exception but the norm. *Journal of Organizational Behavior, 15*(3), 245–259. https://doi.org/10.1002/job.4030150306

Rousseau, D. M. (1989). Psychological and implied contracts in organizations. *Employee Responsibilities and Rights Journal, 2*, 121–139. https://doi.org/10.1007/BF01384942

Rhoades, L., Eisenberger, R., & Armeli, S. (2001). Affective commitment to the organization: The contribution of perceived organizational support. *Journal of Applied Psychology, 86*, 825–836. https://doi.org/10.1037/0021-9010.86.5.825

SAPR. (2015). *Commander's 30-day checklist for unrestricted reports of sexual assault.* http://www.sapr.mil/public/docs/policy/toolkit/Commander_Checklist_for_Unrestricted_Reports_20150122.pdf

Schneider, K. T., Swan, S., & Fitzgerald, L. F. (1997). Job-related and psychological effects of sexual harassment in the workplace: Empirical evidence from two organizations. *Journal of Applied Psychology, 82*(3), 401–415. http://dx.doi.org/10.1037/0021-9010.82.3.401

Shore, L. M., Tetrick, L. E., Lynch, P., & Barksdale, K. (2006). Social and economic exchange: Construct development and validation. *Journal of Applied Social Psychology, 36*(4), 837–867. https://doi.org/10.1111/j.0021-9029.2006.00046.x

Shore, L. M., & Wayne, S. J. (1993). Commitment and employee behavior: Comparison of affective commitment and continuance commitment with perceived organizational support. *Journal of Applied Psychology, 78*(5), 774–780. http://dx.doi.org/10.1037/0021-9010.78.5.774

Skarlicki, D. P., & Folger, R. (1997). Retaliation in the workplace: The roles of distributive, procedural, and interactional justice. *Journal of Applied Psychology, 82*(3), 434–443. http://dx.doi.org/10.1037/0021-9010.82.3.434

Smith, C. P., & Freyd, J. J. (2013). Dangerous safe havens: Institutional betrayal exacerbates sexual trauma. *Journal of Traumatic Stress, 26*(1), 119–124. https://doi.org/10.1002/jts.21778

Smith, R. T., & True, G. (2014). Warring identities: Identity conflict and the mental distress of American veterans of the wars in Iraq and Afghanistan. *Society and Mental Health, 4*(2), 147–161. https://doi.org/10.1177/2156869313512212

Snow, S. (2018, March 1). *Seven marines court-martialed in the wake of Marines United scandal.* Marine Corps Times. https://www.marinecorpstimes.com/news/your-marine-corps/2018/03/01/seven-marines-court-martialed-in-wake-of-marines-united-scandal/

Solinger, O. N., Hofmans, J., Bal, P. M., & Jansen, P. G. (2016). Bouncing back from psychological contract breach: How commitment recovers over time. *Journal of Organizational Behavior, 37*(4), 494–514. https://doi.org/10.1002/job.2047

Stander, V.A., & Thomsen, C.J. (2016). Sexual harassment and assault in the U.S. military: A review of policy and research trends. *Military Medicine, 181*, 20–27. https://doi.org/10.7205/MILMED-D-15-00336

Street, A. E., Gradus, J. L., Stafford, J., & Kelly, K. (2007). Gender differences in experiences of sexual harassment: Data from a male-dominated environment. *Journal of Consulting and Clinical Psychology, 75*(3), 464–474. http://psycnet.apa.org/doi/10.1037/0022-006X.75.3.464

Tajfel, H., & Turner, J. C. (1979). An integrative theory of intergroup conflict. In W. G. Austin & S. Worchel (Eds.), *The social psychology of intergroup relations* (pp. 33–47). Brooks/Cole.

Tannenbaum, S. I., Mathieu, J. E., Salas, E., & Cannon-Bowers, J. A. (1991). Meeting trainees' expectations: The influence of training fulfillment on the development of commitment, self-efficacy, and motivation. *Journal of Applied Psychology, 76*(6), 759–769. http://psycnet.apa.org/doi/10.1037/0021-9010.76.6.759

Tepper, B. J., Henle, C. A., Lambert, L. S., Giacalone, R. A., & Duffy, M. K. (2008). Abusive supervision and subordinates' organization deviance. *Journal of Applied Psychology, 93*(4), 721–732. http://psycnet.apa.org/doi/10.1037/0021-9010.93.4.721

Tomprou, M., Rousseau, D. M., & Hansen, S. D. (2015). The psychological contracts of violation victims: A post-violation model. *Journal of Organizational Behavior, 36*(4), 561–581. https://doi.org/10.1002/job.1997

Turnley, W. H., & Feldman, D. C. (2000). Re-examining the effects of psychological contract violations: unmet expectations and job dissatisfaction as mediators. *Journal of Organizational Behavior, 21*(1), 25–42. https://doi.org/10.1002/(SICI)1099-1379(200002)21:1%3C25::AID-JOB2%3E3.0.CO;2-Z

United States Army Recruiting Command. (2013). *Frequently asked questions about Army recruiting—Army enlistment.* http://www.usarec.army.mil/hq/apa/faqs.htm#costper

Veterans Affairs. (2018). *Military sexual trauma.* https://www.ptsd.va.gov/public/types/violence/military-sexual-trauma-general.asp

Willness, C. R., Steel, P., & Lee, K. (2007). A meta-analysis of the antecedents and consequences of workplace sexual harassment. *Personnel Psychology, 60*(1), 127–162. https://doi.org/10.1111/j.1744-6570.2007.00067.x

Winerip, M. (2013, May 13). Revisiting the military's Tailhook scandal. *The New York Times.* https://www.nytimes.com/2013/05/13/booming/revisiting-the-militarys-tailhook-scandal-video.html.

Zhao, H. A. O., Wayne, S. J., Glibkowski, B. C., & Bravo, J. (2007). The impact of psychological contract breach on work-related outcomes: a meta-analysis. *Personnel Psychology, 60*, 647–680. https://doi.org/10.1111/j.1744-6570.2007.00087.x

CHAPTER 4

"POUR ENCOURAGER LES AUTRES"

Punishment as a Signal of Organizational Decision Frames

Daniel J. Svyantek
Auburn University

Voltaire, in *Candide*, provides a discussion of an interesting historical example of military discipline in the 18th century British Navy between two characters in the novel. One character notes that in England, it pays to shoot an admiral from time to encourage the other admirals (Norris, 2011). On first reading, this seems to be fantastic fiction. Remarkably, however, this appears to actually have happened for the British Navy during the Seven Years War between England and France. Voltaire's characters, therefore, are referring to actual history.

In 1756, during the Seven Years War, Admiral John Byng was in command of a British fleet charged with protecting the island of Minorca against the incursions of the French (Norris, 2011). The British fleet arrived to find the French were besieging the fort controlling the approaches to Minorca. Admiral Byng, seeing this, intended to relieve the siege. Before the British

Organizations Behaving Badly:
Destructive Behavior and Corrective Responses, pp. 59–88

could land troops to relieve the fort, however, the British fleet spotted the approach of a French fleet. Admiral Byng ordered the British fleet to attack the French fleet. The British fleet sailed to confront the French fleet using a traditional fleet formation of the British Navy that was based on successful sea battles in the past. The French fleet, due to its position, had an initial advantage and was able to damage the leading ship of the British fleet without suffering initial damage. Moreover, the British fleet, due to the formation they were in, was unable to do much damage to the ships of the French fleet as the battle progressed. The French fleet eventually withdrew from the battle and the area around Minorca. The British fleet then had entered a period of 4 days of inaction as Byng tried to decide on what to do. He did not attempt to relieve the siege of the fort or pursue the French fleet.

Byng was subsequently relieved of command (Norris, 2011). Popular opinion in England raged against Byng's actions. The strength of this reaction was a factor in the decision by the Royal Navy to court-martial Admiral Byng. The court-martial raised several charges against Byng. All but one charge, the vague charge of not having done his utmost, were dismissed.

Basically, this charge may be interpreted as Byng should have done more in the situation. The charge did not specify what he should have done. This charge, while vague, carried the death penalty (Norris, 2011). Public opinion was so against Byng that no clemency appeals were supported by the King of England. The execution of Admiral Byng was carried out on March 14, 1757.

As noted above, Voltaire noted, that such a punishment was intended as a message for others observing the punishment. The phrase, *pour encourager les autres*, was coined to describe this type of organizational action. The phrase, according to the *Merriam-Webster* (2019) dictionary is defined as meaning a punitive action (e.g., executing a person) taken against an individual as a warning to others. The primary purpose of such a punishment is to change the behavior of observers.

This approach to punishment seems to work. Kinkel and Sandbrook (2018) propose that execution of Admiral Bing played a key role in changing the course of the Seven Years War for the British. This is because the execution of Admiral Byng led other leaders to act differently when confronting subsequent naval situations against the French. The purpose of such a punishment is not necessarily a desired punishment for the actor (for example, few in the Royal Navy supported the execution of Admiral Byng (Norris, 2011)). Such punishment's social purpose—the use of this punishment is to show others in the social system (a) behaviors not supported by the social system and/ or (b) to signal to the observers the appropriate behaviors for the future if similar situations arise again is important in changing organizational behavior. In effect, such actions are organizational change interventions signaling changes in the organizational context of the organization taking such actions.

The remainder of this chapter will investigate the effect of such *pour encourager les autres* actions in organizations. First, the chapter provides a more recent example of this type of action, and subsequent changes in the behavior of members of a social system using the United States Navy as the social system of interest. Second, the chapter Funder's (2001, 2006) approach to understanding and predicting behavior of individuals within a social system will be described. The analysis of this situation will be shown as an excellent example for understanding Funder's approach and this situation. Second, a discussion of the importance of social contexts in supporting behaviors and behavioral styles within organizations will be provided and the role of punishment as an organizational signal for change will be discussed. Third, a proposed mechanism through which immediate decision contexts affect individuals in ambiguous decision environments, and the effects of organizational reward systems (here punishment) may alter decisions will be provided. Finally, the chapter provides conclusions and practical implications.

USS STARK AND THE USS VINCENNES: A MODERN EXAMPLE OF *POUR ENCOURAGER LES AUTRES*?

The U.S. Navy began an active policing of the Persian Gulf during the 1980s. This focus continues today. During the 1980s, there were several incidents threatening, or damaging, U.S. naval ships (Arkin, 1989). First, the USS Stark was struck by two cruise missiles fired by an Iraqi jet on May 17, 1987. Second, the USS Samuel Roberts struck a mine. Third, the USS Vincennes shot down an Iran Air flight, killing 290 civilians, on July 3, 1988.

The remainder of this portion of the chapter centers on the USS Stark and the USS Vincennes incidents because of their underlying similarity. Each involves the captain of a U.S. naval ship making a decision to protect or not protect his vessel from incoming airplanes. Each captain faced uncertainty based on information being received and processed about approaching airplanes. These airplanes may or may not constitute a threat to each ship. The final decision in each situation required the captain to decide whether to fire missiles at the incoming airplanes and destroy the potential threat to each vessel.

The USS Stark began receiving information about a potential threat from an identified, incoming Iraqi military fighter jet on May 17, 1987 (Halloran, 1988). Information was received in time for the captain of the USS Stark to take defensive action. This action would have required firing on the incoming fighter jet in a nonwar situation. The threat evaluation, however, for this fighter was not seen as high. The captain and other officers decided that the incoming jet was not hostile, and no action was taken until too late. The fighter subsequently fired two Exocet missiles at the USS Stark (Wilson, 1987). Both missiles hit the USS Stark and 37 sailors were killed. The U.S. Navy took action against the captain (and other officers) of the U.S. Stark within a month. The captain was relieved of command of the USS Stark (as of June 19, 1987) (Wilson, 1987). In July 1987, the captain was allowed to retire from the U.S. Navy after being reprimanded and censured by the U.S. Navy (Moore, 1987) without a formal court-martial.

The USS Vincennes tracked an incoming Iranian airliner on July 3, 1988 (Halloran, 1988). In this case, based on the information received, Captain Rogers and his officers identified the civilian airliner as a hostile fighter. The USS Vincennes provided a verbal warning to warn the airliner away. When the airliner did not change course, a missile was fired. The missile destroyed the airliner and all on the airliner were killed. The consequences of this action for Captain Rogers were much different than those received by Captain Brindel. Captain Rogers was honored by the U.S. Navy and received medals for his service in the Persian Gulf (although the citations did not mention the downing of the Iranian airliner Moore, 1990).

Funder (2001, 2006) proposed that the understanding and prediction of behaviors exhibited by individuals requires that (a) behavior in question be defined; (b) the individual differences of the actors relevant for the behavior in question be understood; and (c) the contextual differences for actors be defined. Interpreting, and predicting, behavior of individuals requires understanding of all three factors. This approach to understanding behavior in context seems to be particularly relevant for understanding the actions of the captains of the USS Stark and USS Vincennes. Moreover, in this case, Funder's model shows the critical importance of understanding the context for behavior.

First, the basic behavior in question for both captains is the same. The action was the firing of a defensive missile at an incoming potential threat. Each captain faced a decision to take this defensive action or not take this defensive action based on his understanding of incoming information in an ambiguous situation.

Second, each of these captains would have had a long period of socialization (20 plus years) into the culture of the U.S. Navy. This would lead them to be similar in their abilities and other individual differences relevant to a successful climbing of the career ladder to the command a ship. The two captains of these ships, Captain Glenn Brindel (USS Stark) and Captain Will Rogers (USS Vincennes) were both experienced and capable seamen (Halloran, 1988). Captain Brindel, for example, was on the "fast track" in his naval career (Moore, 1987) before the USS Stark incidents. The common experiences of the captains, moreover, would have helped them integrate the organizational culture of the U.S. Navy. This enculturation would have provided the captains with the general information necessary for performing as a naval officer in most situations through organizational processes as the attraction-selection-attrition (ASA) model and person-organization fit. For this situation, the macro-context is of interest because of the influence of this context on individuals across careers would have made the two captains very similar in their approaches to command and problem-solving. This macro-context is the organizational culture of an organization and is critical in understanding general patterns of behavior.

Finally, however, there is the immediate context in which the actual behavior occurs. This is a primary area of difference, and potentially similarity, for the two situations. The behaviors of the two captains illustrate the ambiguity for naval captains during this period in the Persian Gulf (Halloran, 1988). It has been hypothesized that one of the primary issues faced by both captains was that whatever behavior they chose might be the wrong one (Moore, 1987). This was due to the uncertain nature of the rules of engagement for taking defensive action by the U.S. Navy in the Persian Gulf at this time. This situation reflects the immediate decision environment of the Captains Brindel and Rogers and highlights the way organizational reward and punishment systems support patterns of behavior.

The next section will introduce two macro-contextual variables, organizational culture, and organizational climate, which influence behaviors in organizations. Second, a discussion of how individuals within organizations come to be similar will be provided through enculturation into organizational cultures will be discussed. Finally, the role of organizational climate in adaptive organizational behavior and the use of punishment to alter behavior will be evaluated.

ORGANIZATIONAL CONTEXTS AND INDIVIDUAL BEHAVIOR

Organizational culture may be defined by a set of shared values and norms, held by employees, which guides employees' interactions with peers, management, and clients/ customers (Morgan, 1998). *Organizational climate* is more behaviorally oriented in that climates for safety or service, for example, may be found in the workplace (Schneider, 2000). These climates, for example, might represent the specific patterns of interactions and behaviors that support safety or service in the organization. Taken together, these variables help define the context in which workplace behavior occurs. We will address similarities and differences for these two constructs.

Organizational Culture

Organizational culture has been defined in a variety of ways. It has been defined as (a) view culture as the dominant values espoused by an organization (Deal & Kennedy, 1982); and (b) the philosophy that guides organizational policy (Ouchi, 1981; Pascale & Athos, 1981). These definitions tap into parts of the essence of organizational culture, yet they do not capture the full picture of organizational culture because they do not provide a multidimensional, multilevel definition of organizational culture (Nahavandi & Malekzadeh, 1988).

Schein's (1985) model of the three levels of organizational culture is a multidimensional, multilevel definition of culture. First, the most superficial or visible level of culture is artifacts and creations: These represent the physical and social environment of the social situation. The second level of culture is values, norms, and attitudes, or a sense of what "ought to be." The first two levels may be analyzed by a third-party observer. For example, artifacts may signal the real importance of different practices in the organization. For example, consider two organizations espousing the value of their employees to the company. In Organization 1, employee parking is based on first come-first served. No employee at any level of the organization has a reserved parking spot. In Organization 2, the managers and supervisors all have reserved parking spots which are closer to the work areas than the parking for lower-level employees. In which organization are employees really valued? Based on this single artifact, the normal observer would say Organization 1. These two levels have a reciprocal event across time. Change in values may lead to change in artifacts, or vice versa.

Finally, after time and experience in the organization, organizational members acquire the deepest level of organizational culture. These are the unconscious, automatic assumptions uniformly held by all members of the culture. It is these unconscious assumptions which make up the true culture of an organization. Organizational culture, therefore, is the antecedent of other organization-level variables such as organizational climate in most cases.

Schein (1985) proposed that organizational founder(s) are the primary source(s) of the values, which define organizational culture. These values, in turn, are the primary guides for the later development of organizational structure, organizational climates and organizational design as the organization matures. Organizational culture, once established by the founder(s), is maintained over time through organizational socialization practices to assimilate newcomers into the organization.

Therefore, organizational culture may be highly resistant to change and "frozen" in a sense that the assumptions and beliefs established by the founder(s) are maintained although change may be required to improve organizational effectiveness. Organizational culture may be so embedded in the people, processes, and relationships that change is resisted even as the organizational culture ceases to be relevant in a changing environment (Schein, 1985). Barney (1986) described how organizational culture change efforts may fail even when economic performance would increase. Maladaptive behaviors exhibited by individual members of the organization will continue without strong signals of supported, directional change by the organization.

A major reason for the formation of organizational culture is the creation of social order (Trice & Beyer, 1993). Organizational culture allows recurrent behavior patterns among people to develop within organizations. These patterns form the basis of predictable interactions within an organization. Organizational culture provides employees with the contextual information necessary to be successful members of the company to which they belong. Namenwirth and Weber (1987) propose that culture serves four purposes for any social group. These purposes define (1) what it means to be a member of the group; (2) social and economic justice within the group; (3) how the elements of the group are organized to produce a socially "good" group; and (4) how the group makes the materials or services it was formed to produce.

Svyantek and colleagues (Brown & Svyantek, 2001; Svyantek, 1997; Svyantek & Brown, 2000a; Svyantek & Brown, 2000b; Svyantek & Brown; 2001; Svyantek & DeShon, 1993; and Svyantek & Snell, 1999) have proposed that organizational culture has two general functions based on Namenwirth and Weber's (1987) description of the purposes of culture. Namenwirth and Weber's first three purposes are closely linked to how a social group integrates individual members in the social system. These three purposes provide group members with information on what are the valued behaviors within a social situation. This is the integration function of culture (Svyantek, 1997; Svyantek & Brown, 2000a). The integration function represents the core values defining what it means to be a member of the organization. It is these core values which are transmitted across generations of organizational members through organizational processes related to selection, socialization, and reward practices of an organization. This may be considered the "genotype" of the organization. This allows organizations to maintain their core values across time and environmental change. For example, consider the Roman Catholic Church where the core values (e.g., only males may be priests) of the church have lasted for centuries. It is these values which are passed on to new generations of organizational members.

Organizations, however, may need to adapt to changes in the environment for survival purposes. This is the adaptation function of culture (Svyantek, 1997; Svyantek & Brown, 2000a). This function may be thought of as the phenotype of organization. The adaptation function of organizational culture provides the organization with the flexibility to adapt to environmental changes. However, these changes are less fixed in the culture and do not necessarily impact the integration function of the organizational culture (Svyantek, 1997; Svyantek & Brown, 2000). For example, the Roman Catholic Church began having services in the native language of the country instead of Latin in the 1960s. However, the basic patriarchal nature of the core values of the church did not change because of the change in language.

The adaptation function is more plastic than the integration function. But this means that organizational adaptive functions are independent of the core values of the organization and may be copied by other organization. Svyantek and Brown (2000b) show this using the example of the production of the minivan by the automobile industry. Organizations were able to copy and create a popular minivan (adaptive function) no matter the core values of the automobile manufacturer. This means that the integration function and adaptation function of the culture may not be directly related and changes in one function do not necessarily lead to changes in the other (Svyantek, 1997; Svyantek & Brown, 2000a).

Organizational culture, therefore, is the antecedent of other organization-level variables. Organizational culture is maintained over time through organizational socialization practices to assimilate newcomers into the organization. Therefore, organizational culture may be highly resistant to change and "frozen" in a sense that the assumptions and beliefs established by the founder(s) are maintained although change may be required to improve organizational effectiveness. Organizational culture may be so embedded in the people, processes and relationships that change is resisted even as the organizational culture ceases to be relevant in a changing environment (Schein, 1985). However, such an organization may still change in the adaptive function of its culture and survive for at least some time.

Two organizational processes are relevant for understanding how the organizational culture comes to be learned and used by organizational members. These are person-organization fit and the attraction-selection-attrition model. These will be discussed in the next section.

Organizational Processes and the Creation of Organizational Culture

Person-Organization Fit. Person-environment fit is a concept which impacts organizational behavior and organizational performance. There are two primary forms of person-environment fit (Kristof, 1996) to be considered in human resource practices which may have legal implications for a company. These are person-job fit and person-organization fit.

Person-job (PJ) fit is concerned with the degree to which there is a match between an employee's skills and abilities and the requirements of the job the employee holds (Kristof, 1996). The better the match, the more likely the employee is to be a successful employee. As this match decreases and employees do not have the needed skills and abilities to perform the job, employees tend to be frustrated and dissatisfied. This leads to decreases in both individual and organizational performance. This concept of fit is consistent with traditional approaches to human resource practices (e.g., selection and performance evaluation). Defining person-job fit is done in traditional ways by matching the needs of job analyses to the knowledges, skills, and abilities of applicants.

Person-organization (PO) fit is concerned with the degree to which there is a match between employee characteristics and the characteristics of the organization (e.g., organizational culture) in which the employee works (Kristoff, 1996). The better the match, the more likely the employee is to be a successful employee. For example, some organizations value teamwork and some organizations value individual accomplishment. Individuals with a high need for individual accomplishment will have good fit with an organization valuing individual accomplishment: However, their fit will be poor in an organization valuing teamwork. As this match decreases and employee characteristics and values do not reflect organizational characteristics, employees tend to be frustrated and dissatisfied. This leads to decreases in both individual and organizational performance.

Person-organization (PO) fit has been shown to be related to a number of organizational variables including (1) job choice decisions by organizational applicants (Cable & Judge, 1996); (2) organizational attraction of applicants (Judge & Cable, 1997); (3) selection decisions made by recruitment interviewers (Cable & Judge, 1997); (4) employee job satisfaction, job tenure and career success (Bretz & Judge, 1994); and (5) employee's level of task and organizational citizenship performance (Goodman & Svyantek, 1999).

PO fit is the primary mechanism through which individuals and organizations match values, norms, and beliefs. Person-organization fit is defined as "the congruence between patterns of organizational values and patterns of individual values, defined here as what an individual values in an organization, such as being team-oriented or innovative" (Chatman, 1991, p. 459). The emphasis here is on the match of an individual's values, when considered along with the value system in a specific organizational culture, and the potential effects that this match (or lack of match) has on that individual's subsequent behavior and attitudes in the company. The process by which person-organization fit may come to maintain an organizational culture across time; influence organizational human resource practices; and affect employee behavior is illustrated in the ASA model (Schneider, 1987a, 1987b; Schneider et al., 1995). This model will be discussed in the next section.

Attraction-Selection- Attrition Model. Schneider (1987b) proposed that "attributes of people, not the nature of the external environment, or organizational technology, or organizational structure, are the fundamental determinants of organizational behavior" (i.e., "the people make the place") (p. 437). The attraction-selection-attrition (ASA) framework is a mechanism for explaining homogeneity of organizational level variables such as organizational culture found in organizations. Schneider (1987a) stated that this homogeneity is due to three main processes. First, it occurs because people are attracted to places that they prefer (attraction). People will seek out organizational environments in which they are comfortable being a member. The primary human resource practice affected by this is recruitment and there are potential legal implications for organizations here. Second, homogeneity results from people being selected into settings to which they are perceived to be compatible (selection). Organizations tend to select certain individuals who appear to fit with those already there. The primary human resource practice affected by this is selection and there are potential legal implications for organizations here. Third, if people manage to enter an environment that is not a fit for them, they will tend to leave it (attrition) or the organization may terminate them. The behaviors exhibited by individuals with lack of fit may come to be dysfunctional and hinder their individual, or the organization's performance (Svyantek & Brown, 2001). The primary human resource practice affected by this is termination and there are potential legal implications for organizations here.

This model been supported empirically. For example, Schein and Diamonte (1988) found a relationship between three different personality variables and organizational characteristics. People who rated themselves as high on a personality characteristic were more likely to be attracted to an organization that was described as reflecting that characteristic. Similarly, it was found that organizational climate information and personality variables interact in a recruitment situation (Furlong & Svyantek, 1998). Personality variables were found to prime individuals to perceive and select organizational climates in which they will have a high probability of succeeding.

Schneider's ASA framework indicates that particular kinds of people are attracted to certain settings, and those who fit are not as likely to leave the organization. Thus, the ASA framework suggests there will be a restriction in range of individual differences in organizations (i.e., as compared with the general population). This restriction of range results in an organization of people who will also be very similar in behavior, experiences, orientations, feelings and reactions and creates a relatively homogenous group of individuals. This homogeneity, in turn, helps maintain the organizational culture across time. However, it also means that, for those employees joining the organization and exhibiting different patterns of behavior, there may be negative human resources consequences for the employee. This in turn means that there will be potential legal implications for the organization using PO fit in their human resource practices.

Therefore, as noted earlier, the two captains within the USS Stark and USS Vincennes examples are very similar in the both their respective knowledges, abilities and skills and in the norms, beliefs, and values they subscribed to as officers in the U.S. Navy. Person-organization fit and the ASA model operate to create individuals enculturated for similarity within the integration function for organization culture proposed by Svyantek and Brown (2000a). However, there must be some way for organizations and organizational members to adapt to changes in environmental features. These adaptations need not violate the integration function for an organization. The construct of organizational climate is an important one for understanding potential differences in behavior across time and environments. Changes here allow adaptations. The role of organizational climate in organizations is discussed in the next section.

Organizational Climate and the Adaptive Function

Organizational Climate. As noted earlier, organizational climate is more behaviorally oriented in that climates for safety or service, for example, may be found in the workplace (Schneider, 2000). These climates, for example, might represent the specific patterns of interactions and behaviors that support safety or service in the organization. These climates will be created through, and supported by, more specific rules and procedures, and through such human resource practices as the organizational reward system. Schneider (2000) provided a framework for reconciling organizational culture and organizational climate. Organizational climate, according to Schneider, represents the descriptions of the things that happen to employees of an organization. Organizational climate is behaviorally oriented in that climates for safety (cf., Zohar, 1980) or service (Schneider et al., 1998), for example, may be found in the workplace. These climates represent the patterns of interactions and behaviors that support safety or service in the organization. Organizational climate, therefore, is a description of what occurs within the organization. However, when employees are questioned on why these patterns exist, deeper levels of insight are found. The question of why is answered with stories and myths that describe life in the organization and this defines organizational culture. Organizational culture, therefore, is an antecedent of constructs such as organizational climate (Cooke & Szumal, 2000).

There is a reciprocal relationship between behavioral outcomes, organizational climate and organizational culture (Svyantek & Bott, 2006; Svyantek & Brown, 2002). Therefore, changes in organizational culture may cause organizational climate change, leading to changes in the patterns of behaviors and interactions defined by organizational climate. However, the opposite change direction is possible. Enough changes in organizational climates may lead to changes in organizational culture (Schneider, 2002). Therefore, feedback loops exist between organizational culture and organizational climate across time.

However, as noted earlier, the primary reason for investigating organizational climate is to understand how changes occur in such specific practices to allow the organization to adapt to a changing environment, The USS Stark and USS Vincennes example illustrates how the use of the organizational reward system may lead to changes in organizational climate. Punishment in organizations is discussed in the next section.

Punishment as a Social Signal. Punishment may be used for four primary reasons (Trevino, 1992). These four reasons are to signal to observers (a) so that social norms of the group are upheld; (b) the appropriate (or inappropriate) behaviors expected of observers; (c) for the deterrence of misconduct; and (d) to create a perception of the fairness and justness (high or low) of the organization in enforcing rules.

Punishment within organizations is a social event (Trevino, 1992; Butterfield, et al., 2005). Punishment actions within organizations have actors (punishee and punisher) and observers. Punishment's effects on observers support the proposal that there is a reciprocal relationship between organizational culture and organizational climate. For example, in high trust social systems, the use of punishment may against free riders is seen as appropriate by observers. They see the punishment as equitable because it brings cheaters back into line with the norms of the social system (Bailliet & Van Lange, 2013). In low trust social systems this effect does not occur.

The primary difference for the captain of the USS Vincennes, relative to the captain of the USS Stark, is the knowledge of the aftermath for the USS Stark's captain. The USS Stark's captain was censured by the U.S. Navy. He was allowed to resign ending a career path on the fast track to higher levels of command in the US Navy. This aftermath, while not executing the individual as Admiral Byng was, is hypothesized as providing a *pour encourager les autres* example for all other naval officers who might confront such a decision situation. In effect, the decision-making climate of the U.S. Navy was changed by this aftermath. The next section will discuss the manner in which observed change affects the decisions made by individuals in similar situations.

ORGANIZATIONAL CLIMATE AND DECISION-MAKING

The hypothesized mechanism for the effects of the USS Stark aftermath on subsequent officers in similar situation is based on the Tversky and Kahneman model of decision-making. First, this basic model will be discussed. Second, a proposed mechanism by which organizational punishment practices may impact will be described. Finally, the way change in the decision environment affects individuals' with different cognitive frames will be investigated.

The Tversky and Kahneman model of decision making. Decision framing occurs when the manner in which objective information is presented to a decision-maker alters the decisions made by that decision-maker (Kahneman & Tversky, 1979; Tversky & Kahneman, 1981). Decision frames represent the decision-maker's conceptualization of the acts, outcomes and probabilities associated with making a particular choice. Tversky and Kahneman's (1981) research has focused primarily on the effects of gain and loss decision frames. In this research subjects are presented with one of two sets of two options. One set of options is framed in terms of possible gains while the second is framed in terms of possible losses. The two options in each set have equal expected values but one option is stated as a probability while the other is stated as a sure thing. Choice between the two options, in either framing condition, should be random according to an expected value view of decision making. People, however, are risk-averse in situations where the options are framed in terms of possible gains and approximately 80% of subjects choose the option stated as a sure thing. People are risk-taking in situations where options are framed in terms of losses and approximately 80% of subjects choose the probability option. Choices made by subjects in these subjects are dependent on the decision frame received. The effect is hypothesized to be universal across decision type (Kahneman & Tversky, 1979; Kahneman & Tversky, 1984; Tversky & Kahneman, 1981; Tversky & Kahneman, 1986), a subject's past history (Toland & O'Neill, 1983) and different levels of decision-maker expertise (McNeil et al., 1982). The universal influence of decision frames is hypothesized to be analogous to a visual illusion (Tversky & Kahneman, 1986). This is the reflection hypothesis. Individuals, according to this hypothesis, will be risk-averse when information is presented in a gain frame: Individuals, however, will be risk-seeking when the information is presented in a loss frame. The frame itself provides the illusion which supports the two patterns of decision-making for decisions with different frames but the same objective, expected utility for each option presented.

The mechanism by which this occurs is held to be a change in a cognitive reference point against which incoming information is judged. Decisions are based on a comparison of the relative utility of the choices to a reference point adopted by the decision maker. This reference point defines the demarcation between losses and gains for the decision-maker. Different decision frames elicit different reference points. Decision-framing process is a two-stage process. The first stage involves the automatic activation of a risk-seeking or risk-avoiding behavioral reference point by the gain or loss frame received by the decision-makers. According to Tversky and Kahneman (1981), this creates the universal response to decision frames indicated within the reflection hypothesis. The second stage involves a cognitive evaluation of the information presented within a problem. Subjects are seen as being unaware of the way decision-framing potentially affects attractiveness of the various decision options open to them. The context of the decision-making situation acts so that objective perception and judgment, as defined by expected utility of the choice, is impossible for decision- makers in this second phase. This leads to different decisions being made for identical, objective information by multiple decision-makers.

Catastrophe Theory and Decision Framing. Catastrophe theory provides a unique framework for modeling the effects of decision frames on decision-makers. Catastrophe theory has been proposed as a way to explain the sudden shifts in preference in perceptual experiments involving illusions (Stewart & Peregoy, 1983). Decision framing occurs is analogous to such perceptual illusions. Catastrophe theory is a heuristic metaphor for the (a) the process in which decision frames affect decision- makers and (b) the abrupt, nonlinear reversals of preference which occur when decision-makers are given a loss frame after being presented a gain frame (or vice versa). Moreover, catastrophe theory makes a number of predictions which can further our present understanding of decision climates in organizations.

Svyantek et al. (1991) studied the effects of decision frame and change in information related to the objective percentages of loss received by individuals making a series of decisions. The Tversky and Kahneman paradigm has been primarily concerned with single decisions. Using catastrophe theory as a heuristic device helps to understand the way in which decision framing might affect multiple trials of similar decision situations. Svyantek et al. showed, for multiple related decisions, the response set created initially will result in a tendency to either be risk-seeking or risk-averse within decision-makers. The range of risk-seeking or risk-averse decision-making will be determined by two factors. These are (a) the expected value of the options presented an individual and (b) the response set developed by the decision-maker in previous decisions.

This response set enhances the illusion created by the decision frame (gain or loss) received by the decision-maker as probability of success changes.

Figure 4.1 illustrates the way in which decision framing may be modeled using catastrophe theory. The vertical axis represents the percentage of individuals choosing the sure thing option in a decision framing situation (i.e., risk-averse behavior is on the top of the graph which risk-seeking behavior is indicated by being in the bottom half of the graph). The horizontal axis represents the actual expected value for a series of decision options presented to subjects receiving either the gain or loss frame. These values will be equivalent for gain or loss frames (e.g., at Points A, B, and C on Figure 4.1). The only difference is the way in which the expected values are framed.

Individuals receiving a loss frame are hypothesized to develop a risk-seeking response set (lower line). This response set will be most strong when a very large proportion of the sample in question will receive a strongly negative outcome framed as a sure thing such that A represents (most die); B (half die) and C (few die). The solid line on the graph represents the risk-seeking preference frame.

Those receiving a gain frame are hypothesized to develop a risk-aversion response set (top, dotted line). This response set will be most strong when a very large proportion of the sample in question will receive the positive outcome in the sure thing option such that A represents (few saved); B (half saved) and C (most saved).

In some cases, the expected value framed in the options will be the sole determinant of the response made by decision-makers. For example, Points A and C represent such cases. Here the expected values for the sure thing are such that a) individuals with both response sets would pick the option stated as a probability (e.g., Point A might represent a decision where the problem states 10 of 600 are saved or 590 of 600 die in the sure thing option) or b) individuals with both response sets would pick the option stated as a sure thing (e.g., Point C might represent a decision where the problem states that 590 of 600 are saved or 10 of 600 die in the sure thing option). At such extreme values, the dominant response will be the same irrespective of the frame received.

The area of greatest interest is the middle area labeled "Ambiguous Interpretations." In this zone, the expected values of the options received will be such that it is, a priori, difficult to define a dominant option as can be done for extreme values. Here the response set (i.e., current frame and past frames) will be the major determinant of the option chosen by decision-makers. Point B, for example, might state that 300 of 600 are saved or 300 of 600 die in the sure thing option. Therefore, choices made at Point B will be different. The individuals receiving a gain frame would choose the sure thing while those receiving the loss frame would choose

Figure 4.1

A Catastrophe Theory Approach to Decision Framing Across Probability Change

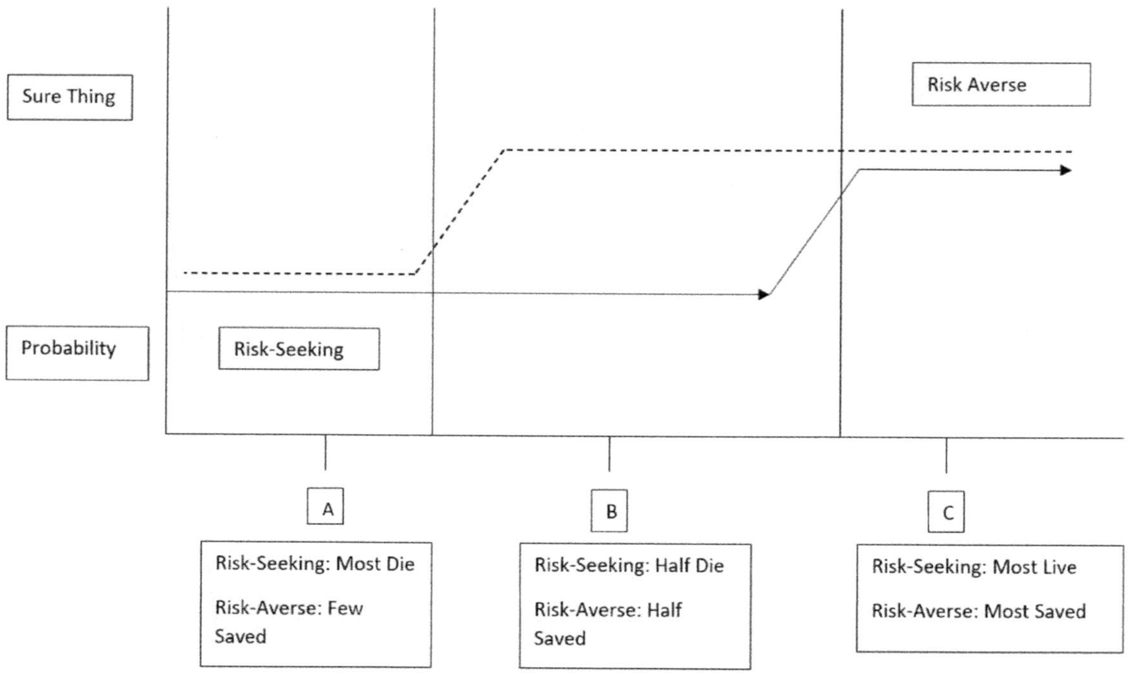

(cf., Svyantek, DeShon, et al., 1996)

the probability option. The tendency to follow the basic results of decision framing research will be strengthened if decision-makers have previously been exposed to choices with extreme expected values framed similarly. This results in an area of expected value where (a) individuals receiving gain or loss frames respond differently; (b) the tendency to respond in one way is influenced by the framing of decisions made in the past; (c) this tendency will create a lag or delay in responding to changes in expected value so that choice differences between frames will and (d) at some point on the expected value continuum, a sudden reversal of preference will occur among decision-makers such that the option hypothesized to be the dominant choice by Tversky and Kahneman will no longer be selected. This sudden reversal of preference will occur without any change in the frame received by subjects. Essentially, for this reversal, the objective information in the decision outweighs the illusion created by the decision frame.

Organizational Frames and Organizational Decisions. The range of options available to decision-makers within organizations is restricted by the context in which the decision occurs (Simon, 1976). Organizational members are motivated to seek out, understand and use relevant information defining behaviors supported by an organization. By creating consistent expectations for the appropriate behavior (e.g., rewarding conservative or risky decision practices), management can increase the predictability of behavior of different individuals in the organization. This particularly can be important when the information provided by the organizational culture, while relevant, does not give the decision-maker the correct solution in an ambiguous situation. Organizations, therefore, create climates for specific decision situations. These climates may change as the organization needs to adapt to the environment. These climates support consistent interpretations across organizations and organizational members. These climates act as an *organizational frame*.

Organizational frames represent the individual's interpretation of the supported decision practices within the organizational environment (Svyantek, Jones, et al.,1991). Organizational frames, when activated by a decision-making problem in a social situation affect decisions in a manner analogous to Tversky and Kahneman's (1981) decision-framing mechanism (Showers & Cantor, 1985), affecting the processing of decision-relevant information by decision-makers and will be particularly important for situations to which the individual is motivated to adapt (Shower & Cantor, 1985). The decision maker within an organizational environment is motivated to learn what decision-making practices the organization supports and are personally adaptive (cf. Sathe, 1985).

A growing body of research illustrates the importance of contextual factors, as well as decision frames, on decision-making. Different social contexts influence the setting of the reference point used by decision-makers (Shoemaker, 1980). Decision options (one a probability and the other a sure thing), with equal expected value, framed as loss situations were presented in a gambling and insurance buying context. The context changed the preferred option of subjects independent of the decision frame. People were more willing to take a chance on losing a large sum by selecting the probability option versus taking a certain smaller loss in the gambling condition (i.e., consistent with Tversky and Kahneman's predictions of risk-seeking for loss frames). In the insurance buying condition, however, subjects took the certain smaller loss by choosing to buy insurance (i.e., were risk-averse). This result was attributed to the evoking of different psychological sets based on social norms in the two situations. Social norms in the insurance case shifted the reference point used by the decision-makers and made them risk-averse while the gambling situation made them risk-seeking. The framing phenomena was shown to be broader than just a universal response to the mode of presentation (i.e., decision frames). In addition, the reflection hypothesis proposed by Kahneman and Tversky (1979) was not supported. Shoemaker's research shows that the hypothesized reflection does not occur because social frames may lead to choice independent of decision frame received.

Framing Effects and Context. Levin et al. (1985) found statistically significant effects for both context (gambling, consumer judgments, and student evaluations) and decision frames on the same decision. Neale and Bazerman (1985) evaluated the influence of decision frames and the confidence level of a negotiator as a contextual influence on student negotiation behavior and found significant main effects for both the decision frames and the confidence levels of the subjects. Davis and Bobko (1986) found significant effects for contextual factors and decision frames on the escalating commitment phenomena. These studies may be interpreted as showing that subjects were influenced by more than just decision frames when faced with a gain or loss situation within a context. Neale et al. (1987) showed that roles, as well as the social context, could influence choices in a manner analogous to decision frames. The extent of the role framing effect was hypothesized to possibly be dependent on how well the role frame is learned. Choice behavior, for the individual with high role knowledge, was shown to be more dependent on the influence of the role frame than the presented decision frames.

The organizational frame will be similar within a class of individuals and will lead to common patterns of decision-making behavior within an organization (and/or role within the organization as Neale et al. (1987) have proposed) as individuals seek to make decisions which match organizational requirement and are personally adaptive. Therefore, the decision-maker observes the consequences of others' decisions in the organization. The captain of the USS Vincennes' organizational frame was different based on the consequences received by the USS Stark's captain.

Organizational frames are held to operate similarly to decision frames. First, the organizational frame is activated and creates a cognitive reference point against which incoming information relevant to the judgment is made. Decisions are based on a comparison of the relative utility of the choices to a reference point adopted by the decision maker.

The need to adapt to the internal organizational environment may lead to judgments (by third-party, objective observers) that organizational decision-makers are unable to make effective decisions. An "effective decision," however, cannot be defined without consideration of both organizational and individual needs in the decision situation and the actual information provided in the situation.

This is illustrated in a study conducted by Svyantek, Jones, et al. (1991). They conducted a study in which individuals received a series of decisions in an in-basket. These decisions were based on the Vroom-Yetton (Vroom & Jago, 1988) model of leadership. These decisions were chosen because the Vroom-Yetton model provides a means for analyzing decisions made by leaders and defining the best solution for the decision. There are five solutions offered the decision-maker using this model. These solutions range from very participative to very autocratic. As part of the in-basket, individuals received information describing the organizational culture of the organization to which they belonged. One culture was a very autocratic organization with top-down decision-making. The second organization was very participative and consensus across levels was important. One decision, according to the Vroom-Yetton model, required the use of the middle solution. Decision-makers in the autocratic culture were more autocratic than the model's solution. Decision-makers in the participative culture were more participative than the model's solution. Therefore, it was found that, according to the model, decision-makers in both simulated organizations made "errors." These "errors" were based on using the organizational frame as a reference point for understanding the decision information proved each individual. Svyantek, Jones, et al. (1991) propose the "average" of many such choices may reflect the decision-making style of an organization. The findings of this study illustrate that the definition of decision quality for a decision-maker within an organizational context reflects more than the objective information presented. The decision-maker here will be rewarded for supporting the "status quo" not for making a decision which is of high, objective quality.

It is this status quo bind that represents the situation in which the captain of the USS Stark found himself. This is discussed in the next section.

Organizational Framing and the USS Stark and USS Vincennes. The catastrophe model of decision framing is hypothesized to be relevant for organizational framing conditions in which specific decision climates are developed by organizations as they adapt to the environment in which they reside. As noted earlier in the description of decision framing, the organizational frame represents a response set which is automatically set based on the captains of the two ships knowledge of Navy culture and observed reward and punishment practices of the Navy.

Figure 4.2 illustrates the differences between the two incidents. The vertical axis represents a binary decision by the captain to defend/ not defend the ship (by firing defensive missiles) in an uncertain, ambiguous situation. The horizontal axis represents the change in information about the incoming planes approach to the ships. This information is received and interpreted by the captain and other important personnel on the two ships. For ease of understanding how the ambiguous information is interpreted by the captains, for this figure the two ships are represented as starting at the same point on the horizontal axis. This point represents the initial point at which the two incoming jets appear on the tracking radar of the two ships. This is a point where neither captain is experiencing a threat. As information is processed, however, both captains reach a point of uncertainty about whether the incoming jet may constitute a potential threat. The captain of the USS Stark frame of reference for interpreting this information is based on his knowledge of the U.S. Navy culture and pertinent information such as current rules of engagement. He decides he requires more information to understand and decide about the level of threat presented by the Iraqi jet. He waits too long. The Iraqi jet fires its missiles, and the USS Stark is struck. The captain of the USS Vincennes is facing a similar situation. His frame of reference is created by his knowledge of the U.S. Navy culture, pertinent information such as rules of engagement, and his knowledge of the punishment received by the USS Stark's captain. This additional information represents the change in the organizational decision climate he uses to make his decision. He fires defensive missiles before the he has clarity on the nature of the incoming jet in the area labeled "Potential Threat." As a result, a civilian airliner is shot down.

Once again, the area of greatest interest is the middle area labeled "Ambiguous Interpretations." In this zone, the incoming information is processed in the second phase of the two phase information processing model proposed by Tversky and Kahneman (1981). This leads to differences in when the defensive actions will be taken. The two captains make their interpretation of the incoming information based on the organizational frame activated in the first phase of the Tversky and Kahneman model. Here the results in the value of incoming information is evaluated against this organizational frame. This leads to the different points of the decision to defend the ship.

Figure 4.2

A Catastrophe Theory of Organizational Framing During the USS Stark and USS Vincennes Incidents

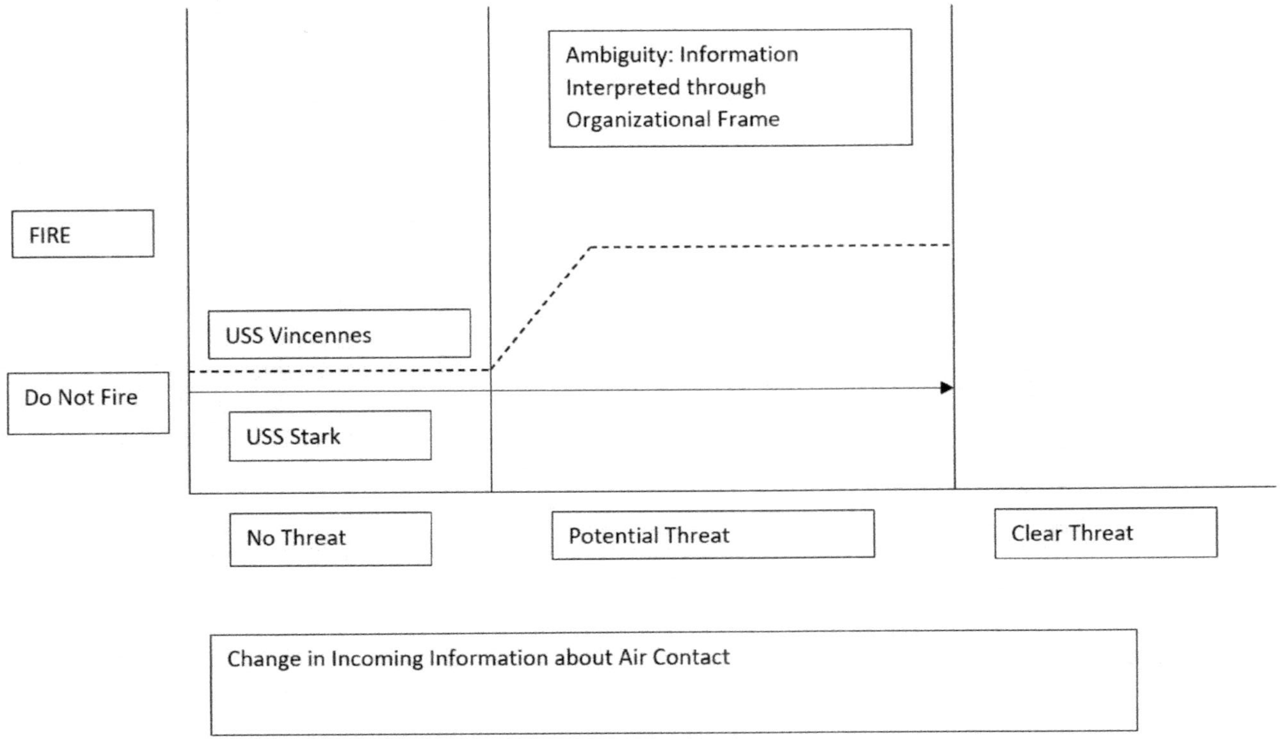

"POUR ENCOURAGER LES AUTRES" ACTIONS IN ORGANIZATIONS

Organizational culture affects behaviors within an organization. Organizational culture defines a *strong situation* (Mischel, 1977) for individuals residing within it. A strong situation provides people with generally accepted rules and guidelines for appropriate behavior. The rules that are present in strong situations constrain people from acting in a manner inconsistent with accepted conduct and behavior. Organizations develop values and norms to set parameters on the behaviors exhibited within an organization. Organizational culture guides organizational policy: The ideal is a pattern of behavior by organizational members which meets the guidelines laid down by the organization even if individual members or groups are not in contact with the organization (Ouchi, 1981). This is the integrative function of organizational culture.

However, as noted earlier, organizations still need to adapt to changing environments. This is the purpose of organizational frames for more specific behaviors (i.e., the adaptive function of culture). Organizational performance evaluation processes, using rewards and punishments, signal supported and unsupported behavior through organizational frames for different types of decision making. The switching of an organizational frame for decision-making purposes may need to occur with rapidity in a changing organizational environment. One method for this is to use *pour encourager les autres* actions. There are several guidelines for the use of these actions.

Effective Use of the *Pour Encourager les Autres* Method

There are principles for making punishment effective on the individual level and organizational level. These principles, as will be shown, interact with each other as both the person receiving the punishment and observers are considered.

Establish a linkage with a specific behavior. The goal of punishment is to reduce the probability that a particular behavior will be produced by an individual (Rachlin, 1976). The individual must (a) understand the relationship between punishment and the presence of the behavior and (b) seek to avoid the punishment on subsequent occasions. Therefore, punishment to be effective, must be clearly linked to a specific behavior and the punishment be aversive enough that behavior not be produced by the individual. These principles hold for observers as well. Observers must perceive the observed punishment as linked to a defined behavior and not to the individual being punished. Without this understanding, the observers cannot learn and change their behaviors. One characteristic of such *pour encourager les autres* actions by organizations, therefore, is that these actions are carried out in public and publicized by the organizations. Admiral Byng was court-martialed, and the results of the court-martial publicized by the national press. His peers in the British Navy observed both the process and the results. Similarly, Captain Brindel being relieved of command and retirement was publicized by the U.S. press. The process and outcome was witnessed by his peers (including Captain Rogers). Therefore, if an organizational member is being made an example of for the benefit of others in similar situation in the future, the behavior and outcome should be clearly linked in the appropriate media used by the organization. Such media may be the press. However, the media may be internal newsletters; announcements at group meetings; or memos received by organizational members. No matter the media, the behavior and outcome must be linked, and this linkage understood by all.

Salience of the person receiving the punishment. It appears that such punishment may be more effective when the person receiving this punishment is high in the organization (Loeffel, 2009). Loeffel (2009) discussed the use of Sippenhaft in the German army during World War II. *Sippenhaft* is the holding of an individual's family responsible for the actions of an individual member of the army. Therefore, the family of an army member who deserted, for example, could face stiff punishment from the Nazi German government. In his description of the usage, however, a key factor that comes is that there were few incidents of this at the lower levels of the hierarchy in the German army. Privates' families, for the most part, were not bothered if the families were perceived as loyal. For higher ranks (e.g., generals), however, the families were more likely to be punished. Therefore, for the *pour encourager les autres* actions to be effective, the individual being punished must be of rank in the organizational hierarch. This appears to have been the case for the USS Stark. The captain and other high-ranking ship officers were punished. The enlisted personnel were not punished. The salience of this punishment is recognized by a wider range of organizational members from multiple levels of the organizational hierarchy. Punishing the captain in a *pour encourager les autres* action, however, was recognized and the frame of reference used changed

Responsibility, authority, and blame. Responsibility for the behavior being punished is critical. Responsibility refers to liability for blame (Trevino, 1992). Observers' make attributions of responsibility for blame. Seven factors are considered in making these attributions. These six are (Trevino, 1992):

1. Causality—this deals with the question of the causes of the observed behavior and outcome. The person being punished must be seen as causing the behavior and outcome through his/her actions or inactions.
2. Intentionality and coercion—this deals with the question of whether the action being punished was intentional or accidental and/or unintentional. One question asked is whether or not the individual could have behaved otherwise. As intentionality attributions increase, the severity of punishment increases.
3. Consequence severity—the more severe the consequences, the more observers believe someone is to blame. This blame is attributed to the person being held responsible.
4. Social roles and status—responsibility is attributed to roles and positions within organizations. Observers more often ascribe responsibility to higher individuals in the situation.
5. Past performance—the performance history of the person being punished is considered. Persons with poor performance history (or other disciplinary actions against them) are held more individually responsible for outcomes of actions. Excellent past performance records may lead to situational attributions by observers and, therefore, required punishments are seen as less by observers.
6. Individual characteristics—individual differences of the person being punished may be relevant for observers. Demographic variables (e.g., gender or race) may interact with other characteristics in the attributions made by observers.
7. Perceived similarity—the more similar the observer perceives she/he is to the individual being punished, the more that punishment severity is affected. Similarity between observer and the individual leads to lower attributions of responsibility.

The situation with the USS Stark shows how these attributions of responsibility by observers are made. Captain Brindel was held responsible for the failure to defend his ship (causality). This, given the situation and the traditions of the sea, is the appropriate individual to hold responsibility. Punishing an enlisted personnel as a scapegoat would probably not have altered the organizational frame used as a frame of reference for judging information received on the USS Vincennes. Second, intentionality was attributed to be low. Captain Brindel, by other officers, seen as a much of a victim of circumstances as an intentional actor. One Pentagon official noted that the USS Stark was a no-win situation for crew and captain (Moore, 1987). The nature of the environment and rules of engagement made it a problem for anyone in the situation. Third, the consequences were severe—Many U.S. sailors died in the incident. Fourth, Captain Brindel held a high-ranking position in the U.S. Navy. His social role and position increased attributions of responsibility. Fifth, Captain Brindel's past performance was excellent. As noted earlier, he was seen as on the career fast track in the U.S. Navy. Finally, his individual characteristics were similar to others in the U.S. Navy, particularly for people in a similar role and position. Therefore, his perceived similarity was likely high.

Equitable punishment. Observers' attributions of responsibility play a key role in determining how they actually see the equitability of the punishment delivered. Punishment must have equity (Butterfield et al., 2005) with the behavior being punished. Punishment of too great severity or not enough severity will affect the future behaviors of observers in similar situations. As noted by earlier, individuals in high trust cultures are more likely to accept punishment as appropriate—this appropriateness is determined by the punishment equitability as well as attributions of responsibility.

Implications. For *pour encourager les autres* actions to work as desired, it has been shown that these actions must be (1) be linked to specific behaviors of interest; (2) the individual being punished must be salient; (3) the responsibility for the action must be attributed to the person receiving the punishment by observers; and (4) the punishment must be deemed equitable to the nature of the behavior being sanctioned by the organization.

CONCLUSION

Organizations create organizational cultures for two purposes. The first is for integration of new organizational members into the system. This function creates the value system which the organization perpetuates through time. This function defines the values held by "us" and is used to differentiate one organization from another. Organizations also, however, must adapt to changing environmental conditions. This adaptation may occur without changing the basic nature of what it means to be a member of the organization. However, fairly specific behaviors will change to allow the organization to compete within its environment better. One technique for creating such an adaptive change is the use of *pour encourager les autres* actions. *Pour encourager les autres* actions change the frames of reference for making judgments in particularly relevant decision situations. This change in frames of reference leads to changes in behavior in situations of ambiguity and uncertainty. These frames of organizational observers with knowledge of the appropriate (or inappropriate) behavior for the ambiguous situation. The cognitive mechanism is seen as analogous to Tversky and Kahneman's (1981) two-phase decision framing model. The first phase occurs when a particular decision or organizational frame is activated by the situation. The second phase is the evaluation of the information in the uncertain situation. Different activated frames will lead to different decisions even though the actual information received is the same.

Another interesting analysis of the USS Stark and USS Vincennes incidents has been conducted by Paris et al. (2000). This analysis focused on the use and assessment of the information being received in the ambiguous, uncertain situation described in Figure 4.2. Better methodologies for analyzing incoming information and communicating this information were proposed as ways to improve ship performance in these situations.

This chapter proposes, however, that no matter how the methodologies for the processing, analysis, and communication of information are improved, errors will still be made in such situations until the appropriate action to take is identified by enough information to remove all uncertainty about the threat (e.g., the area labeled "Clear Threat" on Figure 4.2). The two captains were in a "damned if they do, damned if they don't" situation (Halloran, 1988). They were interpreting received objective information based on their respective, activated organizational frame. Both, therefore, are subject to decision-making errors similar to that described for other organizational framing situations (e.g., Svyantek et al., 1991; Svyantek & Kolz,1996).

The use of the Funder (2001, 2006) model for understanding behavior showed, for this situation, the behavior was the same and the individuals making the decision were very similar. The primary difference is the *pour encourager les autres* actions taken against Captain Brindel. This led to the difference in behavior by Captain Rogers. However, it must be noted that both captains made mistakes (Halloran, 1987) based on the organizational frame used in the decision situation. Captain Brindel's caution was punished leading to Captain Roger's more aggressive evaluation of the situation.

The Funder (2001, 2006) model would support a hypothesis that, if the two captains were switched in their roles. Captain Rogers may have waited too long if he was in command of the USS Stark while Captain Brindel may have shot too soon if he was in command of the USS Vincennes and knew of the *pour encourager les autres* actions taken against Captain Rogers. A similar analysis of another situation has been made. This situation involved the Japanese bombing of Pearl Harbor on December 7, 1941. Admiral Kimmel was initially held solely responsible for the debacle (Twomey, 2019). His peers in the U.S. Navy, however, noted that they would have made the same choices given the information that he had. They recognized that the difference in frames of reference held were more a function of the situation than they were of the person in the situation. This is the nature of *pour encourager les autres* actions. The individual being punished is less important than the message being sent. These actions serve as clear signals to organizational members of when the appropriate behavior to exhibit is changed for specific situations without altering the overall culture of the organization.

REFERENCES

Arkin, W. (1989). Troubled waters: The Navy's aggressive war strategy. *Technology Review (00401692)*, *92*(1), 54. http://spot.lib.auburn.edu/login?url=https://search.ebscohost.com/login.aspx?direct=true&db=edb&AN=8902200180&site=eds-live&scope=site

Barney (1986). Organizational culture: can it be a source of sustained competitive advantage? *Academy of Management Review, 11*, 656–665.

Bretz, R. D., & Judge, T. A. (1994). Person-organization fit and the theory of work adjustment-Implications for satisfaction, tenure, and career success. *Journal of Vocational Behavior, 44*, 32–54.

Brown, L. L., & Svyantek, D. J. (2001). Complex systems, time and graphical analysis of organizational behavior. *The International Journal of Organizational Analysis, 9*, 354–368.

Butterfield, K. D., Trevino, L. K., Wade, K. J., & Ball, G. A. (2005). Organizational punishment from the manager's perspective: An exploratory study. *Journal of Managerial Issues*, *17*(3), 363–382. http://spot.lib.auburn.edu/login?url=https://search.ebscohost.com/login.aspx?direct=true&db=buh&AN=18420530&site=eds-live&scope=site

Cable, D. M., & Judge, T. A. (1996). Person-organization fit, job choice decisions, and organizational entry. *Organizational Behavior and Human Decision Processes, 67*, 294-311.

Cable, D. M., & Judge, T. A. (1997). Interviewer's perceptions of person-organization fit and organizational selection decisions. *Journal of Applied Psychology, 82*, 546–561.

Chatman, J. A. (1991). Matching people and organizations: Selection and socialization in public accounting firms. *Administrative Science Quarterly, 36*, 459–484.

Cooke, R. A., & Szumal, J. L. (2000). Using the Organizational Culture Inventory to understand the operating cultures of organizations. In N. M. Ashkanasy, C. P. M. Wilderon, & M. F. Peterson (Eds.), *Handbook of organizational culture and climate* (pp. 147–162). SAGE.

Davis, M. A., & Bobko, P. (1986). Contextual effects on escalation processes in public sector decision making. *Organizational Behavior and Human Decision Processes, 37*, 121–138.

Deal, T. E., & Kennedy, A. A. (1982). *Corporate cultures*. Addison-Wesley.

Funder, D. C. (2001). Accuracy in personality judgment: Research and theory concerning an obvious question. In B. W. Roberts & R. Hogan (Eds.), *Personality psychology in the workplace* (pp. 121 – 140). American Psychological Association

Funder, D. C. (2006). Towards a resolution of the personality triad: Persons, situations, and behaviors. *Journal of Research in Personality, 40*, 21–34.

Furlong, M. A. & Svyantek, D. J. (1998). The relationship between organizational climate and personality: A contextualist perspective. *Journal of Psychology and Behavioral Sciences, 12,* 43–53.

Goodman, S. A., & Svyantek, D. J. (1999). Person-organization fit and contextual performance: Do shared values matter? *Journal of Vocational Behavior, 55,* 254–275.

Halloran, R. (1988). The downing of Flight 655: A tale of 2 American Skippers, damned if they do and if they don't. *The New York Times.* http://spot.lib.auburn.edu/login?url=https://search.ebscohost.com/login.aspx?direct=true&db=edsgov&AN=edsgcl.175908153&site=eds-live&scope=site

Judge, T. A., & Cable, D. M. (1997). Applicant personality, organizational culture and organizational attraction. *Personnel Psychology, 50,* 359–394.

Kahneman, D., & Tversky, A. (1979). Prospect theory: An analysis of decision under risk. *Econometrica, 47,* 263–291.

Kahneman, D., & Tversky, A. (1984). Choices, values, and frames. *American Psychologist, 39,* 341–350.

Kinkel, S., & Sandbrook, D. (2018). *"Byng's execution played a key role in turning the war around."* BBC History Magazine. http://spot.lib.auburn.edu/login?url=https://search.ebscohost.com/login.aspx?direct=true&db=edb&AN=128059885&site=eds-live&scope=site

Kristof, A. L. (1996). Person-organization fit: An integrative review of its conceptualization, measurement, and implications. *Personnel Psychology, 49,* 1–49.

Levin, I. P., Johnson, R. D., Russo, C. P., & Deldin, P. J. (1985). Framing effects in judgment tasks with varying amounts of information. *Organizational Behavior and Human Decision Processes, 36,* 362–377.

Loeffel, R. (2009). Soldiers and terror: Re-evaluating the complicity of the Wehrmacht in Nazi Germany. *GERMAN HISTORY, 27*(4), 514–530. https://doi.org/10.1093/gerhis/ghp078

McNeil, B. J., Pauker, S. G., Sox, H. C., Jr., & Tversky, A. (1982). On the elicitation of preferences for alternative therapies. *New England Journal of Medicine, 306,* 1259–1262.

Mischel, W. (1977). The interaction of person and situation. In D. Magnusson & N. S. Endler (Eds.), *Personality at the crossroads: Current issues in interactional psychology.* Lawrence Erlbaum.

Moore, M. (1987). Two officers on USS Stark are allowed to quit by Navy. *The Washington Post.* http://spot.lib.auburn.edu/login?url=https://search.ebscohost.com/login.aspx?direct=true&db=edsggo&AN=edsgcl.5079770&site=eds-live&scope=site

Moore, M. (1990). 2 Vincennes officers get medals; citations do not mention downing of Iranian airliner that killed 290. *The Washington Post.* http://spot.lib.auburn.edu/login?url=https://search.ebscohost.com/login.aspx?direct=true&db=edsggo&AN=edsgcl.8960905&site=eds-live&scope=site

Morgan, G. R. (1998). *Organizational theory* (2nd ed.). Addison-Wesley.

Namenwirth, J. Z., & Weber, R. P. (1987). *Dynamics of culture.* Allen & Irwin.

Nahavandi, A., & Malekzadeh, A., (1988). Acculturation in mergers and acquisitions. *Academy of Management Review, 13,* 79–90.

Neale, M. A., & Bazerman, M. H. (1985). The effects of framing and negotiator overconfidence on bargaining behaviors and outcomes. *Academy of Management Journal, 28*, 34–49.

Neale, M. A., Huber, V. L., & Northcraft, G. B. (1987). The framing of negotiations: Contextual versus task frames. *Organizational Behavior and Human Decision Processes, 39*, 228–241.

Norris, D. A. (2011). The remarkable case of the unfortunate Admiral Byng. *History Magazine, 12*(4), 12–13. http://spot.lib.auburn.edu/login?url=https://search.ebscohost.com/login.aspx?direct=true&db=khh&AN=60144717&site=eds-live&scope=site

Ouchi, W. G. (1981). *Theory Z*. Addison-Wesley.

Paris, C., Johnston, J. H., & Reeves, D. (2000). A schema-based approach to measuring team decision making in a Navy Combat Information Center. In C. McCann, & Pigeau, R. (Eds.), *The Human in command: Exploring the modern military experience* (pp. 263–278). Kluwer Academic/Plenum.

Pascale, R. T., & Athos, A. G. (1981). *The art of Japanese management*. Simon & Schuster.

Pour encourager les autres. (2019). In *The Merriam-Webster.com Dictionary*. Retrieved December 4, 2019, from https://www.merriam-webster.com/dictionary/pour%20encourager%20les%20autres

Rachlin, H. (1976). *Behavior and learning*. W.H. Freeman.

Sathe, V. (1985). *Culture and related corporate realities*. Richard d Irwin.

Schneider, B. (1987a). E=f(P,B): The road to a radical approach to person-environment fit. *Journal of Vocational Behavior, 31*, 353–361.

Schneider, B. (1987b). The people make the place. *Personnel Psychology, 40*, 437–453.

Schneider, B. (2000). The psychological life of organizations. In N. M. Ashkanasy, C. P. M. Wilderon, & M. F. Peterson (Eds.), *Handbook of organizational culture and climate* (pp. xvii–xxi). SAGE.

Schneider, B., Goldstein, H. W., & Smith, D. B. (1995). The ASA framework: An update. *Personnel Psychology, 48*, 747–773.

Schneider, B., White, S. S., & Paul, M. C. (1998). Linking service climate and customer perceptions of service quality: Test of a causal model. *Journal of Applied Psychology, 83*(2), 150–163.

Schein, E. H. (1985). *Organizational culture and leadership*. Jossey-Bass.

Schein, V. E., & Diamonte, T. (1988). Organizational attraction and the person-environment fit. *Psychological Reports, 62*, 167–173.

Shoemaker, P.J. (1980). *Experiments of decision under risk: The expected utility hypothesis*. Mrtinus Nijhoff.

Showers, C., & Cantor, N. (1985). Social cognitions: A look at motivated strategies. *Annual Review of Psychology, 36*, 275–305.

Simon, H. A. (1976). *Administrative behavior: A study of decision-making processes in administrative organizations* (3rd ed.). Free Press.

Stewart, I. N., & Peregoy, P. L. (1983). Catastrophe theory modeling in psychology. *Psychological Bulletin, 94*(2), 336–362. https://doi.org/10.1037/0033-2909.94.2.336

Svyantek, D. J. (1997). Order out of chaos: Non-linear systems and organizational change. *Current Topics in Management, 2*, 167–188.

Svyantek, D. J., & Bott, J. P. (2006). Organizational climate, personality interactions and organizational behavior. In J. C. Thomas & D. L. Segal (Eds.), *Comprehensive handbook of personality and psychopathology: Personality and Everyday Functioning* (Volume 1, pp. 412-431). John Wiley& Sons.

Svyantek, D. J., & Brown, L. L. (2001). Stability in the American automobile industry: Insights from alternate representations. *Emergence, 3,* 42–57.

Svyantek, D. J., & Brown, L. L. (2000a). A complex systems approach to organizations. *Current Directions in Psychological Science, 9*(2), 69–74.

Svyantek, D. J., & Brown, L. L. (2000b). Complex systems and the measurement of organizational change. *Current Topics in Management, 5*, 41–62.

Svyantek, D. J., & DeShon, R. P. (1993). Organizational attractors: A chaos theory explanation of why cultural change efforts often don't. *Public Administration Quarterly, 17*, 339–355.

Svyantek, D. J., DeShon, R. P., & Siler, M. T. (1991). The illusion of certainty: A catastrophe theory explanation of decision framing. *Current Psychology: Research and Reviews, 10*, 199–210.

Svyantek, D. J., Jones A. P., & Rozelle, R. (1991). The relative influence of organizational decision frames on decision making. *Advances in Information Processing in Organizations, 4*, 127–145.

Svyantek, D. J., & Kolz, A. R. (1996). The effects of organizational frames and problem ambiguity on decision-making. *Journal of Business and Psychology, 11(2)*, 13–150.

Svyantek, D. J., & Snell, A. S. (1999). Knowledge out of chaos: Using phases spaces for the qualitative evaluation of organizational change. In M. P. Cunha & C.A. Marques (Eds.), *Readings in organization science: Organizational change in a changing context.* (pp 523–540). Instituto Superior de Psicologia Aplicada.

Toland, A., & O'Neill, P. (1983). A test of prospect theory. *Journal of Economic Behavior and Organization, 4*, 53–56.

Trice, H. M., & Beyer, J. M. (1993). *The cultures of organizations*. Prentice-Hall.

Twomey, S. (2016). *Countdown to Pearl Harbor: The twelve days of attack.* Simon and Schuster.

Trevino, L. K. (1992). The social effects of punishment in organizations: A justice perspective. *Academy of Management Review, 17*(4), 647–676. http://spot.lib.auburn.edu/login?url=https://search.ebscohost.com/login.aspx?direct=true&db=edb&AN=4279054&site=eds-live&scope=site

Tversky, A., & Kahneman, D. (1981). The framing of decisions and the psychology of choice. *Science, 211*, 453–458.

Tversky, A., & Kahneman, D. (1986). Rational choice and the framing of decisions. *Journal of Business, 59*, S251–S278.

Vroom, V. V., & Jago, A. G. (1988). *The new leadership: Managing participation in organizations.* Prentice-Hall.

Wilson, G. C. (1987). 3 USS Stark officers replaced; Navy cites failure to react during attack. *The Washington Post.* http://spot.lib.auburn.edu/login?url=https://search.ebscohost.com/login.aspx?direct=true&db=edsggo&AN=edsgcl.4996381&site=eds-live&scope=site

Zohar, D. (1980). Safety climate in industrial organizations: Theoretical and applied implications. *Journal of Applied Psychology, 65*(1), 96–102.

CHAPTER 5

ARMED, NOT READY

Technological Determinism, Discourse, and the Blitzkrieg of Today

Rachel L. Whitman
Auburn University

"The advance of technology is based on making it fit in so that you don't really even notice it, so it's part of everyday life."

—Bill Gates

In the pantheon of human mythos, technology holds a throne that cannot be usurped. Discussions of technology's origin, utility, and influence intwine themselves with discussions of social and economic histories, as tangled in our pasts as in our present. So influential is technology in the course of human affairs that it adopts a sense of agency, casting doubt as to whether its role can be reduced to mere assistance. This begs the question: to what extent does technology influence human civilization?

While the advent of the internet provides a salient example of the impact of technological change, the presence of technology in society is undeniable. The extent of technology's influence *upon* society is far more controversial—

Organizations Behaving Badly:
Destructive Behavior and Corrective Responses, pp. 89–108

as evidenced by the rousing debate surrounding the sociological perspective of technological determinism. Though technological improvements are currently driven by human-led insights in sciences, metallurgy, and craftsmanship, some historic commentary on the role of technology adopts a more causative viewpoint. In particular, technological determinism posits that technology not only influenced the structure of society, but served as the major active force whose characteristics shaped the entirety of human sociotechnical systems throughout history. That is, technological determinism argues that technological developments *determine* society.

Critics of technological determinism are loud and insistent, yet debates of its accuracy continue. Philosophically, technological determinism offers an unsatisfying account of societal progression. However, language bearing technologically deterministic overtones flourishes in organizational discourse (Leonardi & Jackson, 2004). The main influence of technological determinism lies not in its ability to explain history, but in its use by organizations as justification for questionable actions.

The purpose of the current review is not to pass judgment upon the extent to which technology determines society. Rather, this chapter aims to achieve three things:

1. Furnish the reader with an understanding of technological determinism, its tenants, and its counterpoints.
2. Demonstrate that technologically deterministic viewpoints, narratives, and language are rampantly invoked across a wide variety of organizational contexts.
3. Highlight the unique risks posed by technological determinism in today's tech-integrated world.

THE TOOLS OF FATE: TECHNOLOGICAL DETERMINISM

"Technology made large populations possible; large populations now make technology indispensable."

—Joseph Krutch

Defined by its loosest terms, technological determinism is "the idea that technology has important effects on our lives" (Adler, 2007). Outside of this vague, almost-irrefutable notion, agreement upon the formal definition of technological determinism is lacking (Söderberg, 2013). Typically, definitions of technological determinism include two major ideas: that technological innovations follow an inevitable internal logic, and that these innovations ultimately are responsible for determining the shape and structure of society (Wyatt, 2008). Technological determinism is often identified as the philosophy that all meaningful structures and socioeconomic systems are not only connected to, but *caused by* technological development (Winter & Taylor, 1996). However, closer examination of this definition reveals nuances rife with subjectivity.

"Technological"

In order to refute or support claims of technology's influence upon society, one must first establish what "technology" actually refers to. Here—as in much of the conversation surrounding technological determinism—we run into some disagreement. Should technology only refer to the means of production, as interpreted by Marxist proponents of technological determinism? Should it include other devices, such as cell phones, that facilitate production but are not exclusively tied to it? Ultimately, the specification of *what* exactly is determining things eludes identification, potentially encapsulating everything from physical tools to intellectual methods.

Sociological accounts of older civilizations initially relied upon archaeological artifacts, meaning that many historic eras were described primarily according to their physical tools and materials: "The Bronze Age," "The Stone Age," and so forth (Wyatt, 2008). While the reductionism of entire societies to the tools they used is understandable when speculating about nonliterate societies on the basis of limited archaeological evidence, Wyatt (2008) notes that many archaeologists continue to define eras by their material tools long after knowledge of literate culture is obtained. Wyatt frames this reductionism as unjustifiably technologically determinate, but do concede that the physical tools available in a given time period both describe and define the way everyday life is experienced. Anyone who has conducted an internet search for what would once have required physical access to an encyclopedia would likely agree.

While material tools such as spears and guns are rarely disputed as "technology," they are not the only entities deserving of the label. Ascribing too narrow a label to "technology" when considering technological determinism ignores the contributions of inventions in non-mechanistic fields. Studies of the impact of technology benefit from a more inclusive definition (Miller, 1998). Medical advancements in pharmaceuticals—such as antibiotics, insulin, selective serotonin uptake inhibitors—represent developments in biology, chemistry, and experimental design rather than engineering. Yet it is quite apparent that claims of technological determinism would be strengthened by including the likes of penicillin and vaccines among the ranks of "technology," for their influence upon society is immediately apparent and far-reaching (Podolsky, 2010; Rappuoli et al., 2014).

We may perhaps be confident that technology consists of more than machines. Still, if the label of technology is applied too broadly, then our ability to properly debate or refute the claims of technological determinism is weakened (Hirst, 2012). Considering inventions on a smaller scale illustrates such an issue. Should the zipper's impact on clothing and fashion be considered under a technologically deterministic lens? Advances in agricultural equipment have facilitated food production and population increases, so what about the role of devices such as coffee makers?

Adding technical knowledge and processes bloats the definition of technology further, making it harder to disprove deterministic claims. Randomized controlled clinical trials serve as the gold standard for establishing the effectiveness of drugs and behavioral treatments, yet their development is an achievement in experimental design. If everything born by human minds or crafted by human means is technology, is it even possible to parse the strength of causality between society and human creations? Likely not.

As discussed, the limits of technological determinism consist of subjective boundaries set primarily by the interpreter. Ideally, our working definition of technology would consist of more than tools and machines, but avoid venturing so far into the realm of human expression as to include less-tangible developments in art or culture. At such a point, the direction of causality of techno-social relations becomes impossible to detangle. Depending on the magnitude of "determinism" one pairs with their technological specifications, the possibility of parsing out society and technology's joint influence may already be a lost cause.

"Determinism"

The degree to which technology independently shapes human society is encapsulated in the deterministic element of technological determinism. The word "determinism" conveys a causal relationship. By emphasizing the consequences of technology rather than its creation, technological determinism distracts opponents from considering society's influence upon the creation of technology—whatever "technology" may be (Hirst, 2012). As is the case with defining what materials and objects that are referred to, scholars widely disagree on the magnitude of influence and autonomy that technological determinism means to ascribe to its components. That is, to what degree does technology *determine* societal changes? Is technology the *only* force influencing the structure of human systems? Or is it simply a major player?

Here we arrive at the division between "soft" and "hard" forms of technological determinism—though expressing these forms as a continuum likely provides a more accurate representation of the distinction. In its most stringent form, technological determinism states that technology is the *sole* influence driving social change, while softer forms typically pose it as a major—although perhaps not the only—contributing factor (Adler, 2007). Harder forms of technological determinism are accordingly more difficult to support and less popular with social scientists, as they deny that human behavior may impact societal structures (Chandler, 1995). The complete transfer of autonomy from individuals to their devices bears a large burden of proof. Consequently, many scholars reserve the label of technological determinism for the more restrictive, harder forms of the perspective (Wyatt, 2008). In contrast, soft technological determinism tolerates claims that technology is not the sole determinant of societal structures—merely that it poses a strong influence over a civilization's capabilities.

The spectrum of technologically deterministic perspectives is well-quantified in Bimber's (1990) typology, which consists of norm-based, unintended consequences, and logical sequences accounts of technological determinism. In norm-based accounts, technological determinism is a cultural agreement: a decision wherein control over technology is relinquished when efficiency and productivity take higher priority than ethicality. Bimber points to this as a weak form of technological determinism, questioning whether it should even be labeled as such.

The unintended consequences model of technological determinism frames it around the emergence of unexpected social outcomes resulting from technological developments (Bimber, 1990). Proponents who adopt this perspective typically point to the byproducts of technological developments as indication of technology's autonomy: if technology behaves outside the realm of human control by producing outcomes not anticipated or desired by its operators, it must therefore possess a degree of independence.

The logical sequences account of technological determinism provides the "hardest" perspective of Bimber's (1990) categories. In accordance with the technological imperative, the logical sequences account presents technological determinism as a universal law of nature, wherein technology has an internal logic driving its developments independently of its social context. The wheel is developed because it *must* be. Bronze gives way to steel because it is the *logical* next step. This sort of account represents the "hardest" of stances on technological determinism—in that it and is sometimes regarded as the only "true" form of technological determinism (Bimber, 1990).

These characteristics of determinism associated with the logical sequences account include the inevitability of technological progression—

sometimes referred to as the technological imperative (Chandler, 1995). The imperative adopts a linear, near-evolutionary view implying that technology goes extinct when new developments render it obsolete. For some technologies, this tenant possesses a degree of face validity: if you want to contact a relative, would you send a telegram or a text message? However, other technologies exist intergenerationally: hunting rifles and crossbows, wood-burning stoves and geothermal heating, fossil fuel and renewable energy sources (Chandler, 1995). Older technologies do not regularly undergo the same mass extinction events as do biological species—the technology may be used less frequently, but it still exists (Raghaviah, 2012).

As determinism in its most extreme form is antithetical to the existence of human will, "hard" technological determinism is typically less popular with social scientists, who eagerly propose alternative perspectives (Chandler, 1995). Social constructivism in particular resembles a weaker approach to technological determinism, wherein the meaning of technology is not an inherent self-determined characteristic, but impacted by social forces (Rice & Leonardi, 2014). As such, it emphasizes a balanced perspective of sociotechnical interactions. As explained by Jackson and colleagues (2001), "[f]undamental to constructionism is the active effort to privilege neither social nor technical factors in constructing accounts of technology design, development, implementation, or use" (p. 2).

In their review of technological and social emphasis present in research on knowledge management systems, Jackson and colleagues (2001) also found most social constructionist research to orient toward the technical aspects of information and communications technology, rather than social perspectives. Despite social constructionism's emphasis on avoiding technological bias, it seems as though its practical research carries residuals of determinism. The authors propose several explanations for this "tilt" in the research, including the convenience sampling used by studies as well as the novelty of the technology potentially drawing the researcher's attention (Jackson et al., 2001). Additionally, Jackson and colleagues propose that whether an organization was studied during stasis or a period of change may have altered the salience of technology, with the latter situation proposed as drawing more focus to socially-generated organizational processes.

Similar to softer technological determinism and social constructivism, perspectives written by sociotechnical systems theorists also acknowledge how human behavior can affect technology's efficiency (Pasmore et al., 2019). Sociotechnical theories emphasize the interaction of social and technical factors upon organizational performance—noting that attempts to ensure the joint optimization of both factors may result in unintended outcomes at best, and dysfunction at worst (Walker et al., 2008). This latter tenant of sociotechnical systems theory echoes the unintended consequences account of technological determinism proposed by Bimber (1990).

Indeed, sociotechnical systems and technological determinism appear to be two sides of the same coin (Svyantek et al., 2007), a coin that seems to be well-represented in the duality of social constructivism. Like Jackson and colleagues (2001), Svyantek and colleagues (2007) propose that technology and social forces differ in their importance according to the surrounding organizational context—positing that social change is more influential in times of peace and stability. Times of chaos and conflict, however, direct a hyper-focus on the technology available to address it—a phenomenon witnessed clearly in times of war. "Technology opens the door. It is military-economic competition that drags us through" (Dafoe, 2015, p. 1070).

INVOCATIONS OF TECHNOLOGICAL DETERMINISM

"Science and technology revolutionize our lives, but memory, tradition and myth frame our response,"

—Arthur Schlesinger (Historian)

Many words have been spilled in attempts to validate or disprove technological determinism, at the cost of examining the perspective's own influence. That is, less research discusses how an individual's belief in the autonomy or inevitability of technology shapes his or her behaviors in daily life. Similarly, whether technologically deterministic beliefs exert higher-order influences at the institutional level has received little attention.

Regardless of one's views as to the credibility of the *claims* of technological determinism, the magnitude of its influence as a perspective should not be dismissed: even though sociotechnical analysts disregard its stronger claims, technological determinism is still endorsed and evoked by end users of technology in organizations (Wyatt, 2008). As pointed out by Michael L. Smith, "Researchers haven't attempted to identify the needs technological determinism addresses" (Smith, 1994, as cited in Wyatt, 2008). While identifying such psychological needs satisfied by technological determinism would necessitate an empirical investigation, the elements of technological determinism can be reviewed within organizational narratives.

Technological Determinism on the Stage of History

As mentioned previously, military-economic pressure strongly incentivizes technologically-deterministic viewpoints, making it an ideal setting to examine any resulting rhetoric (Dafoe, 2015). The nature of war amplifies the salience of technology's impact: the idiom "bring a knife to a gun fight" epitomizes the deterministic—and often correct—assumption that one's tools are of crucial importance in determining the outcome of conflict. On the whole, war changes the structures of society and its citizens both at the micro and macro levels (Modell & Haggerty, 1991). It is unsurprising that the interconnectedness of armament technology, wartime pressures, and resulting social change offers a breeding ground for debates about technological determinism.

This chapter examines the second World War for two reasons. The first is that World War II (WWII) represented a dramatic loss of life, with a death toll nearly four times higher than World War I (WWI) for American soldiers alone (DeBruyne & Leland, 2015). The long-lasting impact of WWII upon soldiers (Hunt & Robbins, 2001; Robson et al., 2009), civilians (Gráda, 2019; Ichino & Winter-Ebmer, 2004), and societal structures—for example, the increase of women in the American workforce (Goldin, 1991)—makes its technology a prime candidate for establishing technological determinism.

The second reason for examining discussions of WWII relates to the manner in which it shaped our cultural understanding of technology (Miller, 1998). Improvements in tank design freed battle from the tedious advancements of WWI's trench warfare, and the development and use of the atomic bomb cemented WWII as pivotal for the role of technology in war (Ohler, 2017). As such, the prominence of technology utilized has inadvertently turned WWII into a stage for the post hoc validation of technological determinism.

At risk of being general, this chapter will not attempt to vet the role of every piece of technology used by allied and axis forces in WWII. Relating a proper understanding of the context, mechanics, and strategy of the numerous nuanced events comprising the second World War necessitates a great deal more expertise and space. Many scholars have procured excellent analyses in incredible detail (McCarthy & Syron, 2002; Mitcham, 2001) and readers of technically-inclined minds would be well-served to peruse their work further. However, an accessible example of the consequences of invoking technological determinism may be found in the discussion and dissection of the military movements of Nazi Germany. In particular, the prevalence of the "German Super Soldier" myth will be examined in the context of technological determinism.

Actions of the Nazi army—the *Wehrmacht*—in the early stages of WWII were initially decisive and destructive enough to claim Nazi territory unlike any advances seen in the trench-bound nature of the first World War (Ohler, 2017). Some of this credit is undoubtedly due to the use of the German's Panzer tank divisions. The series of six Panzer tanks manufactured and deployed during WWII boasted superior engineering that proved devastating in action. While the first two Panzers developed were lighter tanks with somewhat underpowered armor and weaponry, they fought alongside the far better equipped Pz. 4—the Nazi's most-produced tank that outclassed the U.S. Sherman in regards to firepower, armor, and efficiency (Hopkins, 2013; "Panzer," 2017). While produced in smaller quantities than the Panzer IV, the Pz. 5 Panther proved even more impressive: "With the possible exception of the [Soviet-made] T-34, the Panther was probably the finest tank built by any country during the war" ("Panzer," 2017).

The bold, mechanical movements of the Panzer divisions—although ultimately finding defeat at the hands of the Soviets—inspired no small amount of analysis. "The casual student of WWII does not need to read much to be exposed to a pervasive adulation of the *Wehrmacht*" (Brown, 1986). Much of this seemed to view the Nazi forces—if not favorably—then at least with a degree of awe or respect. In his dissection of Colonel Trevor N. Dupuy's *Numbers, Prediction, and War*, retired Brigadier General John S. Brown (1986) pointed out that the statistic most flaunted as evidence of *Wehrmacht* superiority—that each German soldier possessed the same effectiveness as 1.55 American ones—was computed on the basis of biased sampling, an overinclusion of Panzer divisions relative to their proportion in the *Wehrmacht*, and a disregard for circumstances limiting weaponry effectiveness.

Despite the discourse painting German forces—particularly Panzers—as technologically superior and therefore more efficient that Allied forces, Brown (1986) demonstrated that the effectiveness of American armor and infantry was roughly equivalent to German Panzers. If adjustments are made for the fact that the *Wehrmacht* consisted mostly of infantry—which Brown calculates as less effective than its American counterpart—then the effectiveness of the U.S. Army winds up superior to that of the Germans, Panzers or no (Brown, 1986). Given the outcome of WWII, this may not be surprising.

The mythos surrounding the Nazi *Wehrmacht* extends beyond the domain of its technologically-advanced tanks. A blitzkrieg also occurred at the neurological level, spurred by the quantities pharmaceutically-produced methamphetamine that swept through the country and armed forces. Although the extent to which methamphetamine was utilized in the Nazi forces is subject to some disagreement, the effect of its presence extends far beyond the end of the war.

Entering WWII, Germany positioned itself as an influential developer and producer of pharmaceuticals, vitamins, and stimulants (Metzner, 2004; Reinold & Hoberman, 2014). Amphetamines were first synthesized in 1937 by Temmler and patented under the name Pervitin; following hasty trials it was thrust into German doctor's laps as part of an intense marketing campaign (Ohler, 2017). The marketing campaign extolled the virtues of

Pervitin, which included alertness, the reduction of fatigue, and decreased sensitivity to pain (Levine et al., 1948). Pervitin also resulted in a loss of appetite and increased visual and auditory perception (Levine et al., 1948).

The increased focus granted by Pervitin paired neatly with the post-WWI push for productivity in Germany. Productivity surpassed health in importance; any illness was to be addressed with minimal interruption to ones work—a phenomenon known as "*schonungskrank,*" or "managed illness" (Cocks, 2007). Initially prescribed as an enhancer, the question was not *should* Pervitin be used but rather *who* should use it (Forst, 1939; Snelders & Pieters, 2011). Initial uncontrolled studies on the drug's effectiveness emphasized that reactions to the drug varied between individuals, with some patients complaining of difficulty breathing with a tightness in the chest, but this generally resolved within 15 minutes (Defalque & Wright, 2011; Levine et al., 1948). Even with the requirement of additional rest following the mental stimulation of Pervitin, the drug found high demand in citizens who saw value in the additional productivity it offered (Snelders & Pieters, 2011). Soldiers in particular found additional benefits in mental stimulation while constantly battling fatigue throughout the war—though it was allegedly taken for everything from boosting one's mood to curing hangovers (Defalque & Wrigh, 2011; Racine, 2019). Thus, Pervitin became a "chemical whip used to raise industrial and military productivity" (Anthony et al., 1941, as cited in Cocks, 2007).

A cheap substance, Pervitin remained popular amongst civilians until 1939, when fears about addiction prompted the Reich Health Office to restrict use by requiring a prescription to purchase the drug (Lewy, 2008). Military use, however, did not seem to diminish: 64 million tablets were distributed to the *Luftwaffe* and *Wehrmacht* between April 1940 and December 1940 (Brown, 1986). While the Nazi Air Division did not favor use of Pervitin while flying due to the risk of hyperventilation, the pills were included in *Luftwaffe* bail-out bags, which were eventually discovered when British forces captured Nazi pilots (Delfaque & Wright, 2011; Ohler, 2017). This had the unintended side effect of encouraging rumors of German experimentation in the development of super soldiers.

Indeed, discussion of Nazi warfare in the 1940s and later carries traces of technologically deterministic suggestions that the drugs themselves were responsible for much of the Nazi's success: "In early 1941, German newspapers quoted reports in the British press and from the BBC attributing the brilliant German military success to the use of stimulants and claiming that German pilots captured in England carried Pervitin" (Defalque & Wright, 2011, p. 22). The Blitzkrieg, in particular, bolstered these rumors. Allied soldiers swapped stories of ruthless Nazi enemies who needed no sleep, and instead ripped through the European countryside untethered by human limitations (Ohler, 2017). Following the rapid conquering of territory, German propaganda attempted to tie the victory to the superiority of Nazi soldiers—Ohler (2017), however, points to Pervitin as the deciding factor. Internally, it seems as though the *Wehrmacht* agreed: "The Reich Ministry for Arms and Ammunition ... had even classified Pervitin as 'decisive for the outcome of the war'" (Ohler, 2017, p. 101).

Interestingly, it is widely accepted that American and British forces also utilized pharmaceutical stimulants: the use of Benzedrine is suspected but few primary sources remain intact to substantiate this claim (Racine, 2019; Weindling, 2016). However, myths of German superiority continued to circulate, entangled in accounts of drug use. Brown (1986) noted this myth may be given credence due to a sort of histographical bias: while historians possessed abundant access to records from all levels of the English-speaking British and American forces, the only accounts written in English from the German forces tended to originate from officers, who possessed a higher-order view of the *Wehrmacht*'s maneuverings. "The lower in an institution one descends, the more inchoate its activities may appear" (Brown, 1986, p. 16). Brown (1986) also notes that the myth of German superiority may likely have been exaggerated by the French and British as means of offsetting responsibility for their comparatively lackluster performance.

Regardless, some researchers have gone so far as to credit Nazi drug use—particularly by Hitler, who was administered an unknown number of substances throughout the war before pharmaceutical supply chains were destroyed—with the fatal decision to split the warfront and engage the Soviets during the Russian winter (Ohler, 2017). Ohler's claim that Operation Barbarossa stemmed from Hitler's drug-fueled incoherence was criticized by Weindling in 2016 as reducing all of Germany's performance issues down to addiction—a critique that seems to recognize the technologically deterministic argument put forth by Ohler (2017). Ohler's claims do possess some face validity in that Operation Barbarossa was never part of some overaching program for world domination, and was only implemented as a last resort when it became clear that Soviet desires for territory were incongruent with German plans (Koch, 1983).

After the war, association of the Nazi regime with experimental drug enhancements continued, shifting toward the use of anabolic steroids in professional sports. While synthetic Testosterone was first developed in 1935 by German and Croatian scientists, no concrete evidence exists supporting its use during the 1936 Olympics or WWII—despite a wide network of citations suggesting they did (Reinold & Hoberman, 2014). Instead, Reinold and Hoberman (2014) determined beliefs that German athletes and Nazi soldiers doped with anabolic steroids originated from Nicholas Wade's 1972 report in *Science* magazine, where he credited German soldiers with the first use of anabolic steroids as performance enhancers—albeit as "hearsay evidence" (Reinold & Hoberman, 2014). Following this single claim, the doping theory wormed its way into dozens of peer-reviewed articles—proliferating unchecked as questions of the ethicality of testosterone use in the Olympics rose (Reinold & Hoberman 2014).

The rumor of Nazi doping is precisely that—a rumor. However, the fact that it was accepted without question for so long leads one to wonder as to why it was so believable. Reinold and Hoberman (2014) proceeded to hypothesize that the linkage of testosterone with the Nazi soldiers occurred due to the perceived hyper-masculinization of the regime: "Male domination in the Nazi style has set a standard no other masculine style has been able (or willing) to match. For masculine megalomania on this scale, only the male hormone will do" (p. 879). Doping rumors thus represented another theme in the technologically-deterministic narratives surrounding the Third Reich.

TECHNOLOGICAL DETERMINISM IN ORGANIZATIONAL NARRATIVES

The discussion of drug use in Nazi Germany at times possessed overtones of technological determinism, particularly in regards to Pervitin's use in sustaining—and ultimately degrading—the performance of the *Wehrmacht*. Allied and Nazi alike forces seemed to view the use of Pervitin as decisive for the outcome of the Blitzkrieg, increasing the perceived effectiveness of the *Wehrmacht*. Brown's supposition that Allied forces overemphasized the seeming superiority of Nazi troops to alleviate responsibility—and thus blame—for the Nazi's unchecked takeover of Western Europe aligns with the use of technological determinism in organizational narratives.

Organizational narratives consist of rhetoric, stories, and expectations that communicate organizational culture and inform employees as to appropriate and expected values (Meyer, 1995). While one might expect such narratives to be uniform across an institution, they can in fact be contradictory, such that employees in one department possess entirely different narratives from those in another (Tunby Gulbrandsen & Norholm Just, 2013). Therefore, organizational values as expressed to the public through relations departments may not widely reflect the values of other components of the organization. These organizational stories and myths play into the culture of the organization, making them a significant component that should not be disregarded (Bolman & Deal, 1984).

Technological determinism possesses several qualia that make it a compelling feature of organizational narratives. Determinism's tendency to reify technological progress as a material entity, serves to paint technology as a "harbinger of social progress"—some mythical entity whose arrival and integration is not only preordained, but to our ultimate benefit (Hirst,

2012; Leonardi & Jackson, 2004). Technological determinism may therefore be evoked in an inspirational fashion, as deterministic terminology's "prophetic connotations" with progress make it particularly convincing (Chandler, 1995). This optimistic slant seems to work: the general public views technologically determinism favorably (Winner, 1997).

The technological imperative is particularly useful in reshaping organizational narratives around technological change: "persuasive writers can make it seem like natural common sense ... presented as an unproblematic given" (Chandler, 1995). It is no surprise that governmental agencies have used technological determinism to justify military spending (Stowsky, 2003). Managers, too, adopt technologically deterministic language to promote change in their organizations, a strategy that has the dual benefits of portraying the change as natural while also removing their responsibilities as a change agent (Leonardi, 2008).

While upper management might use technological determinism as a justificatory tool, employee reactions may not contain such enthusiasm. Change itself is notoriously difficult to manage (Pellettiere, 2006). Attempts to implement new technology are often met with resistance, particularly when integration requires changing business practices (Grant et al., 2006). This means that change implemented on account of technologically deterministic visions may spell disaster for organizations, despite the "assured productivity" often advertised by developers of new technology (Edwards, 1995). Technological determinism may also encourage business decisions on a larger level, whose results may be more disastrous.

The U.S. West-Qwest Merger

The disastrous merger of communications giants U.S. West and Qwest is perhaps the quintessential example of technologically deterministic rhetoric used to force together otherwise-incompatible organizations. Leonardi and Jackson (2009) provide an excellent review of antecedents, conflicts, and consequences of the ill-fated endeavor, which will be briefly relayed here. The $40 billion USD merger represented the first such combination of a telecommunications company (U.S. West) and an Internet start-up (Qwest Communications International). The core technologies of the two companies differed substantially, leading to skepticism as to the feasibility of combining such different companies (Leonardi & Jackson, 2004).

In addition to the core technologies of each organization differing, their respective discourses surrounding the role of their technologies in relation to their organizational goals differed (Leonardi & Jackson, 2004). U.S. West emphasized maintaining a strong presence in their regional territory, thus prizing customer and employee loyalty. This contrasted with Qwest's territory-less emphasis on speed, efficiency, and keeping up with the latest in data transfer technology (Leonardi & Jackson, 2009). This latter perspective came packaged with the assertion that newer technology equated superior technology and thus a superior organization—a technologically deterministic perspective that enabled Qwest's complete organizational dominance over U.S. West (Leonardi & Jackson, 2009).

Despite U.S. West's significantly larger size, Qwest was able to effectively snuff out all traces of its organizational culture—alienating their loyal consumer base and losing lifelong employees in the process (Leonardi & Jackson, 2009). This was accomplished through criticisms of U.S. West's analog communications technology as inferior to Qwest's newer fiber optics; attacks on the core technology of the older company thus served as a proxy for criticisms of its organizational culture (Leonardi & Jackson, 2009). The materiality of the technological service offered by the two companies granted the semblance of objectivity to Qwest's claims; the emergence of digital information transmission seemed well-poised to replace analog methods, echoing themes of inevitability and technoprogress (Chandler, 1995). The corresponding cultural domination of Qwest over U.S. West was met with a $3.3 billion USD loss the following quarter (Leonardi & Jackson, 2004). Participating in the progression of technology, it seems, was not enough to satisfy U.S. West's numerous lifelong employees and disenfranchised consumer base.

THE BLITZKRIEG OF TODAY

In many situations, adopting a technologically-deterministic viewpoint poses little risk. The humorous theory of *resistentialism* illustrates this through our human tendency to view technology as animated and autonomously deviant—characteristics exemplified through advice such as "never let the printer know you're in a hurry," lest it jam to spite you (Chandler, 1995). As seen in the U.S. West—Qwest merger, however, narratives of technological determinism may be used to justify organizational decisions that lead to a loss in employees, resources, and even culture. It is not unreasonable to suppose that technological determinism may facilitate organizational misbehavior, or the prioritization of mechanical resources over human ones. However, narratives of technological determinism possess implications that may leave the organization vulnerable in another fashion entirely.

The rise of cloud computing and the Internet of Things (IoT) poses new risks to customers, employees, and organizations. With additional connectivity comes additional vulnerability in exposure, as organizations must choose between availability of information and its security. Critical societal infrastructure systems are particularly vulnerable to compromised control, given the centrality of the services provided: telecommunications, healthcare, and economic services all must balance security with speed of access in today's interconnected world (Abouzakhar, 2013). Achieving this balance has proved difficult for: the average cost of a malware attack for organizations is $2.4 million USD—with the number of large-scale breaches increasing by 27% each year (Sobers, 2019). These costs are inflicted through reputation loss, turnover, and diminished business; cybercrime damages estimated to reach $6 trillion USD each year by 2021 (Sobers, 2019)

Information security breaches originate from a number of sources, both inside and outside the organization. Employees and other organizational "insiders" pose the greatest threat to information security by far, and may compromise the organization intentionally or accidentally (Loch et al., 1992; Im & Baskerville, 2005; Warkentin & Wilson, 2009). Training may improve employee awareness of cybersecurity policy, but motivation and reinforcement through organizational culture are necessary to ensure compliance with good security habits (Gundu, 2019).

The establishment of an organizational culture espousing the importance of cybersecurity habits may be incongruent with technologically-deterministic narratives. The underlying themes of determinism serve to minimize human influence in the realm of technology: assertions that technology is an autonomous force, that technological advancements are inevitable, all imply that *human actions matter less*. Any minimization of the role of human behavior in securing an organization's information is concerning. Beliefs in the central tenants of technological determinism therefore pose a risk to organizational security, particularly given that individuals who believe in the autonomy of technology may silence or deter expression of views to the contrary (Chandler, 1995).

The primary danger of technological determinism to today's society is therefore the risk that associated reductions in human responsibility and autonomy in sociotechno relationships may encourage disengagement in good cybersecurity hygiene. Such risks may be higher if the organizational culture is saturated with narratives of determinism. Technology is *necessary but insufficient* for achieving information security when not accompanied by mindful user behavior, but the tenants of technological determinism imply otherwise.

Given that attitudes are influential upon behavior (Glasman & Albarracin, 2006), it is in the organization's interests for employees to possess attitudes affirming not only the importance of cybersecurity, but the employee's own ability to keep the organization safe. While themes of inevitability invoked in technologically deterministic rhetoric intend to convince the recipient to acquiesce with the progress of technological change, it also endows technology with a godlike sense of autonomy. Managers who invoke deterministic rhetoric are able to defer responsibility of any proposed changes, as determinism implies that the technology itself would be the cause of any unfavorable outcomes. With the autonomy of technological systems therefore comes a consequential release of responsibility. From this perspective, an employee may view their role in contributing to organizational cybersecurity as less important than the security tools—ad blockers, spam filters, firewalls—in play. If such attitudes contribute to reduced security hygiene, then they may place the organization at increased risk for a breach of information.

While the effect of technological determinism possesses theoretical support for a negative association with cybersecurity culture and compliance, such relationships still require empirical validation. Research attention directed at the consequences of deterministic attitudes in organizations would be well-suited to explore the claims discussed within this chapter. In particular:

1. Given that technologically-deterministic language is employed during public organizational mergers at the executive level, is technological determinism present in narratives at other levels of organizations?
2. Are individual attitudes toward the validity of technological determinism related to attitudes about (a) organizational technology or (b) cybersecurity technologies?
3. Are attitudes about the validity of technological determinism related to engagement with good cybersecurity behaviors?
4. Do organizational contextual factors, individual differences, or job type interact with any of the above relationships?

The connection between technological determinism and cybersecurity attitudes remains full of potential for theoretical and empirical research alike. By considering the potential for organizational narratives—particularly those extolling the autonomy and inevitability of technological progress—we may hopefully move toward a better understanding of the interactions between society, technology, and human behavior.

CONCLUDING REMARKS

Technological determinism's validity and definition is widely debated, but its prominence is evident. Its use as a heuristic to promote technological progress may prove troublesome, given its devaluation of human control over technosocial change. These fundamental characteristics enable the leveraging of the perspective as a means of discouraging critical analysis of the implementation of new technologies, but also may manifest in general attitudes of technology. If such attitudes result in a lessened sense of accountability for predominantly technologic procedures, organizational insiders may assume technological controls are sufficient for ensuring the security of information systems—when the reality could not be further from the truth. Technological determinism's validity is questionable, but we should consider researching its potential to impact organizations when endorsed as such. The language of organizations is crucial to conveying its culture—and the implications of technological determinism must be weighed before being woven into the next narrative of change. Organizational security may depend upon it.

REFERENCES

Abouzakhar, N. (2013). Critical infrastructure cybersecurity: A review of recent threats and violations. *Proceedings of the 12th European Conference on Information Warfare and Security*, 1–10.

Adler, P. S. (2007). Technological determinism. In S. Clegg, & J. R. Bailey (Eds.), *International encyclopedia of organization studies*. SAGE.

Anthony, A., Parade, G. W., Muralt, A. V., Müller, E. A., Eichholtz, F., & Hellpach, W. (1941). Symposium on fatigue and measures of combating fatigue. *Deutsche Medizinische Wochenschrift, 67*(49), 1327–1332.

Bimber, B. (1990). Karl Marx and the three faces of technological determinism. *Social Studies of Science, 20*(2), 333–351.

Bolman, L. G., & Deal, T. E. (1984). *Modern approaches to understanding and managing organizations*. Jossey-Bass.

Brown, J. S. (1986). Colonel Trevor N. Dupuy and the mythos of Wehrmacht superiority: A reconsideration. *The Journal of Military History, 50*(1), 16.

Chandler, D. (1995). *Technological or media determinism*. https://www.wolearn.org/pluginfile.php/45/mod_page/content/23/chandler2002_PDF_full.pdf

Cocks, G. (2007). Sick heil: Self and illness in Nazi Germany. *Osiris, 22*(1), 93–115.

Dafoe, A. (2015). On technological determinism: A typology, scope conditions, and a mechanism. *Science, Technology, & Human Values, 40*(6), 1047–1076.

DeBruyne, N. F., & Leland, A. (2015). *American war and military operations casualties: Lists and statistics*. Congressional Research Service Washington United States.

Defalque, R. J., & Wright, A. J. (2011). Methamphetamine for Hitler's Germany: 1937 to 1945. *Bulletin of Anesthesia History, 29*(2), 21–24.

Edwards, P. N. (1995), "From 'impact' to social process: Computers in society and culture." In S. Jasanoff, G. E. Markle, J. C. Peterson, & T. Pinch (Eds.), *The handbook of science and technology studies* (pp. 257–285). SAGE.

Eichholtz, F. (1941). Ermüdungsbekämpfung: Über stimulanten. *Deutsche Medizinische Wochenschrift, 67*, 1356

Encyclopaedia Britannica. (2017, November 23). *Panzer*. https://www.britannica.com/technology/panzer

Forst A. W. (1939), 'Frage-Kasten.' *Münchener Medizinische Wochenschrift, 86*, 1440.

Glasman, L. R., & Albarracin, D. (2006). Forming attitudes that predict future behavior: A meta-analysis of the attitude-behavior relation. *Psychological Bulletin, 132*(5), 778.

Goldin, C. D. (1991). The role of World War II in the rise of women's employment. *The American Economic Review*, 741–756.

Gráda, C. Ó. (2019). *The famines of WWII.* https://voxeu.org/article/famines-wwii

Grant, D., Hall, R., Wailes, N., & Wright, C. (2006). The false promise of technological determinism: the case of enterprise resource planning systems. *New Technology, Work and Employment, 21*(1), 2–15.

Gundu, T. (2019, February). Acknowledging and reducing the knowing and doing gap in employee cybersecurity complaince. In *ICCWS 2019 14th International Conference on Cyber Warfare and Security* (pp. 94–102). Sol Plaatje University.

Hirst, M. (2012). One tweet does not a revolution make: Technological determinism, media and social change. *Global Media Journal-Australian Edition, 6*(2), 1–11.

Hopkins, N. (2013). *A poor defense: Sherman Tanks in WW2.* University of Illinois Archives. https://archives.library.illinois.edu/blog/poor-defense-sherman-tanks-ww2/

Hunt, N., & Robbins, I. (2001). The long-term consequences of war: the experience of World War II. *Aging & mental health, 5*(2), 183–190.

Ichino, A., & Winter-Ebmer, R. (2004). The long-run educational cost of World War II. *Journal of Labor Economics, 22*(1), 57–87.

Im, G. P., & Baskerville, R. L. (2005). A longitudinal study of information system threat categories: The enduring problem of human error. *DATA BASE for Advances in Information Systems, 36*(4), 68–79.

Jackson, M. H., Poole, M. S., & Kuhn, T. (2002). The social construction of technology in studies of the workplace. In L. A. Lievrouw & S. Livingstone (Eds.), *Handbook of new media: Social shaping and consequences of ICTs* (pp. 236–253). SAGE.

Koch, H. W. (1983). Hitler's 'Programme' and the genesis of Operation 'Barbarossa'. *The Historical Journal, 26*(4), 891–920.

Leonardi, P. M. (2008). Indeterminacy and the discourse of inevitability in international technology management. *Academy of Management Review, 33*(4), 975–984.

Leonardi, P. M., & Jackson, M. H. (2004). Technological determinism and discursive closure in organizational mergers. *Management, 17*(6), 615–631.

Leonardi, P. M., & Jackson, M. H. (2009). Technological grounding: Enrolling technology as a discursive resource to justify cultural change in organizations. *Science, technology, & human values, 34*(3), 393–418.

Levine, J., Rinkel, M., & Greenblatt, M., (1948). Psychological and physiological effects of intravenous Pervitin. *The American Journal of Psychiatry, 105*(6), 429–434

Lewy, J. (2008). The drug policy of the Third Reich. *Social History of Alcohol and Drugs, 22*(2), 144–167.

Loch, K. D., Carr, H. H., & Warkentin, M. E. (1992). Threats to information systems: Today's reality, yesterday's understanding. *MIS Quarterly, 17*(2), 173–186.

McCarthy, P. & Syron, M. (2002). *Panzerkrieg: The rise and fall of Hitler's tank divisions.* Carroll & Graf.

Metzner, R. (2004). Nazis on speed: Drogen im 3. Reich. *Journal of Psychoactive Drugs, 36*(2), 289–290.

Meyer, J. C. (1995). Tell me a story: Eliciting organizational values from narratives. *Communication Quarterly, 43*(2), 210–224.

Miller, C. R. (1998). Learning from history: World War II and the culture of high technology. *Journal of Business and Technical Communication, 12*(3), 288–315.

Mitcham, S. W. Jr. (2001). *Panzer legions: A guide to the German army*. Greenwood.

Modell, J., & Haggerty, T. (1991). The social impact of war. *Annual Review of Sociology, 17*(1), 205–224.

Ohler, N. (2017). *Blitzed: Drugs in the Third Reich*. Houghton Mifflin Harcourt.

Pasmore, W., Winby, S., Mohrman, S. A., & Vanasse, R. (2019). Reflections: Sociotechnical systems design and organization change. *Journal of Change Management, 19*(2), 67–85.

Pellettiere, V. (2006). Organization self-assessment to determine the readiness and risk for a planned change. *Organization Development Journal, 24*(4), 38–43.

Podolsky, S. H. (2010). Antibiotics and the social history of the controlled clinical trial, 1950–1970. *Journal of the history of medicine and allied sciences, 65*(3), 327–367.

Racine, N. (2019). Blood, meth, and tears: The super soldiers of World War II. *History Matters: An Undergraduate Journal of Historical Research, 16*, 7–21.

Raghaviah, J. (2012) *Technology in history: An overview* (Working Paper No. 27). Retrieved from Centre for Socio-economic & Environmental Studies Website: http://csesindia.org/wp-content/uploads/2018/08/TECHNOLOGY-IN-HISTORY-AN-OVERVIEW.pdf

Rappuoli, R., Pizza, M., Del Giudice, G., & De Gregorio, E. (2014). Vaccines, new opportunities for a new society. *Proceedings of the National Academy of Sciences, 111*(34), 12288–12293.

Reinold, M., & Hoberman, J. (2014). The myth of the Nazi steroid. *The International Journal of the History of Sport, 31*(8), 871–833.

Rice, R. E., & Leonardi, P. M. (2014). Information and communication technologies in organizations. *The SAGE Handbook of Organizational Communication: Advances in Theory, Research, and Methods,* 425–448.

Robson, D., Welch, E., Beeching, N. J., & Gill, G. V. (2009). Consequences of captivity: Health effects of far East imprisonment in World War II. *QJM: An International Journal of Medicine, 102*(2), 87–96.

Smith, M. L. (1994). Recourse of empire: Landscapes of progress in technological America. In Smith, M. R. & Marx, L. (Eds.), *Does technology drive history? The dilemma of technological determinism* (pp. 37–52). MIT Press.

Snelders, S., & Pieters, T. (2011). Speed in the Third Reich: Metamphetamine (Pervitin) use and a drug history from below. *Social History of Medicine, 24*(3), 686–699.

Sobers, R. (2019). *60 Must-Know Cybersecurity Statistics for 2019.* https://adaptus.com/60-must-know-cybersecurity-statistics-for-2019/

Söderberg, J. (2013). Determining social change: The role of technological determinism in the collective action framing of hackers. *New Media & Society, 15*(8), 1277–1293.

Stowsky, J. (2003). *Secrets or shields to share? New dilemmas for dual use technology development and the quest for military and commercial advantage in the digital age.* UCAIS Berkeley Roundtable on the International Economy, UC Berkeley.

Svyantek, D. J., Mahoney, K. T., & Cullen, K. L. (2007). Social Innovation During a Period of Technological Stasis. *Refining Familiar Constructs: Alternative Views in OB, HR, and I/O*, 259–288.

Tunby Gulbrandsen, I., & Nørholm Just, S. (2013). Collaboratively constructed contradictory accounts: Online organizational narratives. *Media, Culture & Society, 35*(5), 565–585.

Walker, G. H., Stanton, N. A., Salmon, P. M., & Jenkins, D. P. (2008). A review of sociotechnical systems theory: a classic concept for new command and control paradigms. *Theoretical issues in ergonomics science, 9*(6), 479–499.

Warkentin, M., & Willison, R. (2009). Behavioral and policy issues in information systems security: the insider threat. *European Journal of Information Systems, 18*(2), 101–105.

Weindling, P. (2016). History: addiction and the Reich. *Nature, 538*(7623), 38–39.

Winner, L. (1997). An excerpt from" technological determinism: Alive and kicking? *Bulletin of Science, Technology & Society, 17*(2-3), 49–50.

Winter, S. J., & Taylor, S. L. (1996). The role of IT in the transformation of work: a comparison of post-industrial, industrial, and proto-industrial organization. *Information Systems Research, 7*(1), 5–21.

Wyatt, S. (2008). Technological determinism is dead; Long live technological determinism. In E. J. Hackett, O. Amsterdamska, M. Lynch, & J. Wajcman (Eds.), *The handbook of science and technology studies* (3rd ed., pp. 165–180). MIT Press.

CHAPTER 6

COGNITIONS ASSOCIATED WITH ORGANIZATIONAL DEVIANT BEHAVIORS

Thomas Wilmore
Auburn University

The revelation of scandals in massive organizations, such as Enron, Tyco, and WorldCom, in early 2000s prompted increased research in the area of business ethics (Ferrell & Ferrell, n.d.). Despite the increase in research and heightened sensitivity regarding unethical behavior in organizations, deviant behaviors in organizations continue to occur and cost organizations around the world billions of dollars each year. The Association of Certified Fraud Examiners estimated that occupational fraud costs organizations over $7.1 billion between January 2016 and October 2017 (Association of Certified Fraud Examiners, 2018).

Though large-scale ethical atrocities, such as those at Enron and WorldCom, occur very seldomly, a few very large scandals have occurred in prominent organizations in recent years. The Wells Fargo account scandal serves as one of those scandals. In late 2016, news of the Wells Fargo account scandal became widespread after the United States Consumer Financial Protection Bureau, the Office of the Comptroller of the Currency,

Organizations Behaving Badly:
Destructive Behavior and Corrective Responses, pp. 109–125

and the City and County of Los Angeles collectively fined the company $185 million for establishing over one million unauthorized bank accounts (Wolff-Mann, 2019). After the fines, Wells Fargo's stock price suffered, and on September 26, 2016, the company's stock hit its lowest point since February of 2014 (Egan, 2016). Wells Fargo's troubles did not end there, however. In March of 2017, an estimate of 3.5 million unauthorized accounts hit the press (Wolff-Mann, 2019). Following the scandal, Wells Fargo admitted to firing 5,300 low-level employees over the creation of unauthorized accounts, and the CEO at the time, John Stumpf, left the company (Wolff-Mann, 2019). The scandal not only negatively impacted those within the company, it also harmed hundreds of thousands of the bank's customers (Wells Fargo, 2017). A 2017 third-party review of Wells Fargo's banking accounts found that roughly 190,000 of the unauthorized accounts incurred fees and charges (Wells Fargo, 2017). In response, Wells Fargo paid millions of dollars in compensation to these customers (Wells Fargo, 2017).

This chapter will examine practices that Wells Fargo engaged in that potentially led its employees to commit this scandalous behavior, focusing on three individual processes associated with unethical behavior in organizations: perceptions of unfairness, perceived norms, and a bottom-line mentality. Based on interviews with former Wells Fargo employees (Arnold, 2016a), these processes appear likely to have played a role in the company's account scandal. Finally, this chapter will offer some advice on how to prevent deviant behavior from occurring in organizations.

Perceptions of Fairness/Justice

Perceptions of organizational injustice may have played an important role in the Wells Fargo account scandal. Interviews with a few of Wells Fargo's former employees suggest that employees felt that the company set unfair expectations for them and that managers treated them unfairly (Arnold, 2016a). For example, one former employee who worked at the company for five years said she thought the expectation to sell twenty products a day during one sales push called "Jump into January" seemed impossible (Arnold, 2016a). The same former employee also said two of her managers would come to her desk, reprimand her, and tread past her coworkers (Arnold, 2016a). Research points to a positive association between perceptions of unfairness and unethical behavior (Schweitzer & Gibson, 2008) and between perceptions of unfairness and intentions to behave unethically (Kickul, 2001). When employees judge situations as unfair, they likely experience negative emotions (Allred, 1999). When employees then engage in unethical behavior, they experience greater happiness and reduced anger (Schweitzer & Gibson, 2008). Based on the experiences described above by former Wells Fargo employees, it would come as no surprise if employees' perceptions of unfairness at Wells Fargo prompted them to engage in illegal practices to "balance the scales" and to reduce their negative emotions. The following portion of this chapter will discuss organizational justice theories, possible applications of those theories to the case of the Wells Fargo account scandal, and ways in which organizations can foster high organizational justice perceptions among their employees.

Equity Theory. J. Stacey Adams first proposed equity theory in the 1960s. According to this theory, employees try to maintain equity between their work inputs and the compensation they receive for those inputs against the inputs and compensation of other workers (Adams, 1963). If employees feel that inequity exists between their work inputs-to-compensation ratio and that ratio of their coworkers, employees will view their situations as unfair according to equity theory. This theory could apply to the case of Wells Fargo. Prior to the widespread news of the account scandal, Wells Fargo tied employee bonuses to sales numbers (Tayan, 2019). Personal bankers could receive bonuses of around 15 to 20% of their salary, and bank tellers could receive bonuses of up to 3% percent of their salaries (Tayan, 2019). In addition to those actually selling to customers, district managers also could receive bonuses of $10,000 to $20,000 if their branches met their sales targets according to several Wells Fargo employees (Glazer & Rexrode, 2016). If Wells Fargo employees believed they contributed significantly more to the branch meeting its sales targets than their district manager but received a lesser reward from the outcome than their district manager, equity theory would predict they would perceive injustice. Since its introduction in the 1960s, however, some have criticized equity theory for not incorporating more factors that influence people's perceptions of fairness. For example, some have claimed the theory needs to include information concerning the effects of procedures on perceptions of fairness, rather than simply focusing on material outcomes (Cropanzano & Folger, 1989).

Referent Cognitions Theory. In order to incorporate the effect of procedures on perceptions of fairness, Folger devised the referent cognitions theory (RCT) (Folger, 1986). According to RCT, an individual perceives a situation as unfair when he or she believes a more favorable outcome would have resulted from a procedure that should have been used (Folger, 1986). To investigate RCT, Cropanzano and Folger (1989) had undergraduate research participants complete two tasks: a computer matching game and a card matching game. The experimenter, a female graduate student, informed participants that she would use their results on only one of the tasks to determine eligibility for an extra credit unit (Cropanzano & Folger,

1989). The experimenter told and reminded all the participants that the first task they worked on would not contribute to the extra credit decision (Cropanzano & Folger, 1989). After completing the first task, Cropanzano and Folger (1989) separated the participants into high-referent and low-referent conditions by informing half of the participants (i.e., the high-referent group) that using the first task for evaluation would have resulted in them receiving the extra credit unit, while telling the other half (i.e., the low-referent group) that using the first task would not have resulted in them receiving the credit. In addition to creating high-referent and low-referent conditions, Cropanzano and Folger also separated the participants into two decision conditions: a subject-decision group and an experimenter-decision group. The participants in the subject-decision group had the opportunity to choose which of the two games they wanted to serve as the basis for the reward decision prior to performing either of the tasks, while the experimenter simply informed those in the experimenter-decision group that she would assign them the reward-decision task (Cropanzano & Folger, 1989). The researchers separated the participants into the two decision groups to study the "should" component of RCT (Cropanzano & Folger, 1989). All of the participants received news that they did not score high enough to receive the extra credit unit after completing the second task, but those in the experimenter-decision group could blame the experimenter for not assigning them the task that "should" have been used in the extra credit decision (Cropanzano & Folger, 1989). Those in the subject-decision group did not have the same incentive to blame the experimenter for the negative outcome because they chose the reward-decision task themselves (Cropanzano & Folger, 1989). The results of the Cropanzano and Folger study support RCT. Only the participants in the high-referent, experimenter-decision group perceived the situation as unfair, supporting the interaction between outcomes and procedures in fairness evaluations (Cropanzano & Folger, 1989). In addition to providing support for RCT, the Cropanzano and Folger study also provides insight into how job autonomy as well as having a voice may affect fairness evaluations in the workplace. Based on the results of the study, workers who feel as though they have greater input in decisional processes may have higher perceptions of procedural justice than those who do not (Cropanzano & Folger, 1989). Lind et al. (1990) also found that giving individuals a voice led to higher fairness judgments. Unfortunately, it does not appear that Wells Fargo gives its employees much of a voice (Flitter & Cowley, 2019). In fact, employees expressed the ability to raise grievances with managers as one of their biggest concerns in a survey consisting of over 27,000 employees in Wells Fargo's IT department in 2018 (Flitter & Cowley, 2019). Screwfix, a hardware company based in the United Kingdom, on the other hand, serves as a prime example of an organization that does well at giving its employees a voice (Maier,

2016). This company gives employees the opportunity to provide feedback on management, interactions with customers, ideas for improvement, et cetera every two weeks (Maier, 2016). The company importantly also listens to the feedback and used employees' suggestions to develop a new customer card (Maier, 2016). If Wells Fargo managers and those who worked for the company's ethics hotline would have encouraged and listened to comments made by employees, the company might have prevented the scandal from spreading much earlier on (Arnold, 2016b). One former Wells Fargo employee named Jeremy claims that he told his manager that employees were opening unauthorized accounts for customers in 2007, but rather than work to fix the problem, Jeremy claims that the company pushed him to quit his job (Arnold, 2016b).

Interactional Justice and Communication. Though RCT incorporates both distributive and procedural justice, the theory neglects the social factors that play a role in individuals' fairness evaluations. The concept of interactional justice focuses more on the social components taken into consideration when assessing the fairness of a situation. Interactional justice contains two components: informational justice and interpersonal justice (Colquitt, 2001). Informational justice involves the explanations provided for a given outcome, while interpersonal justice involves the extent to which those involved in executing the procedures or determining the outcomes treat those impacted by the decision with dignity and respect (Colquitt, 2001). Though some point to the high correlation between procedural justice and interactional justice as evidence that the two should not be viewed as separate constructs (Cropanzano & Greenberg, 1997), other studies support the separation of these constructs. In Skarlicki and Folger's (1997) study, the authors found a three-way interaction of distributive justice, procedural justice, and interactional justice on organizational retaliatory behavior (ORB). They also found that at high levels of interactional justice, the two-way interaction of distributive justice and procedural justice on ORB was not significant, indicating that high interactional justice can offset the effects of low distributive and low procedural justice on deviant behaviors in organizations (Skarlicki & Folger, 1997). Moorman (1991) found that of the three types of justice (i.e., procedural, distributive, and interactional), only interactional justice had a significant relation to organizational citizenship behavior. These studies support a view of interactional justice as a distinct type of justice, rather than as simply a part of procedural justice.

Ways Organizations Can Foster Justice Perceptions. The Skarlicki and Folger (1997) study mentioned above illustrates the importance of interactional justice in reducing retaliatory behaviors in organizations, but the study does not provide information regarding how organizations can foster high interactional justice perceptions among their employees. Communication relates to both interpersonal and informational justice and can impact justice perceptions (Kernan & Hanges, 2002). Patient and Skarlicki (2010) looked at the association between empathy expressed by managers in delivering the news of a layoff and interactional justice. The authors found that trait empathetic concern in written communication and empathetic induction in face-to-face communication positively predicted interpersonal and informational justice perceptions (Patient & Skarlicki, 2010). Based on the interviews with former Wells Fargo employees, at least some of Wells Fargo's managers lacked empathy in their interactions with employees, reprimanding them for not meeting sales numbers and pushing them to meet sales numbers in demeaning one-on-one meetings (Arnold, 2016a). One former Wells Fargo employee compared the one-on-one meetings to a trip to the principal's office, and she also said the managers would tell her, "If you don't meet your solutions, you're not a team player. If you're bringing down the team, then you will be fired, and it will be on your permanent record" (Arnold, 2016a). This kind of behavior likely reduced interactional justice perceptions among employees at Wells Fargo and may have contributed to some of the employees' decisions to commit fraud.

With regard to the impact supervisor-focused justice perceptions can have on employees, Colquitt et al. (2013) found that supervisor-focused justice perceptions generally had stronger effects on employees' attitudes and behaviors than organization-focused justice and that supervisor-focused justice appeared more changeable than organization-focused justice. In light of these results, the authors suggested that organizations could look at traits that predict adherence to justice rules when making selecting decisions for supervisory employees (Colquitt et al., 2013). Both empathy and emotional stability have been shown to predict adherence to justice rules (Masterson et al., 2005; Mayer et al., 2007). Colquitt et al. (2013) also propose organizations could offer supervisors training in justice principles, citing that this training has been shown to increase fairness perceptions (Skarlicki & Latham, 2005).

Organizational Culture and Organizational Climate

Organizational culture refers to a set of shared values and norms employees within an organization hold that guide their interactions with peers, leaders, and consumers (Morgan, 1998). Organizational culture permits regular behavior patterns among people to form, and these patterns lay the foundation for predictable interactions within an organization (Svyantek & Bott, 2004). Organizational climate represents those specific patterns of interactions and behaviors that occur within an organization (Svyantek & Bott, 2004). Organizational culture and organizational climate impact employees' behaviors by defining a strong situation (Mischel, 1977), which precludes people from behaving in a manner contrary to approved conduct and behavior (Svyantek & Bott, 2004). Organizations create norms and values to establish boundaries on the behaviors exhibited within the organization (Svyantek & Bott, 2004). The following portion of this chapter will detail how norms within an organization can work to influence ethical decision-making.

Perceived Norms

Perceived norms also may have played a role in the Wells Fargo scandal. Numerous studies have indicated that perceived norms can play a role in unethical behavior, and in the case of Wells Fargo, at least two former employees who worked for the company between 2004 and 2011 claimed that deceptive sales practices were ubiquitous and even occurred in the company's headquarters (Arnold, 2016a). This section will look at two types of perceived norms, descriptive norms and injunctive norms; reasons descriptive norms likely had a large impact in the case of the Wells Fargo account scandal; and potential ways to reduce unethical behavior in organizations through the use of norms.

Descriptive Norms. Descriptive norms constitute the perceptions of what most people do, while injunctive norms refer to perceptions of what most people approve or disapprove of (Cialdini et al., 1990). Cialdini et al. (1990) performed several studies looking at the effects of perceived norms on littering behavior. In their studies, Cialdini et al. (1990) used the environment surrounding the participants as the descriptive norm. A clean environment would signify to the participant that most people do not litter there, while a littered environment would signify most people do litter there (Cialdini et al., 1990). The researchers also utilized the behavior of a confederate to increase the salience of the environment to the participants (Cialdini et al., 1990). In their first study, a confederate either littered in front of or simply walked by the participant across the two environments: clean and littered (Cialdini et al., 1990). The behavior of the confederate functioned to make the state of the environment salient to the participant or, in other words, activate the descriptive norm (Cialdini et al., 1990). The researchers found that participants littered the most when in a littered environment after witnessing the confederate litter and littered the least when in a clean environment after witnessing the confederate litter (Cialdini et al., 1990). This finding suggests that the participants' focus on the descriptive norm impacted their behavior as opposed to simply the assessment of the behavior's impact on the environment because the participants did not litter the least in the cleanest environment (i.e., the clean environment in which the confederate simply passes by and does not litter) (Cialdini et al., 1990).

Though the Cialdini et al. (1990) studies only looked at littering behavior, the results of their studies comport with the results of studies looking at other forms of unethical behavior (Gino et al., 2009; Kobis et al., 2015). For example, Kobis et al. (2015) found a significant correlation between perceived descriptive norms and bribery in a corruption game in their first two studies. The researchers also found in their third study that participants who received an anti-corruption descriptive norm prime engaged in bribery significantly less than those who received no prime or a pro-corruption descriptive norm prime (Kobis et al., 2015). The findings of this study indicate that descriptive norms may serve not only as aids for post hoc justifications for unethical behavior (e.g., "I did something wrong, but everyone else was doing it too."), but also as guides for corrupt behavior (Kobis et al., 2015), as Cialdini et al. (1990) found with regard to littering behavior.

In the case of Wells Fargo, newcomers in the organization may have used the descriptive norm of creating unauthorized accounts to guide their behavior. These norms probably had the greatest impact on those relatively new to Wells Fargo because these individuals likely experienced the most uncertainty about organizational expectations. Research shows people more likely adhere to descriptive norms when ambiguity is high (Connor et al., 1999). The particular susceptibility of newcomers at Wells Fargo to descriptive normative influence also stems from two theoretical perspectives: Bandura's social learning theory and social identity theory. According to Bandura's social learning theory, individuals learn vicariously by observing others' behaviors and the consequences of those behaviors and by modeling others' behaviors (Bandura, 1971). If new employees at Wells Fargo saw coworkers creating fake accounts and avoiding chastisement and receiving bonuses by doing so, they may have decided to model this behavior. Social identity refers to the portion of an individual's self-concept that comes from perceived membership in a social group (Tajfel, 1981). According to the social identity theoretical perspective, unethical norms could lead people to behave unethically because of their desire to act in accordance with their group identity (O'Fallon & Butterfield, 2012). New hires at Wells Fargo may have been influenced by the descriptive norm of creating unauthorized accounts due to their desire to identify with the group, a desire likely amplified by the feelings of anxiety associated with their new position (Hogg, 2012). In their study, O'Fallon and Butterfield (2012) found evidence supporting a social learning theoretical perspective and social identity theoretical perspective regarding the relationship between observed peer unethical behavior and observers' unethical behavior.

In addition to affecting newer employees, descriptive norms may have also influenced the behavior of more established employees at Wells Fargo through relative deprivation theory. The relative deprivation theoretical perspective shares similarities with equity theory. According to this theoretical perspective, if individuals see others performing unethical behavior and receiving more favorable outcomes than themselves, they will feel a sense of relative deprivation and experience negative emotions (Bernstein & Crosby, 1980). In order to reduce these negative emotions, they may engage in the same unethical behaviors as their peers. The relative deprivation perspective could certainly explain why some of Wells Fargo's employees decided to engage in illegal sales practices. If employees saw their peers making unauthorized accounts and receiving desirable outcomes by doing so, they may have felt compelled to also make unauthorized accounts to rid themselves of unpleasant emotions stemming from their perceptions of relative deprivation. The O'Fallon and Butterfield (2012) study mentioned previously also found that relative deprivation partially mediated the relationship between observed peer unethical behavior and observers' unethical behavior.

Injunctive Norms versus Descriptive Norms. In addition to studying the effects of descriptive norms on littering behavior, Cialdini et al. (1990) also studied the effects of injunctive norms on littering behavior. They found that participants littered significantly less after being presented with an injunctive norm prime (i.e., a recycling prime) than after being presented with less related primes (Cialdini et al., 1990). The researchers also found that injunctive norms affected littering behavior across more situations than descriptive norms (Cialdini et al., 1990). Results of other studies also show that perceived injunctive norms impact behavior in different situations than descriptive norms. Kredentser et al. (2012) found that injunctive norms impacted behavioral intentions more when participants had the ability to cognitively elaborate, while descriptive norms impacted behavioral intentions more when participants could not cognitively elaborate. The results of another study conducted by Jacobsen et al. (2011) showed that reduced willpower, or self-regulatory capacity, reduced conformity to an injunctive norm but increased conformity to a descriptive norm, despite both norms advocating for the same behavior. These studies indicate that injunctive norms influence behavior in a more deliberative fashion, while descriptive norms impact behavior in a more automatic way.

Though Wells Fargo may have tried to make the injunctive norms of the company more salient by having a code of ethics and an ethics hotline, their sales culture created a recipe for reliance on descriptive norms. Research has shown that people rely more on automatic ways of thinking when under time pressure or when experiencing a great deal of cognitive load (Kruglanski & Webster, 1996). As previously mentioned, descriptive norms appear to influence behavior more automatically than injunctive norms. Therefore, employees under the immense sales pressure at Wells Fargo may have been particularly susceptible to the influence of the perceived descriptive norm of unauthorized account creation.

Ways to Reduce Unethical Behavior Using Perceived Norms. If employees' unethical behavior at Wells Fargo arose at least in part from biased, inaccurate perceptions of norms as ex-CEO John Stumpf claims (Glazer & Rexrode, 2016), obtaining information regarding employees' behaviors throughout the company via anonymous surveys or other methods and making that information widely available could have reduced that behavior (Morris et al., 2015). A conducted study by Hallsworth et al. (2014) showed that informing taxpayers that 9 out of 10 people had already complied with the tax law in full made them four times more likely to comply with the law. Organizations may also attempt to nudge employees to behave ethically by having employees sign their names at the top of honesty agreement forms prior to performing an action. At Wells Fargo, this policy could take the form of having employees sign their name in agreement to act in accordance with the ethical guidelines of the company prior to setting up an account for a customer. One study found that having individuals sign self-report documents at the top rather than at the bottom increased the likelihood of honest reporting (Shu et al., 2012). The results of another study conducted by Yam et al. (2014) indicate that a lack of cognitive resources reduces individuals' ability to violate more salient injunctive norms. Having employees signify their agreement to act ethically by signing their name prior to an action should, therefore, work to reduce unethical behavior by increasing the cognitive effort needed to justify unethical behavior as well as the salience of injunctive norms. The evidence regarding the efficacy of this type of nudging is mixed, however. The United Kingdom's Behavioural Insights Team found that moving the signature for an honesty agreement on a tax form to the top of the form may have actually increased fraudulent claims of a discount among Manchester residents (Behavioural Insights Team, 2012), and Cagala et al. (2019) found that having college students sign no-cheating agreements actually increased their likelihood of cheating. Making students sign no-cheating agreements may have increased cheating behavior by weakening the social norms associated with academic integrity (Calgala et al., 2019).

Organizations may also use ethics or whistleblower hotlines to increase the salience of the injunctive norms of the organization and deter unethical behavior. Wells Fargo did in fact have an ethics hotline, and some employees used it to communicate that they witnessed other employees creating unauthorized accounts (Arnold, 2016b). At least some of the employees who reported incidents to the hotline claim the company did not take action after they called the hotline, however, and some even claim their managers retaliated against them for reporting bad behavior (Arnold, 2016b). Regardless of the validity of the claims of retaliation, the ethics hotline at Wells Fargo could not work to deter unethical behavior if employees believed the company would retaliate against them or dismiss their claims of misconduct. The way in which Wells Fargo used its ethics hotline may have also impacted procedural justice perceptions in the organization. As discussed in the section of this chapter on procedural justice and RCT, giving employees a voice can increase justice perceptions (Lind et al., 1990). Employees at Wells Fargo who felt the company did not listen to their concerns about unethical behavior and denied them a voice, however, may have experienced reductions in perceived procedural justice. On a positive note, organizations, therefore, may be able to use ethics hotlines to deter unethical behavior by increasing injunctive norm salience as well as by positively impacting justice perceptions.

Bottom-line Mentality

Several studies have indicated a positive association between a bottom-line mentality (BLM) and unethical or antisocial behavior (Kim, 2018; Mesdaghinia et al., 2018). Kim (2018) proposed and found support for the role of BLM in the association between a calculative mindset and unethical behavior. In this model, a calculative mindset, or the tendency to quantify qualitative values, leads to a bottom-line mentality, or a state in which one neglects considerations not pertaining to the bottom-line outcomes when making a decision (Kim, 2018). This bottom-line mentality, in turn, leads to unethical behavior (Kim, 2018). Wells Fargo's excessive focus on meeting sales goals may have led both managers and lower-level employees to adopt a bottom-line mentality. Greenbaum et al. (2012) found a positive relationship between supervisor BLM and employee BLM. Therefore, the bottom-line mentality of district and branch managers may have trickled down to lower-level employees.

Bottom-line Mentality and Incentive Structures. In order to reduce the likelihood of employees adopting a bottom-line mentality, organizations could refrain from rewarding and punishing employees on the basis of meeting specific sales numbers and could instead reward employees for engaging in certain behaviors that will benefit customers and the company in the long run. Dayton Semerjian, General Manager of Global Customer Success at CA Technologies, suggests tying compensation to behaviors such as engaging in training, creating closed loops with customers, and coming up with new ideas to improve customers' experience (Benjamin, 2016). If an organization desires to tie pay to performance outcomes, it may be tempted to link compensation to customer satisfaction ratings to circumvent the pitfalls of tying compensation to sales numbers. However, this scheme can also lead to a variety of problems. A survey of 1,000 frontline employees by Medallia Institute found that employees were 50% more likely to report that their coworkers coached customers to give them higher scores and twice as likely to report that their coworkers engaged in practices to prevent unhappy customers from replying to customer satisfaction surveys when compensation was tied to customer satisfaction ratings (Benjamin, Gochyyev, et al., 2016). Employees may also view the practice of tying compensation to customer ratings as unfair because customers may incorporate factors outside of the employee's control into their rating decision, such as a slow IT system or product deficiencies (Benjamin & Doerr, 2017).

If organizations want to tie compensation to performance, such as customer satisfaction ratings, Benjamin and Doerr (2017) suggest they may want to do so over a longer period of time to reduce the likelihood of employees perceiving the decision as unfair. One objection to long-term incentive structures revolves around people's tendency to engage in temporal discounting, or a devaluing of rewards as temporal distance increases (Green, Fry, & Myerson, 1994). One may fear this discounting could reduce the reward system's ability to promote goal-oriented behavior. One positive aspect of a long-term incentive structure, however, is its potential to emphasize to employees that the organization has a fixation on growth and development (Benjamin & Doerr, 2017). Though factors that impact the relationship between a calculative mindset and unethical behavior remain largely unknown, Kim (2018) found that long-term orientation significantly moderated the relationship between a calculative mindset and unethical behavior. By rewarding growth and development, organizations may help foster long-term orientation in their employees and reduce the likelihood that a calculative mindset and, ultimately, a bottom-line mentality will adversely influence employees' behaviors..

CONCLUSION

This chapter covered how perceptions of unfairness, bad norms, and a bottom-line mentality could have contributed to the Wells Fargo account scandal. This chapter also offered potential solutions to prevent unethical behavior from occurring in organizations via these three cognitive routes, including increasing empathy in communication, using measures of emotional stability and empathy in selection decisions for supervisors, providing supervisors with training in justice rules, giving employees greater voice in decisional processes, utilizing descriptive and injunctive norms, and changing incentive systems.

Deviant behaviors in organizations not only cost organizations billions of dollars each year, but also harm both organizations' internal and external stakeholders. With the increase in globalization and the use of technology in organizations, properly deterring deviant behaviors in organizations may pose an even greater challenge. Some research suggests that increased psychological distance increases the likelihood that people will make unethical decisions (Wood et al., 2013). Because technology and globalization increase the psychological distance between those who commit deviant behavior and those harmed by such behavior, these trends may increase the likelihood that members of organizations engage in unethical behavior. These observations underscore the importance of continued research to better understand the antecedents of unethical behavior in organizations and how to better deter this behavior in organizations.

REFERENCES

Adams, J. S. (1965). Inequity in social exchange. *Advances in Experimental Social Psychology, 2*, 267–299. https://doi.org/10.1016/S0065-2601(08)60108-2

Allred, K. G. (1999). Anger and retaliation: Toward an understanding of impassioned conflict in organizations. In R. J. Bies, R. J. Lewicki, & B. H. Shepard (Eds.), *Research on negotiations in Organizations* (Vol. 7). JAI Press.

Arnold, C. (Host). (2016, October 4). *Former Wells Fargo employees describe toxic sales culture, even at HQ* [Radio broadcast episode]. https://www.npr.org/2016/10/04/496508361/former-wells-fargo-employees-describe-toxic-sales-culture-even-at-hq

Arnold, C. (Host). (2016, October 21). *Workers say Wells Fargo unfairly scarred their careers* [Radio broadcast episode]. https://www.npr.org/2016/10/21/498804659/former-wells-fargo-employees-join-class-action-lawsuit

Association of Certified Fraud Examiners. (2018). *Report to the nations 2018 global study on occupational fraud and abuse.* https://www.acfe.com/uploadedFiles/ACFE_Website/Content/rttn/2018/RTTN-Government-Edition.pdf

Bandura, A. (1971). *Social learning theory*. General Learning Press.

Behavioural Insights Team. (2012). *Applying behavioural insights to reduce fraud, error and debt*. Tech. rep., Cabinet Office, London. http://38r8om2xjhhl25mw24492dir.wpengine.netdna-cdn.com/wp-content/uploads/2015/07/BIT_FraudError-Debt_accessible.pdf

Benjamin, B. (2016, November 21). *How to get your execs bought into CX* [Blog post]. Retrieved from https://www.medallia.com/blog/creating-executive-alignment/

Benjamin, B., & Doerr, B. (2017, August 24). *How to pay employees based on customer feedback*. Forbes. https://www.forbes.com/sites/groupthink/2017/08/24/how-to-pay-employees-based-on-customer-feedback/#4255e5820b3

Benjamin, B., Gochyyev, P., Sopadijeva, E., & Contra, K. (2016). *Learning before earning: How to incentivize frontline employees to deliver great customer service.*

https://go.medallia.com/rs/669-VLQ-276/images/Medallia-Learning-Before-Earning.pdf

Bernstein, M., & Crosby, F. (1980). An empirical examination of relative deprivation theory. *Journal of Experimental Social Psychology, 16*, 442–456. https://doi.org/10.1016/0022-1031(80)90050-5

Cagala, T., Glogowsky, U., & Rincke, J. (2019, August 5). *Does commitment to a no-cheating rule affect academic cheating?* https://www.academia.edu/7894139/Does_Commitment_to_a_No-Cheating_Rule_Affect_Academic_Cheating

Cialdini, R. B., Reno, R. R., & Kallgren, C. A. (1990). A focus theory of normative conduct: Recycling the concept of norms to reduce littering in public places. *Journal of Personality and Social Psychology, 58*, 1015–1026. http://media.cbsm.com/uploads/1/AFocusTheoryofNormativeConduct.pdf

Colquitt, J. A., Rodell, J. B., Zapata, C. P., Scott, B. A., Long, D. M., Conlon, D. E., & Wesson, M. J. (2013). Justice at the millennium, a decade later: A meta-analytic test of social exchange and affect-based perspectives. *Journal of Applied Psychology, 98*, 199–236. http://dx.doi.org/10.1037/a0031757

Colquitt, J. A. (2001). On the dimensionality of organizational justice: A construct validation of a measure. *Journal of Applied Psychology, 86*, 386–400. https://dx.doi.org/10.1037//0021-9010.86.3.386

Connor, M., Warren, R., Close, S., & Sparks, P. (1999). Alcohol consumption and the theory of planned behavior: An examination of the cognitive mediation of past behavior. *Journal of Applied Social Psychology, 29*, 1676–1704. http://dx.doi.org/10.1111/j.1559-1816.1999.tb02046.x

Cropanzano, R., Byrne, Z. S., Bobocel, D. R., & Rupp, D. E. (2001). Moral virtues, fairness heuristics, social entities, and other denizens of organizational justice. *Journal of Vocational Behavior, 58*, 164–209. https://dx.doi.org/10.1006/jvbe.2001.1791

Cropanzano, R. & Folger, R. (1989). Referent cognitions and task decision autonomy: Beyond equity theory. *Journal of Applied Psychology, 74*, 293–299. http://dx.doi.org/10.1037/0021-9010.74.2.293

Cropanzano, R., & Greenberg, J. (1997). Progress in organizational justice: Tunneling through the maze. In C. L. Cooper & I. T. Robertson (Eds.), *International review of industrial and organizational psychology*: 1997 (pp. 317–372). Wiley & Sons.

Egan, M. (2016, September 26). *Wells Fargo stock sinks to 2-1/2 year low.* CNN Business. Retrieved from https://money.cnn.com/2016/09/26/investing/wells-fargo-stock-fake-account-scandal.html

Ferrell, O. C., & Ferrell, L. (n.d.). *Historical developments in business ethics: Then to now.* https://danielsethics.mgt.unm.edu/pdf/Historical%20Development%20of%20Business%20Ethics.pdf

Flitter, E., & Cowley, S. (2019, March 9). Wells Fargo says its culture has changed. Some employees disagree. *The New York Times.* https://www.nytimes.com/2019/03/09/business/wells-fargo-sales-culture.html

Folger, R. (1986). A referent cognitions theory of relative deprivation. In J. M. Olson, C. P. Herman, & M. P. Zanna (Eds.), *Relative deprivation and social comparison: The Ontario symposium* (Vol. 4, pp. 33–55). Hillsdale, NJ: Erlbaum.

Gino, F., Ayal, S., & Ariely, D. (2009). Contagion and differentiation in unethical behavior: The effect of one bad apple on the barrel. *Psychological Science, 20*, 393–398. https://doi.org/10.1111/j.1467-9280.2009.02306.x

Glazer, E., & Rexrode, C. (2016, September 13). Wells Fargo CEO defends bank culture, lays blame with bad employees. *Wall Street Journal*. https://www.google.com/amp/articles/wells-fargo-ceo-defends-bank-culture-lays-blame-with-bad-employees-1473784452

Green, L., Fry, A. F., & Myerson, J. (1994). Discounting of delayed rewards: A life-span comparison. *Psychological Science, 5*, 33–36. http://www.jstor.org/stable/40062338

Greenbaum, R. L., Mawritz, M. B., & Eissa, G. (2012). Bottom-line mentality as an antecedent of social undermining and the moderating roles of core self-evaluations and conscientiousness. *Journal of Applied Psychology, 97*, 343–359. http://dx.doi.org/10.37/a0025217

Hallsworth, M., List, J. A., Metcalfe, R. D., & Vlaev, I. (2014). *The behavioralist as tax collector: Using natural field experiments to enhance tax compliance* (NBER Working Paper No. 20007). Retrieved from National Bureau of Economic Research website: https://www.nber.org/papers/w20007

Hogg, M. A. (2012). Uncertainty-identity theory. In Van Lange, P. A. M., Kruglanski, A. W., & Higgins, E. T. (Eds.), *The handbook of theories of social psychology* (Vol. 2, pp. 62–80). SAGE.

Jacobsen, R. P., Mortensen, C. R., & Cialdini, R. B. (2011). Bodies obliged and unbound: Differentiated response tendencies for injunctive and descriptive social norms. *Journal of Personality and Social Psychology, 100*, 433–448. http://dx.doi.org/10.1037/a0021470

Kernan, M. C., & Hanges, P. J. (2002). Survivor reactions to reorganization: Antecedents and consequences of procedural, interpersonal and information justice. *Journal of Applied Psychology, 87*, 916–928. http://dx.doi.org/10.1037/0021-9010.87.5.916

Kickul, J. (2001). When organizations break their promises: Employee reactions to unfair processes and treatment. *Journal of Business Ethics, 29*, 289–307. https://doi.org/10.1023/A:1010734616208

Kim, J. (2018). Calculative mindset and unethical behavior: Examining roles of BLM and time orientation. *Academy of Management Proceedings, 2018*(1). https://doi.org/10.5465/AMBPP.2018.13403abstract

Kobis, N. C., van Proijen, J-W, Righetti, F., Van Lange, P. A. M. (2015). Who doesn't?—The impact of descriptive norms on corruption. *PLoS ONE, 10*(6), e0131830. https://doi.org/10.1371/journal.pone.0191830

Kredentser, M. S., Fabrigar, L. R., Smith, S. M., & Fulton, K. (2012). Following what people think we should do versus what people actually do: Elaboration as a moderator of the impact of descriptive and injunctive norms. *Social Psychological and Personality Science, 3*, 341–347. https://doi.org/10.1177/1948550611420481

Kruglanski, A. W. & Webster, D. M. (1996). Motivated closing of the mind: "Seizing" and "freezing." *Psychological Review, 103*, 263–283. http://dx.doi.org/10.1037/0033-295X.103.2.263

Lind, E. A., Kanfer, R., & Earley, P. C. (1990). Voice, control, and procedural justice: Instrumental and noninstrumental concerns in fairness judgments. *Journal of Personality and Social Psychology, 59*, 952–959. http://dx.doi.org/10.1037/0022-3514.59.5.952

Maier, S. (2016). *5 companies getting employee engagement right.* https://www.entrepreneur.com/article/285052

Masterson, S. S., Byrne, Z. S., & Hao, H. (2005). Interpersonal and informational justice: Identifying the differential antecedents of interactional justice behaviors. In S. W. Gilliand, D. D. Steiner, D. P. Skarlicki, & K. van den Bos (Eds.), *What motivates fairness in organizations* (pp. 79–103). Information Age Publishing.

Mayer, D. M., Nishii, L., Schneider, B., & Goldstein, H. (2007). The precursors and products of justice climates: Group leader antecedents and employee attitudinal consequences. *Personnel Psychology, 60*, 929–963. http://dx.doi.org/10.1111/j.1744-6570.2007.00096.x

Mesdaghinia, S., Rawat, A., & Nadavulakere, S. (2018). Why moral followers quit: Examining the role of leader bottom-line mentality and unethical pro-leader behavior. *Journal of Business Ethics, 159,* 491–505. https://dx.doi.org/10.1007/s10551-018-3812-7

Mischel, W. (1977). The interaction of person and situation. In D. Magnusson & N. S. Endler (Eds.), *Personality at the crossroads: Current issues in interactional psychology* (pp. 333–352). Erlbaum.

Moorman, R. H. (1991). Relationship between organizational justice and organizational citizenship behaviors: Do fairness perceptions influence employee citizenship? *Journal of Applied Psychology, 76*, 845–855. http://dx.doi.org/10.1037/0021-9010.76.6.845

Morris, M. W., Hong, Y., Chiu, C., & Liu, Z. (2015). Normology: Integrating insights about social norms to understand cultural dynamics. *Organizational Behavior and Human Decision Processes, 129*, 1–13. https://www.sciencedirect.com/science/article/pii/S0749597815000084

O'Fallon, M. J., & Butterfield, K. D. (2012). The influence of peer unethical behavior on observers' unethical behavior: A social cognitive perspective. *Journal of Business Ethics, 109*, 117–131. https://www.jstor.org/stable/23259305

Patient, D. L., & Skarlicki, D. P. (2010). Increasing interpersonal and informational justice when communicating negative news: The role of the manager's empathetic concern and moral development. *Journal of Management, 36*, 555–578. https://doi.org10.1177/0149206308328509

Schweitzer, M. E., & Gibson, D. E. (2008). Fairness, feelings, and ethical decision-making: Consequences of violating community standards of fairness. *Journal of Business Ethics, 77*(3), 287–301. https://doi.org/10.1007/s10551-007-9350-3

Shu, L. L., Mazar, N., Gino, F., Ariely, D., & Bazerman, M. H. (2012). Signing at the beginning makes ethics salient and decreases dishonest self-reports in comparison to signing at the end. *Proceedings of the National Academy of Sciences of the United States of America, 109*, 15197–15200. https://doi.org/10.1073/pnas.1209746109

Svyantek, D. J., & Bott, J. P. (2004). Organizational culture and organizational climate measures: An integrative review. In J. C. Thomas (Ed.), *Comprehensive handbook of psychological assessmen: Industrial and organizational assessment* (Vol. 4., pp. 507–524). John Wiley & Sons.

Skarlicki, D. P., & Folger, R. (1997). Retaliation in the workplace: The roles of distributive, procedural, and interactional justice. *Journal of Applied Psychology, 82*, 434–443. http://dx.doi.org/10.1037/0021-9010.82.3.434

Skarlicki, D. P., & Latham, G. P. (2005). How can training be used to foster organizational justice? In J. Greenberg & J. A. Colquitt (Eds.), *Handbook of organizational justice* (pp. 499–522). Erlaum.

Tajfel, H. (1981). *Human groups and social categories*. Cambridge University Press.

Tayan, B. (2019). *The Wells Fargo cross-selling scandal.* (Rock Center for Corporate Governance at Stanford University Closer Look Series: Topics, Issues and Controversies in Corporate Governance No. CGRP-62 Version 2). Retrieved from the Stanford Graduate School of Business website: https://www.gsb.stanford.edu/sites/gsb/files/publication-pdf/cgri-closer-look-62-wells-fargo-cross-selling-scandal.pdf

Wells Fargo. (2017, August 31). *Wells Fargo reports completion of expanded third-party review of retail banking accounts, paving way to complete remediation effort.* https://newsroom.wf.com/press-release/wells-fargo-reports-completion-expanded-third-party-review-retail-banking-accounts

Wolff-Mann, E. (2019). Wells Fargo scandal: The complete list. *Yahoo Finance.* https://www.google.com/amp/s/finance.yahoo.com/amphtml/news/wells-fargo-scandals-the-complete-timeline-141213414.html

Wood, M. O., Noseworthy, T. J., & Colwell, S. R. (2013). If you can't see the forest for the trees, you might just cut down the forest: The perils of forced choice on "seemingly" unethical decision-making. *Journal of Business Ethics, 118*, 515–527. https://dx.doi.org/10.1007/s10551-012-1606-x

Yam, K. C., Chen, X., & Reynolds, S. J. (2014). Ego depletion and its paradoxical effects on ethical decision making. *Organizational Behavior and Human Processes, 124*, 204–214. https://doi.org/10.1016/j.obhdp.2014.03.008

CHAPTER 7

WHEN BULLIES GET JOBS

Workplace Bullying in Local Governments

Regan E. Gaskin and Erin L. Borry
University of Alabama at Birmingham

INTRODUCTION

Osama Saleh reported being harassed by a security guard at his workplace. The guard would verbally abuse Saleh, telling him to "go back to Yemen" and calling him a "dirty Arab" (Gould, 2014). The situation turned dangerous when the security guard attacked Saleh and left him with a fractured cheekbone. The employer claimed that the alleged bullying actions were just "banter" between the two coworkers. However, a court did not agree, and because management did not act to stop the harassment, the company was ordered to pay $4.7 million to Saleh (Gould, 2014).

The National Institute for Occupational Safety and Health (2005) reported that between 1993 and 1999, 1.7 million violent acts were committed per year against people who were at work or on duty. In 1993, the National Institute for Occupational Safety and Health (NIOSH) stated that in the prior year, there were 1,000 workplace murders, 6 million threats, and

Organizations Behaving Badly:
Destructive Behavior and Corrective Responses, pp. 127–147

around 2 million physical assaults on workers (Van Aalten, 1994). More recently, in 2017, the Workplace Bullying Institute (WBI) estimated that 61% of US employees were aware of abusive behavior in the workplace. Additionally, 19% of those surveyed reported experiencing abusive behavior and another 19% reported witnessing abusive behavior in the workplace (Namie, 2017). Overall, an estimated 60.3 million U.S. workers are affected by workplace bullying each year (Namie, 2017).

These statistics indicate that workplace bullying is an issue in the United States, yet the academic literature has not explored it much. Largely, literature addresses workplace aggression, violence, assault, harassment, and abuse, all of which could be bullying, but do not encompass all bullying behaviors. In addition, research on workplace bullying in the United States focuses on workers in the private sector (Manners & Cates, 2016; Vega & Comer, 2005), and while research on public sector bullying exists, it focuses on other countries (Venetoklis & Kettunen, 2016; Hutchinson & Eveline, 2010; Lewis & Gun, 2007).

This chapter seeks to understand the prevalence of and attitudes toward bullying in local government organizations through an original survey. Results indicate that local government employees are aware of what workplace bullying is and that it does occur in local governments. These findings should be used to encourage organizations, lawmakers, and researchers to continue to examine workplace bullying in the United States. The remainder of this chapter is organized as follows: first, a literature review explores what we know about workplace bullying, specifically in government organizations. Next, we present the method of data collection and analysis, followed by results. Finally, we explore the study's limitations and avenues for future research.

LITERATURE REVIEW

Workplace bullying is a serious issue. It is sometimes is labeled as harassment, exclusion, or impairing someone's ability to work (Glasø & Notelaers, 2012). One reason the phenomenon continues to be misunderstood is because it is often dismissed as workplace pranks or harmless teasing (Branch & Murray, 2015), or as something that only occurs among children and adolescents (Randall, 1997).

Bullying Defined

Bullying has been broadly defined as "the aggressive behavior arising from the deliberate intent to cause physical or psychological distress to other" (Randall, 1997, p. 22). Workplace bullying, specifically, has been described as a situation in which one or more people persistently, and repeatedly, perceive themselves as being victims of negative actions from superiors or coworkers, and where the victims have difficulty defending themselves against those actions (Einarsen & Skogstad, 1996; Olweus, 1993). In 2014, the Workplace Bullying Institute defined bullying as the "repeated mistreatment; abusive conduct that is: threatening, humiliating, or intimidating, work sabotage, or verbal abuse" (Namie, 2014). Both definitions include the repeated nature of negative behaviors, but they do not fully encompass the phenomenon. For example, the first definition states that a victim has "difficulty defending themselves." An individual could experience bullying, and be able to defend themselves by reporting the incident to a supervisor who resolves the issue quickly. The second definition gives examples of workplace bullying, which can limit what is considered bullying, especially because this definition does not include mention of physical bullying. Seemingly, the lack of a cohesive definition causes managers and leaders to struggle when handling incidents of workplace bullying (Randall, 1997). However, researchers have continued to explore the dimensions of workplace bullying and its effects on individuals and organizations (Einarsen et al., 1994; Lutgen et al., 2006; Namie, 2014). Despite this lack of consensus around its definition, workplace bullying continues to be an issue and has detrimental effects on those in the workplace.

While harassment of those belonging to protected classes is illegal under Title VII of the Civil Rights Act of 1964 and subsequent nondiscrimination laws (EEOC, n.d.), not all bullying can be considered harassment in the legal sense (Nagele-Piazza, 2018). Bullying can occur regardless of one's race, gender, or sex, for example, and thus not be considered harassment because a protected status is not involved (Randall, 1997). Furthermore, harassment can be considered a single incident, whereas bullying tends not to be isolated incidents, but repetitive (Randall, 1997). Therefore, harassment and bullying share many similar behaviors, but differ in time and motive, and laws protecting against workplace harassment may not protect against workplace bullying.

Bullying in the Workplace

Research into workplace bullying is a more recent development when compared to other workplace behavioral phenomena. Early research on workplace behavior focused on harassment and other well-known negative workplace behaviors (Brodsky, 1976). Brodsky's (1976) work focused on workers' compensation claims related to injuries experienced because of workplace harassment. Overall, Brodsky found that workplace culture was a significant factor in these types of injury cases. Later, Andrea Adams (1992) wrote *Bullying at Work: How to Confront and Overcome it*, which included the first documented use of the term workplace bullying.

It was only in the 1990s that research about workplace bullying gained momentum: studies arose about workplace bullying in European countries (Randall, 1997). In 2000, Helge Hoel and Cary Cooper surveyed employees in more than 70 public, private, and voluntary sector organizations, covering about one million employees. Using data from more than 5,300 responses, they found that 10.5% of employees reported having been bullied in the prior 6 months, though to varying degrees of frequency. More than 6% reported that they had been bullied "now and then," and fewer than one percent reported being bullied every day. Another study found that workplace bullying did affect people differently based on race and age (Einarsen & Skogstad, 1996). This same study found that 74.7% of respondents indicated being bullied by a manager, whereas 36.7% reported being bullied by colleagues. In addition, large organizations, male-dominated organizations, and industrial-focused organizations had the highest rates of victimization. Older workers reported being victims more than younger workers, and Asian employees were more likely to be bullied than Whites However, men were reported to be bullies at a significantly higher rate (Einarsen & Skogstad, 1996).

A later study about workplace bullying in Finnish ministries found that about 20% of respondents reported being the victim of task-related bullying several times per month, while 11% reported being the victim of personal bullying (Venetoklis & Kettunen, 2015). They also found that women were more likely to experience bullying and that supervisors are not likely to be victims. In addition, of those who reported being the victim of bullying in the prior 12 months, 60% indicated the issue had not been resolved. More recently, an American study found that almost a quarter of Americans experience workplace bullying (Namie, 2017). Women are more likely to be victimized, men are more likely to be the perpetrators, and 65 percent of victims lose their jobs in order to stop the bullying (Namie, 2017).

Victims of workplace bullying have varied experiences. For example, an employee may feel they are being bullied if they are excluded from work-related activities. However, another employee may not consider that behavior bullying, but instead view a supervisor yelling at them to be bullying. Because of this variation, researchers have difficulty creating an all-encompassing definition (Lutgen-Sandvik et al., 2006). Moreover, workplace bullying actions are referred to as different terms in other parts of the world. For example, "mobbing" (Leymann et al., 1990), "bullying" (Einarsen & Skogstad, 1996; Rayner, 1997; Vartia, 1996), "victimization"

(Einarsen & Raknes, 1997), and "psychological terror" (Leymann, 1990) all refer to instances of systematic mistreatment of an individual. A lack of agreed-upon language has impaired researchers' abilities to contextualize the behaviors associated with workplace bullying. This presents difficulty for researchers who explore bullying in the workplace, and for managers to respond to bullying behaviors.

Negative Impacts of Workplace Bullying

Workplace bullying can negatively affect the quality of human relationships in an organization (Einarsen et al., 1994, Glasø & Notelaers, 2012). This phenomenon affects not only victims, but also organizations and witnesses.

Several studies have shown workplace bullying has a harmful impact on *victims'* health and well-being (Bowling & Beehr, 2006; Brousse et al., 2008; Lapierre et al., 2005, Glasø & Notelaers, 2012). Common negative side effects of bullying include social isolation, low self-esteem, depression, anxiety, among others. The side effects of are not limited to psychological problems, but also physiological, such as concentration difficulties, chronic fatigue, and sleep problems (Bowling & Beehr, 2006; Zapf et al., 1996; Leymann 1990).

Workplace bullying leads to turnover, resulting in costs to the *organization* (Rayner, 1997), including reduced productivity (Hoel et al., 2003), absenteeism (Kivimäki et al., 2000), decreases in worker satisfaction and commitment, and increases in intention to leave (Glasø & Notelaers, 2012). Furthermore, bullying can adversely impact *witnesses* (Workplace Bullying Institute, n.d.). Witnesses may suffer because they may develop a fear of becoming a target of bullying behaviors, incorrectly handling the situation, or losing their job if they intervene (Workplace Bullying Institute, n.d.). Witnesses may also deal with guilt if they do not intervene. This can lead to a sense of share and personal worthlessness, which are similar emotions felt directly by bullying victims (Workplace Bullying Institute, n.d.). In addition, a side effect of workplace bullying is strain on non-work-related relationships, such as family and friends (Randall, 1997).

Research Questions

As noted, extant research on the topic workplace bullying largely focuses on private organizations, and not on government organizations, especially at the local level. In addition, research has largely been conducted outside of the United States. As such, the present research asks:

1. Does workplace bullying occur in local governments?
2. Which workplace bullying behaviors are prevalent?
3. Do local government employees perceive their organizations as having a policy against workplace bullying?
4. What are the perceived outcomes of workplace bullying?

DATA AND METHODS

Given that previous research has largely assessed workplace bullying through self-report measures, this research takes the same approach. An online survey was distributed to employees in two local governments in the Southeastern United States. The first author contacted seven local city managers about distributing the survey to its employees. Four city managers responded: two indicated they could not participate because of current legal issues with the topic, and two agreed to extend the survey to their employees.

City managers of the two participating cities were e-mailed an invitation for distribution to employees. This invitation included a short description of the study, a template for the city manager to use when they reach out to their employees, a link to the survey, and a consent form. Once the employees received the link to the survey, they were able to complete the survey in any location with e-mail and internet access. Upon accessing the survey link, participants were notified of their rights, including to anonymity and confidentiality, and were provided the opportunity to opt out. Respondents were then asked if they worked for a local government, spoke English, and were over the age of eighteen. If a respondent answered "no" to any of these questions, they were directed to the end of the survey and thanked for their time; all others were shown the survey. The participating cities were asked to send out a reminder e-mail three weeks after the first e-mail. The reminder e-mail contained the same information as the previous invitation, modified for context. This process led to 18 responses, 9 from each city.

Measures

The survey focused broadly on the employee's experiences and attitudes towards workplace bullying and covered several topic areas, including workplace characteristics, attitudes about and experiences with workplace bullying, and perceptions of bullying policies.

Workplace Characteristics. The first section of survey focused on the participants' workplace and the role they fill in their organization. Participants were first asked to indicate in which city and department they work. Participants were also asked how many years they have worked in government and how many years they have worked for their current employer. Finally, they were asked if they were a supervisor; if they were, they were asked to indicate the number of years they have been a supervisor at their current organization.

Attitudes and Opinions of Workplace Bullying. Respondents were then asked a series of questions about workplace bullying, including whether they have ever been a witness to, victim of, or perpetrator of workplace bullying, as drawn from (Society of Human Resource Management [SHRM], 2016). If they answered yes, they were also asked how recent these events were. These questions were asked twice: first without any priming about the definition of workplace bullying, and second with an explanation of it. The second set of questions appeared after the language in Figure 7.1.

Experiences with Workplace Bullying. With the definition of workplace bullying and examples, participants were asked to then indicate if they have ever been a witness to, victim of, or perpetrator of the specific types of workplace bullying. If yes, they were asked to indicate when the most recent incident occurred. Regarding the most recent workplace bullying incident they witnessed, respondents were also asked to indicate who the victim and

Figure 7.1

Language Provided to Respondents About Workplace Bullying

The term "workplace bullying" refers to unreasonable behavior by a person (or group of people) that intimidates, degrades, offends, threatens, or humiliates a worker (or group of workers). Workplace bullying negatively affects the physical or psychological health of the targeted employee(s). Workplace bullying generally involves repeated, unreasonable actions, but it can also be a single, severe action. National data suggest that many behaviors can contribute to workplace bullying.

This issue is complicated. No single behavior is necessarily evidence of bullying. Workplace bullying often involves an abuse or misuse of power. However, many bullying situations involve employees bullying their peers.

Workplace bullying is not a tough, but fair supervisor; a tough union advocate; a reclusive coworker (Williams & Ruiz, 2012).

Examples of "workplace bullying" are:

1. Verbal abuse-shouting, swearing, name calling
2. Malicious gossiping and/or spreading lies/rumors about workers
3. Threats or intimidation
4. Cruel comments or teasing
5. Ignoring/excluding workers
6. Unduly harsh or constant criticism
7. Aggression
8. Abuse of authority
9. Unjustified interference with work performance
10. Use of technology for bullying
11. Physical assaults

perpetrator were: supervisor/manager, coworker, subordinate, client, or other, with an option to indicate who.

Participants were also asked if and how they intervened in the last time they witnessed workplace bullying. If they reported they did intervene, they were asked whether they spoke up to the perpetrator, told a supervisor or human resources (HR), or "other," to which they could add information. Finally, participants were given the opportunity to share their experiences regarding workplace bullying in an open-ended question. This question was asked in hopes of collecting qualitative data, which to the authors knowledge has not been analyzed in the local government setting.

Policy. To understand what workplaces are doing about bullying, participants were asked four questions about workplace bullying policy in their organization. The purpose of these questions was to examine whether employees perceived that their workplaces already had documented policies in place and how they were communicated. Respondents could indicate yes, maybe, or no to policies being communicated in the employee handbook, during orientation, in the code of conduct, on the organization's website, through specialized anti-bullying training, during staff meetings, and through communications from either HR or management (SHRM, 2016). While these questions ask respondents to indicate how policies are presented to them, these responses reflect perceptions, rather than the actual existence of such policies.

Participants were also asked who handles their organization's response to workplace bullying reports, including HR, management, immediate supervisors (of victim or perpetrator), legal counsel, security, and a specialized committee for workplace bulling (SHRM, 2016). Respondents were allowed to indicate they were not sure and an "other" option.

Perceived Outcomes. To understand the perceived effects of bullying, participants were asked about the outcomes experienced by the organization after workplace bullying incident. Respondents were able to indicate yes, maybe or no to the following outcomes experienced by the organization after bullying incidents: decreased morale, trust in coworkers, trust in management, trust in HR, and productivity, and increased stress, turnover, and absenteeism (SHRM, 2016).

STUDY FINDINGS

Sample Demographics

A total of 18 employees—nine from each municipality—participated in the survey. Because the city managers did not provide a total number of employees to which they sent the survey invitation, a response rate cannot be estimated. Overall, the sample is diverse in terms of gender, but is homogenous in terms of race: nine respondents (50%) are women, seven men, and two did not answer; 94% of the sample identified as White (one respondent is Black and one preferred not to answer).

Twenty-seven percent of the sample have worked in government for fewer than 10 years, 16% have worked between 10 and 19 years, and 38% have worked in government for 20 years or more. Additionally, 11 participants (61%) are supervisors, while the remaining seven are not. Table 7.1 displays which departments in which the participants currently work. Thirty-three percent of the sample reported working in the police department; half of the sample work in either police or fire and rescue. Other respondents reported working in libraries, parks and recreation, the city managers' office, and finance. Two did not report their department. Participants were not asked for their job titles in an effort to keep responses anonymous.

Attitudes and Opinions of Workplace Bullying

Participants were asked several questions about workplace bullying without any definition or explanation. Table 7.2 displays the results of these questions. Ninety-four percent of participants said they were familiar with the term workplace bullying. Overall, less than half of the respondents reported witnessing or being a perpetrator of workplace bullying.

Experiences With Workplace Bullying

Respondents indicated whether they had been a victim of workplace bullying at their current organization. Table 7.3 displays the participants' responses on which type of workplace bullying they had experienced.

Table 7.1

Departments in Which Respondents Work

Department	Frequency
Police	6
Fire & Rescue	3
Library	2
Parks and Recreation	2
City Manager's Office	2
Finance	1
Missing/No response	2
Total	18

Table 7.2

Attitudes of Workplace Bullying

	Yes	Maybe	No
Are you familiar with the term "workplace bullying?"	17	1	0
Do you believe you have witnessed "workplace bullying" while working at your current organization?	5	3	10
Do you believe you have been the perpetrator of "workplace bullying" while working at your current organization?	1	4	13

Less than half of the participants reported experiencing workplace bullying actions. The most prevalent types of workplace bullying were "verbal abuse," "malicious gossiping and/or spreading lies/rumors," "cruel comments or teasing," and "abuse of authority," with four respondents each indicating they have experienced such bullying. Respondents were less sure about whether they were victims of "threats or intimidation," "ignoring/excluding workers," and "aggression," as respondents indicated "maybe" at the same or higher level of frequency than "yes." Additionally, one participant reported they maybe had been physically assaulted at their current organization.

Table 7.3

Types of Workplace Bullying Experienced by Respondents

	Yes	Maybe	No
1. Verbal abuse-shouting, swearing, name calling	4	0	14
2. Malicious gossiping and/or spreading lies/rumors about workers	4	2	12
3. Threats or intimidation	2	2	14
4. Cruel comments or teasing	4	2	12
5. Ignoring/excluding workers	2	3	13
6. Unduly harsh or constant criticism	3	2	13
7. Aggression	1	4	13
8. Abuse of authority	4	2	12
9. Unjustified interference with work performance	3	2	13
10. Use of technology for bullying	2	0	16
11. Physical assaults	0	1	17

Table 7.4 displays when was the last time participants were victims of specific workplace bullying behavior. While no more than five respondents indicated experiencing a particular type of bullying, most incidents appeared to have happened within the last five years, but not in the last year. By far, more respondents reported being victims of workplace bullying within the last five years, but not in the last year. Two respondents reported being a victim of a physical assault in the last five years. Only four incidents of workplace bullying occurred within the last year, as indicated by these results.

Respondents were asked if they were perpetrators of any of the various types of bullying behaviors. of any of the various types of bullying behaviors. One respondent each indicated they verbally abused, spread rumors or malicious gossip, and ignored or excluded workers. More respondents indicated they might have engaged in bullying behaviors: two respondents indicated they maybe ignored/excluded workers and interfered with work performance. Verbal abuse, cruel comments and teasing, and harsh criticism was "maybe" perpetrated by one respondent each. None of these incidents appeared to have happened in the last year, and instead, in the last five.

A different picture emerges when asked about witnessing bullying at work; responses are shown in Table 7.5. More respondents reported witnessing workplace bullying at their current organization than being victims

Table 7.4

Time of Most Recent Workplace Bullying Victimization

	In the last 5 years	In the last year
1. Verbal abuse-shouting, swearing, name calling	4	1
2. Malicious gossiping and/or spreading lies/rumors about workers	4	1
3. Threats or intimidation	4	0
4. Cruel comments or teasing	3	1
5. Ignoring/excluding workers	4	0
6. Unduly harsh or constant criticism	3	1
7. Aggression	4	0
8. Abuse of authority	5	0
9. Unjustified interference with work performance	5	0
10. Use of technology for bullying	4	0
11. Physical assaults	2	0

or perpetrators. Thirty-eight percent of respondents reported witnessing "malicious gossiping and/or spreading lies/rumors about workers," and 33% reported being witness to "verbal abuse-shouting, swearing, name calling," "threats or intimidation," "cruel comments of teasing," and "unduly harsh or constant criticism." Additionally, 27% of participants witnessed "ignoring/excluding workers," "abuse of authority," and "unjustified interference with work performance." Nobody reported being witness to physical assault. In terms of when respondents witnessed bullying, most indicated they witnessed it in the last five years, but not in the last year (half of the sample). Two respondents each indicated being witness in the last year, six months, and month. Three did not respond.

Finally, with regards to their experiences, participants were asked who the perpetrator was in the most recent workplace bullying incident. 55% of participants (10) reported that the victim in the most recent incident they witnessed was a coworker, and 22% (4) reported that it was a subordinate. Thirty-eight percent (n = 7) of respondents indicated reported that the perpetrator in the more recent incident was a supervisor/manager, 33% (n = 6) reported it was a coworker, and one person reported it was a subordinate. Six respondents (33%) reported intervening in the most recent incident of workplace bullying they

Table 7.5

Types of Workplace Bullying Incidents Witnessed by Respondents

	Yes	Maybe	No
1. Verbal abuse-shouting, swearing, name calling	6	2	10
2. Malicious gossiping and/or spreading lies/rumors about workers	7	4	7
3. Threats or intimidation	6	1	11
4. Cruel comments or teasing	6	3	9
5. Ignoring/excluding workers	5	2	11
6. Unduly harsh or constant criticism	6	0	12
7. Aggression	3	3	12
8. Abuse of authority	5	2	11
9. Unjustified interference with work performance	5	1	12
10. Use of technology for bullying	2	1	15
11. Physical assaults	0	0	18

witnessed; five said they spoke to the perpetrator, and one reported that they told their supervisor.

Workplace Bullying Policy

Table 7.6 displays responses regarding workplace policies on bullying. Fifty percent reported that their city has a documented form of workplace bullying policy in the employee handbook. Overall, most participants either were not sure or reported that their city did not have a documented policy in other forms such as during in person situations such as staff meetings, orientation, or training.

Table 7.6

Documented Workplace Bullying Policy

	Yes	Maybe	No
1. In the employee handbook	9	2	3
2. During employee orientation	3	6	5
3. In the organization code of conduct	5	7	2
4. On the organization's website	3	1	10
5. During staff meetings	2	2	10
6. Through communications (e.g., e-mails, flyers, pamphlets) from HR	2	2	10
7. Through communications (e.g., e-mails, flyers, pamphlets) from management	3	2	9
8. Through bullying prevention training	3	1	10

When it comes to handling workplace bullying incidents, as shown in Table 7.7, respondents indicate that managers and supervisors typically are responsible. In addition, over half of respondents reported that the organizational response to workplace bullying policy depends on the specific circumstances.

Perceived Outcomes of Workplace Bullying

Table 7.8 shows the outcomes workplace bullying has had on the workplace culture, as perceived by the survey respondents. Fifty percent of the respondents reported decreased morale and trust among coworkers, and

Table 7.7

Organizational Response To Alleged Bullying Incidents

	Frequency
1. Response depends on the specific circumstances	9
2. Internal investigation	3
3. Written warning	5
4. Performance improvement plan	3
5. Referral to an EAP (employee assistance program) or counseling	2
6. Suspension	2
7. Termination (zero tolerance)	3
8. Mandatory anger management training	3
9. Demotion	1
10. Other	3

Table 7.8

Perceived Organizational Outcomes Of Workplace Bullying

	Yes	Maybe	No
Decreased			
Morale	9	1	3
Trust among coworkers	9	2	2
Productivity	8	2	3
Trust in management	6	3	4
Trust in human resources	3	5	4
Increased			
Stress and/or depression levels	8	2	3
Turnover	5	3	4
Absenteeism	5	4	3

eight employees (44%) reported decreased productivity. Thirty-three percent of respondents stated that workplace bullying resulted in decreased trust in management. Forty-four percent reported increased stress/depression levels, while 27% reported increased turnover and increased absenteeism. For all categories there were missing and "maybe" responses.

This is similar to outcomes covered in the previous studies, which found that victims suffered from depression, and that increase in turnover and absenteeism were common outcomes of workplace bullying (Rayner, 1997; Hoel et al., 2003; Kivimäki et al., 2000).

Finally, respondents were given a chance to elaborate on an experience they had with workplace bullying. One female supervisor noted that a previous supervisor was "a terrible bully." A second female supervisor talked about her experienced with a subordinate who "has played some immature jokes on another employee," who in turn, reported it. She noted speaking to the bully and "warned him not to do things that affect another employees [sic] job and let him know that if the other person does not think its [sic] funny then it is not a joke and becomes harassment." This response is interesting because she refers to the jokes that one employee made as harassment. If the jokes were based on another employee's protected characteristics, then this situation would meet the legal definition of harassment. However, the participant could be using the term harassment in a looser way. Additionally, she mentioned that the jokes interfered with the target employee's work. This is consistent with previously described definition of bullying and its impacts.

Lastly, a female employee noted that while her workplace is "very liberal" with "liberal employees," sometimes "comments are … directed at those with more conservative values and its [sic] wrong." While it is unclear whether this constitutes bullying behavior—for example, it's unknown if these comments are said *to* people—it is important to note that this participant believes that this type of behavior is an example of workplace bullying.

To conclude, the results show that workplace bullying does occur in local governments but does not occur often. While all listed bullying behaviors were either witnessed or committed, those that were less violent, such as gossiping or exclusion, were more prevalent. Furthermore, most employees stated that their city had a documented policy on workplace. However, most employees reported that the documentation was only given in a written form rather than through face-to-face communication. Additionally, employees perceive negative workplace impacts as a result of bullying in the workplace.

DISCUSSION

Workplace bullying is a phenomenon that has negative effect on not only victims, but anyone involved, including the organization as a whole (Bowling & Beehr, 2006; Brousse et al., 2008; Lapierre et al, 2005; Glasø & Notelaers, 2012, Eron et al., 1987; Nielsen & Einarsen, 2012; Hoel et al., 2003; Kivimäki et al., 2000; Glasø & Notelaers, 2012; Randall, 1997). Between January 2009 and December 2015, 18 state-level court cases referred to workplace bullying specifically (Richardson, Hall, et al., 2016). Comparatively, 93 federal court cases between January 2009 and October 2014 referenced workplace bullying (Richardson, Joiner, et al., 2016). Therefore, workplace bullying is an issue with legal consequences and can affect all types of organizations. These behaviors, and their resulting consequences, should be of interest to managers, consultants, and human resource professionals (Mata, 2016).

To the authors' knowledge, there is a dearth of inquiry into workplace bullying in the public sector, especially in the United States and at the local government level. To fill this gap, this present study asked if and which types of workplace bullying occurred in local governments, as well as the perceptions by employees of workplace bullying policies and effects on the organization. Surveys completed by employees of two local governments indicate that workplace bullying—of various types and severity—and that communications about workplace bullying policies could be improved. In addition, respondents indicated that they perceived workplace bulling to have negative organization effects.

Almost all participants in this study indicated they were familiar with "workplace bullying," and while a smaller number of participants indicated being a victim, perpetrator, or witness to bullying, it is clear that employees are familiar with it as an issue. The most common bullying behaviors witnessed were nonviolent behaviors, such as malicious gossiping/spreading rumors, verbal abuse, threats/intimidation, cruel comments, and harsh criticism. Some participants stated that bullying behaviors occurred within the last month (11%), but a majority reported that these behaviors had occurred with five years (50%).

Participants in this study indicated that their organization has policies in place to address workplace bullying, but results are mixed on how those policies are communicated. A majority of respondents reported receiving a written policy, such as in an employee handbook, but there seemed to be little verbal communication about this policy, such as in the form of training. While written policies are generally viewed as more legitimate than unwritten policies (see, e.g., DeHart-Davis, 2017), issues such as workplace bullying may be worth addressing periodically through verbal emphasis or training. According to SHRM, a good policy would include an objective of the policy, definitions, and examples of what is considered workplace bullying. It should also expand on what evidence is needed to report workplace bullying and who should employees report incidents of workplace bullying to. Moreover, the policy should outline how the organization will proceed with investigating and reprimanding incidents of workplace bullying. A policy should give employers and employees should have a clear understanding of what qualifies and bullying and the process that employees should expect if they report or are reported (Society of Human Resource Management, 2016). Future research on workplace bullying in the public sector should explore workplace policies and their effectiveness.

This study also asked respondents to indicate their perceptions of the effects of workplace bullying. Previous literature has explored the outcomes of workplace bullying on individuals, witnesses, perpetrators, and organizations (Bowling & Beehr, 2006; Brousse et al., 2008; Lapierre et al., 2005; Glasø & Notelaers, 2012; Eron et al., 1987; Nielsen & Einarsen, 2012; Hoel et al., 2003; Kivimäki et al., 2000; Randall, 1997). Participants indicated that they perceived decreased trust in management and coworkers as well as decreased morale and productivity. They also indicated that bullying seems to increase turnover, absenteeism, and depression and stress. These results are similar to outcomes reported by previous studies (Rayner, 1997; Hoel et al., 2003; Kivimäki et al., 2000). This suggests that the outcomes of workplace bullying are similar in the public and private sectors, but future research should explore more directly the organizational and individual effects of workplace bullying in the public sector.

Limitations

While this study generates interesting conclusions and future research questions, it does have limitations. The most critical limitation is the small and limited sample, which limits the generalizability of its findings. However, respondents in this small sample did indicate that workplace bullying is prevalent in their organizations. While this could indicate that bullying behaviors are common, it may also be a reflection of the organizational cultures in which the participants work. In addition, the sample is racially homogenous, which may not capture bullying in the same way that a racially-diverse sample (especially of a racially-diverse organization) would. The lack of diversity could reflect the relative homogeneity of the population of the cities themselves. Future research should strive for larger, more representative samples from which to generalize findings. Research should also consider how race, gender, and organizational status influence perceptions of and experiences with bullying.

Notably, one likely contributor to the small sample is that two cities declined to participate because of legal issues related to workplace bullying. Both cities indicated these issues were ongoing at the time of the invitation, which highlights the importance of understanding and preventing bullying in the workplace. After these cities have resolved the legal issues—or after any organization adopts anti-bullying policies—they may want to survey their employees for at least two reasons: first, to gauge if workplace bullying is (still) a perceived problem and how often it happens; and second, to examine if employees are aware of the organization's policies and procedures regarding bullying in the workplace.

Second, this study relies on self-report surveys, which may be influenced by response biases (Donaldson & Grant-Vallone, 2002). One type of response bias is self-report bias, whereas participants underreport negative behaviors and overreport positive behaviors (Donaldson & Grant-Vallone, 2002). They may also answer questions in the way they think the researcher wants (Donaldson & Grant-Vallone, 2002). These data may also be susceptible to social desirability bias. This bias occurs when a participant gives a socially desirable response instead of answering truthfully (Grimm, 2010). While this could explain why there were so few participants that reported being perpetrators, there were still many participants who reported being a victim or witness. Likely, such bias led to *under*reporting of such behaviors. Future research should consider utilizing different data, such as interviews, incident reports, policy examinations, and surveys that collect information from multiple people about the same event to help mitigate the effects of these biases.

Third, this study focuses on survey responses by employees in these local governments. Participating cities were not asked to provide their policies or about how they are communicated, and thus perceptions about these policies cannot be confirmed. Future research should consider the gap between perceptions about policies and the policies themselves; large gaps may indicate a communication issue on behalf of the organization. In addition, studies should consider how communication of policies—as well as the policies themselves—have an impact on the prevalence of reported bullying incidents.

CONCLUSION

To prevent workplace bullying, it is critical to understand how and how much it occurs. This itself presents a challenge: understanding and conceptualizing of workplace bullying and victim experiences can vary significantly (Randall, 1997). Furthermore, is it difficult to address issues of workplace bullying because there is often a lack of proper documentation (Earnshaw & Morrison, 2001). For victims to receive any compensation, they must prove that their injuries were not caused from a non-work-related source (Earnshaw & Morrison, 2001).

At present, there is no federal anti-workplace bullying policy in the United States. Some states have made efforts. For example, Tennessee is the only state to have a workplace bullying law. The 2014 Tennessee Healthy Workplace Act encourages public employers to prevent bullying behavior in the workplace by implementing a model policy created by the

Tennessee Advisory Commission on Intergoverment (Dade & Schuering, 2014). Another 29 states and two territories in the United States have passed Healthy Workplace legislation. While these laws do not explicitly deal with workplace bullying, they do punish employers for encouraging hostile work environments (Dade & Scheuring, 2014). However, these laws press organizations to be aware of workplace bullying behaviors and how such behaviors may violate existing law, even if present laws do not explicitly prohibit bullying.

Despite efforts by lawmakers to prevent hostile work environments, efforts aimed specifically at anti-workplace bullying in the United States continue to be limited. Efforts are similarly limited in understanding the state and effects of workplace bullying, both in public and private sectors for individuals and organizations. This research has established that at least some employees report bullying in the workplace, sounding the alarm for organizations, lawmakers, and researchers alike to act.

REFERENCES

Adams, A. (1992). *Bullying at work: How to confront and overcome it*. Virago.

Bowling, N. A., & Beehr, T. A. (2006). Workplace harassment from the victim's perspective: A theoretical model and meta-analysis. *Journal of Applied Psychology, 91*(5), 998–1012.

Branch, S., & Murray, J. (2015). Workplace bullying. *Organizational Dynamics, 44*(4), 287-295. https://doi.org/10.1016/j.orgdyn.2015.09.006

Brodsky, C. (1976). *The harassed worker*. Lanham, MD: Lexington Books.

Brousse, G., Fontana, L., Ouchchane, L., Boisson, C., Gerbaud, L., Bourguet, D., Perrier A., Schmitt A., Michel Llorca, P., & Chamoux, A. (2008). Psychopathological features of a patient population of targets of workplace bullying. *Occupational Medicine, 58*(2), 122–128.

Dade, J. M., & Schuering, E. R. (2014). States continue to propose antibullying legislation but fail to act. *Employment Relations Today, 41*(3), 61–70.

DeHart-Davis, L. (2017). *Creating effective rules in public sector organizations*. Georgetown University Press.

Donaldson, S. I., & Grant-Vallone, E. J. (2002). Understanding self-report bias in organizational behavior research. *Journal of Business and Psychology, 17*(2), 245–262.

Earnshaw, J., & Morrison, L. (2001). Should employers worry? Workplace stress claims following the John Walker decision. *Personnel Review, 30*(4), 468–487.

EEOC. (n.d.). *Laws enforced by EEOC*. https://www.eeoc.gov/statutes/laws-enforced-eeoc

Einarsen, S., Raknes, B. R. I., & Matthiesen, S. B. (1994). Bullying and harassment at work and their relationships to work environment quality: An exploratory study. *European journal of work and organizational psychology, 4*(4), 381–401.

Einarsen, S., & Skogstad, A. (1996). Bullying at work: Epidemiological findings in public and private organizations. *European Journal of Work and Organizational Psychology, 5*(2), 185–201.

Einarsen, S., & Raknes, B.I. (1997). Harassment in the workplace and the victimization of men. *Violence and Victims, 12*(3), 247–263.

Eron, L. D., Huesmann, L. H., Dubow, E., Romanoff, R., & Yarmel, P. W. (1987). Aggression and its correlates over 22 years. In N. H. Crowell, R. J. Blanchard, I. Evans, & C. R. O'Donnel (Eds.), *Childhood aggression and violence: Sources of influence, prevention and control*. Academic Press.

Glasø, L., & Notelaers, G. (2012). Workplace bullying, emotions, and outcomes. *Violence and Victims, 27*(3), 360–377.

Gould, T. (2019, May 15). *Company's on the hook for $4.7 million in bullying case.* https://www.hrmorning.com/articles/companys-on-the-hook-for-4-7-million-in-bullying-case/

Grimm, P. (2010). Social desirability bias. *The SAGE Encyclopedia of Social Science Research Methods*. SAGE.

Hoel, S., & Cooper, C. (2000). *Destructive conflict and bullying at work*. University of Manchester.

Hoel, H., Einarsen, S., & Cooper, C. L. (2003) *Organizational effects of bullying. Bullying and Emotional Abuse in the workplace: international perspectives in research and practice*. Taylor and Francis.

Hutchinson, J., & Eveline, J. (2010). Workplace bullying policy in the Australian Public Sector: Why has gender been ignored? *Australian Journal of Public Administration, 69*(1), 47–60.

Kivimäki, M., Elovainio, M., & Vahtera, J. (2000). Workplace bullying and sickness absence in hospital staff. *Occupational and Environmental Medicine, 57*(10), 656–660.

Lapierre, L. M., Spector, P. E., & Leck, J. D. (2005). Sexual versus nonsexual workplace aggression and victims overall job satisfaction: A meta-analysis. *Journal of Occupational Health Psychology, 10*(2), 155–169.

Lewis, D., & Gunn, R. (2007). Workplace bullying in the public sector: Understanding the racial dimension. *Public Administration, 85*(3), 641–665.

Leymann, H. (1990). Mobbing and psychological terror at workplaces. *Violence and Victims, 5,* 119–126.

Leymann, H. (1990). Mobbing and psychological terror at workplaces. *Violence and Victims, 5*(2), 119–126.

Lutgen-Sandvik, P., & Tracy, S. J., & Alberts, J. K. (2006). Burned by bullying in the American workplace: Prevalence, perception, degree and impact. *Journal of Management Studies, 44*(6), 837-862.

Manners, I., & Cates, S. (2016). Bullying in the workplace: Does it exist in United States. *International Journal of Business & Public Administration, 13*(2), 99–114.

Mata, L. S. (2016). *Workplace bullying: A phenomenological study of its human and organizational productivity effects among military personnel* (Doctoral dissertation). Capella University.

Nagele-Piazza, L. (2018, April 11). *Workplace bullying and harassment: What's the difference?* https://www.shrm.org/resourcesandtools/legal-and-compliance/state-and-local-updates/pages/workplace-bullying.aspx

Namie, G. (2014). *2014 WBI U.S. Workplace Bullying Survey.* https://www.workplace-bullying.org/wbiresearch/wbi-2014survey/

Namie, G. (2017). *2017 WBI U.S. Workplace Bullying Survey.* https://www.workplace-bullying.org/wbiresearch/wbi-2017-survey/

Nielsen, M. B., & Einarsen, S. (2012). Outcomes of exposure to workplace bullying: A meta-analytic review. *Work & Stress, 26*(4), 309–332. https://doi.org/10.1080/02678373.2012.734709

Olweus, D. (1993). *Bullying at school: What we know and what we can do*. Blackwell.

Occupational Safety & Health Administration. (2005). *Workplace violence.* https://www.osha.gov/archive/oshinfo/priorities/violence.html

Randall, P. (1997). *Adult bullying: Perpetrators and victims*. Routledge.

Rayner, C. (1997). The incidence of workplace bullying. *Journal of Community & Applied Social Psychology*, 7(3), 199–208.

Richardson, R. E., Hall, R., & Joiner, S. (2016). Workplace bullying in the United States: An analysis of state court cases. *Cogent Business & Management, 3*(1). https://doi.org/10.1080/23311975.2016.1256594

Richardson, R., Joiner, S., & Hall, R. (2016). The status of workplace bullying in federal court cases. *Academy of Business Research Journal, 1*(2016), 117–131.

Society of Human Resource Management. (2016). *Workplace Bullying Policy.* https://www.shrm.org/resourcesandtools/tools-and-samples/policies/pages/cms_018350.aspx

Van Aalten, C. B. (1994). Violence in the workplace. *The NCO Journal, 4*(2), 16–17.

Vartia, M. (1996). The sources of bullying—Psychological work environment and organizational climate. *European Journal of Work and Organizational Psychology, 5*(2), 203–214.

Vega, G., & Comer, D. R. (2005). Sticks and stones may break your bones, but words can break your spirit: Bullying in the workplace. *Journal of Business Ethics, 58*(1-3), 101–109.

Venetoklis, T., & Kettunen, P. (2016). Workplace Bullying in the Finnish Public Sector: Who, me? *Review of Public Personnel Administration, 36*(4), 370–395.

Williams, E. E., & Ruiz, Y. (2012). *Workplace Bullying Survey Final Report* (pp. 1–24, Rep).

Workplace Bullying Institute. (n.d.). *Impact of workplace bullying on coworkers.* https://www.workplacebullying.org/individuals/impact/coworkers/

Zapf, D., Knorz, C., & Kulla, M. (1996). On the relationship between mobbing factors, and job content, social work environment, and health outcomes. *European Journal of Work and Organizational Psychology, 5*(2), 215–237.

CHAPTER 8

PREDICTING ETHICAL BEHAVIOR

A Person-Situation Approach

Elizabeth Ritterbush
DDI

Adam Smith
Kincentric> A Spencer Stuart Company

Rachel Whitman and Daniel J. Svyantek
Auburn University

Ethics and morality have been issues discussed philosophically for thousands of years by humans. This discussion has increasingly become more empirical with the rise of social sciences. Globalization and access to media has made immoral or unethical acts, especially as they relate to business, increasingly more salient during the late 20th and early 21st centuries. This has led to calls to increase organizational transparency and for a renewed emphasis on reducing unethical behavior. The National Business

Organizations Behaving Badly:
Destructive Behavior and Corrective Responses, pp. 149–180

Ethics Survey (Ethics Resource Center, 2013) reported a decline (4% in two years) in unethical behavior within organizations. However, we are unable to speculate whether this decrease is due to one data point or is reflective of a greater trend. Therefore, though this is positive news, more should be done to study how organizations facilitate ethical, or inhibit ensure unethical, behavior. More work is clearly needed to investigate the predictors of ethical and unethical behavior in organizations.

An interesting perspective for understanding ethical behavior is found in the discussion of how the person and situation influences behaviors in organizations. Funder (2001) has proposed that to understand behavior three variables must be studied. First, the person who will perform the behavior must be understood. Second, the situation in which the person resides must be understood. Finally, behaviors that the individual are asked to perform must be understood. This is particularly true for behaviors in which choice exists. Funder has noted that by understanding these three factors, personality and social psychology may be integrated. A brief description of how this integration occurs is provided in the next section.

PERSON AND SITUATIONAL INFLUENCES ON ORGANIZATIONAL BEHAVIOR

The Historical Debate

The mission of personality psychology is to account for the characteristic patterns of thoughts, emotions, behaviors, and the psychological mechanisms that generate these thought patterns (Funder, 2001). However, personality psychology is being informed by the realization that social contexts impact the behaviors of individuals within them.

There are two primary theoretical approaches to personality (Mischel & Shoda, 1998): The trait and social-cognitive approaches. The first approach is the dispositional or trait theory approach to personality (Mischel & Shoda, 1998). This approach proposes the existence of broad, stable traits, factors, or behavioral dispositions as its basic units. Its fundamental goal is to characterize individuals in terms of a comprehensive, but finite and preferably small, set of stable dispositions that remain relatively invariant across situations. These traits are distinctive for the individual and determine a wide range of important behaviors. The second approach, the social-cognitive approach construes personality as a system of mediating units (e.g., encodings, expectancies, and goals) and psychological processes that *interact* with the situation in which an individual resides in the expression of personality.

The dispositional approach is most commonly reflected in the Big Five (Funder, 2001; Mischel & Shoda, 1998). Currently, the Big Five model of personality forms the common currency of personality research (Funder, 2001). This model is the dominant theoretical approach to investigating personality in many areas within I/O psychology, including career success (e.g., Boudreau et al., 2001; Seibert & Kraimer, 2001), leadership (e.g., Judge & Bono, 2000), selection (e.g., Barrick & Mount, 1991; Hurtz & Donovan, 2000), organizational commitment (e.g., Allen & Meyer, 1990) and organizational citizenship behaviors (e.g., Podsakoff et al., 2000; Organ & Ryan, 1995). Across studies and meta-analytically, conscientiousness has been most consistently linked to job performance (Barrick & Mount, 1991; Hurtz & Donovan, 2000; Mount & Barrick, 1995; Salgado, 2002). However, the relationship between these variables has been moderate at best. Meta-analytic results indicate a mean sample-weighted correlation of .10 (Salgado, 2002) to .18 (Mount & Barrick, 1995). In a more recent meta-analysis conducted by Hurtz and Donovan (2000) on explicit measures of the Big Five, the estimated true validity of conscientiousness in predicting job performance was .20. This validity was highest for sales positions (.26) and customer service jobs (.25). Therefore, from these results, it can be concluded that the personality traits (i.e., the Big Five) are moderately predictive of overall job performance.

Formal job descriptions describe activities that contribute to task performance (Borman & Motowidlo, 1993). Employees also augment organizational effectiveness through behaviors that are not directly related to their chief task functions. These acts are important because they form the organizational, social, and psychological context for task activities and procedures. These activities have been labeled discretionary behaviors (Zeithaml et al., 1990), contextual performance (Borman & Motowidlo, 1993) or organizational citizenship behaviors (Bateman & Organ, 1983; Smith et al., 1983). Organ (1997) has proposed that Borman and Motowidlo's (1993) term, contextual performance, may be the most accurate for describing such activities.

Since these extra-role behaviors are considered discretionary, researchers have tried to link personality traits empirically to contextual performance (e.g., Borman & Motowidlo, 1993; Borman et al., 2001; Ilies et al., 2006; Organ & Ryan, 1995). Hurtz and Donovan (2000) examined the predictive validities of the Big Five for two aspects of contextual performance: Job dedication and interpersonal facilitation. Conscientiousness once again emerged as the strongest predictor (.15–.18).

In addition, Hogan et al. (1998) showed that the relationship between personality and contextual performance is affected by the purpose of the contextual performance rating. Specifically, contextual performance appraisal in jobs with no advancement potential versus performance appraisal for jobs with opportunities for promotion. In the former case, conscientiousness scores are predictive of contextual performance, while in the latter case, ambition/surgency scores were predictive of contextual performance. These results are interpreted as showing the relationship between personality and contextual performance is dependent on the reasons for performing the behavior.

Therefore, situational influences are affecting the performance of behavior. The finding that personality does not predict contextual performance to the same degree as the prediction for task performance is troublesome. This is especially true because contextual performance is considered more volitional than task performance. These somewhat inclusive findings for personality prediction, however, may simply reflect an over-emphasis on effects of personality independent of the situation. The social-cognitive model would argue that, at some level, personality is adaptive to the situation, thereby explaining the lack of consistent findings for personality by itself. This leads to the proposal that organizational behavior may only be understood by describing both the person and the situational influences interacting to create a behavioral pattern. This will be shown to be particularly important for ethical behavior in this chapter.

The two approaches, the social cognitive and dispositional, reflect a deeper question about human behavior. This debate concerns whether the person performing a behavior or the situation in which the behavior occurs is the primary cause of a human behavior. An understanding of the person, situation and the behaviors being performed are required for a clear understanding of human behavior (Funder, 2001). One potential source for explaining the linkage of the person and situation to behavior is Mischel's Cognitive-Affective Processing System (CAPS) model of personality (Funder, 2001). The CAPS model integrates the social-cognitive and dispositional approaches to understanding personality. The CAPS model is concerned with how these cognitions and affects change in their salience, or activation, over time and *in relation* to different situations (Mischel & Shoda, 1998). Personality generates the distinctive stable patterns of behavior characteristic of the individual, but an individual's personality does not operate in isolation. Personality interacts with the social world; thus, expression of personality is therefore contextualized. This model explains why the level of prediction of contextual performance by personality in isolation is moderate at best. The performance of behavior, therefore, depends on both situational features and on the cognitive-affective organization comprising the personality of the individual (Mischel & Shoda, 1998). Personality leads to behavioral profiles which specify what an individual will do in each situational context the individual encounters (Funder, 2001). An organizational construct, person-organization fit, provides a model for how members of organizations may form the behavioral profiles described by the CAPS model.

Person-Organization Fit and Behavior in Organizations

Person-environment fit is defined as the compatibility between individuals and their environment (van Vianen, 2018). Person-environment fit may be thought of as having are two primary factors. These are person-job fit (PJ) and person-organization (PO) fit (Kristof, 1996).

Person-job fit is concerned with the degree to which there is a match between an employee's skills and abilities and the requirements of the job the employee holds (Kristof, 1996). The better the match, the more likely the employee is to be a successful employee. As this match decreases and employees do not have the needed skills and abilities to perform the job, employees tend to be frustrated and dissatisfied. This leads to decreases in both individual and organizational performance.

Person-organization fit shows how people and situations create behavioral profiles for volitional behaviors which may not be directly linked to task performance (e.g., contextual performance or ethical behavior) is concerned with the degree to which there is a match between employee characteristics and the characteristics of the organization (e.g., organizational culture) in which the employee works (Kristoff, 1996). The better the match, the more likely the employee is to be a successful employee. For example, some organizations value teamwork and some organizations value individual accomplishment. Individuals with a high need for individual accomplishment will have good fit with an organization valuing individual accomplishment: However, their fit will be poor in an organization valuing teamwork. As this match decreases and employee characteristics and values do not reflect organizational characteristics, employees tend to be frustrated and dissatisfied. This leads to decreases in both individual, and organizational, satisfaction and performance.

Fit can take two forms. Fit may be complementary or supplementary (Kristof-Brown et al., 2005). Person-job fit is typically thought of as complementary fit and relates to the knowledges, skills, and abilities of the different employees in a setting (van Vianen, 2018). Person-organization fit relates to the match of the values held by individuals within the organizational setting (van Vianen, 2018). Here the match affects behaviors in which the individual has the freedom to choose how to act. Therefore, person-organization fit may be critical as a model of understanding ethical behavior.

There are four primary organization-level variables, which help define the context of workplace behavior for individuals (Morgan, 1998). These variables each provide organizational members with information on preferred behaviors of an organization. One, *organizational culture*, is particularly important for volitional behaviors such as ethical behaviors. Organizational culture may be defined by a set of shared values and norms, held by employees, which guides employees' interactions with peers, management, and clients/customers (Morgan, 1998).

Svyantek and his colleagues (Svyantek, 1997; Svyantek & Brown, 2000) have proposed a two-factor model of organizational culture. The aspect of organizational culture of interest for this discussion is its integrative function. Here the group defines 1) what it means to be a member of the group; (2) social and economic justice within the group; (3) how the elements of the group are organized to produce a socially "good" group (Namenwirth & Weber, 1987). It is this integrative function which may have the strongest influence in volitional behaviors.

Summary

As noted above, Funder (2001) has proposed that to understand behavior three variables must be studied. First, the person who will perform the behavior must be understood. Second, the situation in which the person resides must be understood. Finally, behaviors that the individual are asked to perform must be understood. This is particularly true for behaviors in which choice exists. The remainder of this chapter explores the influence of all three factors on ethical behavior. The first study explores the way in which personality traits affect ethical behaviors within different decision contexts. There is no direct manipulation of the situation itself. Building on the results of this study, the second study assesses the effects of personality and the situation together on different behaviors.

STUDY 1

Ethics and morality have been issues of importance for hundreds of years. The rise of globalization and access to media has made immoral or unethical acts, especially as they relate to business, increasingly more salient. This has led to calls to increase organizational transparency and for a renewed emphasis on reducing unethical behavior. The National Business Ethics Survey (Ethics Resource Center, 2013) reported a decline (4% in two years) in unethical behavior within organizations. However, we are unable to speculate whether this decrease is due to one data point or is reflective of a greater trend. The methods used did not ask for behaviors regarding specific decisions/scenarios or their outcomes. Therefore, though this is positive news, more should be done to ensure the reduction of unethical behavior. More work is needed to investigate the predictors of immoral or unethical behavior.

Ethical Decision Making

A review of research (Craft, 2013) cited the primary foundational theories of ethical decision making as those explicitly dealing with morality (cf. Rest, 1994) and Jones (1991). These provide a working framework for understanding the processes related to ethical decision making. Rest's (1994) model included a four-step process for decision making which involves (1) recognizing the issue as a moral one, (2) making a judgment about the morality of the situation, (3) deciding to act upon the moral concerns over other concerns, and (4) then actually acting on any moral concerns (Rest, 1986, as cited in Craft, 2013). Each stage of this process may be affected by Jones's theory of moral intensity.

Jones's (1991) theory proposed that ethical issues can be defined by their moral intensity. Moral intensity is comprised of six elements. The first element is the *magnitude of consequences* which comprises all potential benefits or harms to individuals in the situation. The second element is that of *social consensus* which is related the social norms regarding the context. *Probability of effect* relates to the expected probability of the suspected consequences actually occurring. *Temporal immediacy* relates to the length of time present between the event and the expected outcome. This facet is targeted at those effects that are related to temporal discounting. *Subjective proximity* (social, cultural, psychological, and physical) to the victim or beneficiary of a moral/immoral also plays a role in ethical decision making. Lastly the *concentration of effect*, or the diffusion of consequences of an event, also plays a role in the actor's evaluation of a moral or ethical dilemma. Both this framework and that expressed by Rest (1986) provide a lens through which to categorize and attempt to integrate research on ethical dilemmas. Indeed, much of the research categorized by Craft (2013), O'Fallon and Butterfield (2005), and Lehnert et al. (2015) was classified using these theories.

In 2003, Kelley and Elm used Jones's (1991) theory as a basis for an examination of organizational factors that affected moral intensity of various situations. Kelley and Elm found an interaction between temporal immediacy, probability of effect, and magnitude of consequences post hoc. No support for the original factor structure as presented by Jones was found. However, this research was limited by a primarily qualitative design. The current research seeks to expand on this research by carefully examining ethical decision scenarios that manipulate and combine various situational contexts. Research of this kind will enable us to take a closer look at the potential antecedents of ethical decision making. It may also help to explain previous research (e.g., Dalton & Radtke (2013) which found organizational culture to have a significant effect on the tendency to engage in ethical behavior.

Within the literature there are two broad views regarding what predicts unethical or immoral behavior. Some researchers focus on individual differences, such as personality. Other theorists and researchers focus on situational predictors, such as organizational culture and societal norms/pressures. However, research using either of these viewpoints is often limited by a failure to include a variety of variables and contemplate the possibility of more complex models. More complex views of the individual differences that facilitate unethical tendencies is extremely important for the development of hiring and selection processes, especially as the general populous becomes increasingly more aware of nefarious business practices.

Personality

Previous research has indicated that conscientiousness is an important predictor of integrity and extra-role behaviors at work (Smith et al., 1983). This may be due in part to the likelihood of engaging in rule-following behavior when an individual has high levels of this trait. While the rule-abiding aspect of this trait may be highly relevant to situations that are guided more by rules than by social norms (e.g., organizational contexts), this trait appears to be no less important for predicting behavior from a social perspective. Other researchers have found conscientiousness to be more predictive of honest and accurate reporting than previously developed integrity measures (Horn et al., 2004). Although some argue that such findings are indicative of construct overlap between honesty, integrity, and conscientiousness (Becker, 1998), these findings are no less relevant to a work setting. Given that conscientiousness has been found to be an incredibly strong predictor of both job performance and integrity (Sackett & Wanek, 1996), it is important to consider the added benefit of using this trait as an antecedent of ethical behavior in addition to other personality traits. Thus:

> **H1:** Conscientiousness will be a significant predictor of ethical decision making across contexts.

The current research also investigates the effects of the Honesty-Humility trait of the HEXACO model (Lee et al., 2005). This trait has quickly arisen as the best singular predictor of integrity. The Dark Triad (i.e., Narcissism, Machiavellianism, and Psychopathy) has been theorized to be at the negative pole of the Honesty-Humility Scale (Lee & Ashton, 2014). Other researchers have found that Machiavellianism (Dalton & Radtke, 2013) and psychopathy (Stevens et al., 2012) are negatively related to integrity. One of the unique features of all of these traits is their relation to social and/or antisocial behaviors. Each of the dark triad traits in some way represents individuals that act against social norms. Honestly-Humility on the other hand is characterized partly by fairness and has adopted some of the facets which were previously related to the Five Factor model trait of agreeableness (Lee et al., 2008; Miller et al., 2011). If we are to assume that Jones's suppositions regarding moral intensity of ethical decisions (Jones, 1991) are at least partly true, then it is expected that these personality traits will predict more of the variance in ethical scenarios that focus on social characteristics of the situation as opposed to those that do not. Thus:

H2: Honesty-Humility and Agreeableness with be positively related to ethical decision making.

H3: The Dark Triad traits (particularly Machiavellianism and Psychopathy) will be negatively related to ethical decision making.

H4: Honesty-Humility, Agreeableness, Machiavellianism, and Psychopathy will have stronger relationships to ethical decisions that emphasize a social component as opposed to those that do not.

Context

Theorists such as Jones (1991) have argued that ethical decisions may be based primarily on the context in which they occur. Jones is not the first to speculate such ideas. Indeed, some of the greatest and most foundational ethical theorists across time, such as Aristotle and Kant, argued that the situational context of the decision being made is an important aspect of the subjective ethicality of such a decision (e.g., Solomon, 2004). This may help to explain the lack of a clear definition for ethical decision making. Indeed, morals and values vary not only between situations, but between cultures as well (Becker & Fritzsche, 1987). It is especially important that research in this area take into consideration a wide array of situations that may involve ethical and/or unethical decision making.

In 2001, Funder proposed that behavior cannot be predicted based on the knowledge of an individual's personality alone. The context of the situation is equally as important. However, relatively few studies have taken an integrative approach by examining personality and situational context simultaneously (Funder, 2001). Along a similar vein, Mischel (2004) argued that while aggregating information across contexts may be useful for answering some questions, it is by no means the end all be all. Ignoring the situational context and focusing purely on personality as a predictor fails to account for the variance in behaviors that we see for individuals with similar personalities across situations. Although, individuals may act the same way in near duplicated situations they may not act the same way in all situations requiring a certain trait (e.g., conscientiousness).

Previous researchers have noted that factors in the work environment may interact with personality to affect individual behaviors (Tett & Burnett, 2003). Tett and Burnett (2003) proposed that features such as job demands, distractions, releasers, and facilitators are all likely to affect the expression of various personality traits. These signals or cues may be present at the organizational, social, or task levels relative to the individual engaging in that behavior. Certain environmental cues may be more or less likely to illicit expression of various personality traits due to the strength of the cue itself. For instance, an interview with a stranger for a new job may illicit more socially desirable behavior than an interview with a current boss. Therefore, individual behaviors are likely to be situationally specific wherein various traits would be expressed differently depending on the situational context. Thus:

> **H5:** The predictive ability of personality traits on ethical decision making will differ depending on the context of the situation.

More specifically, not all ethical decisions implicitly involve social aspects. Consider the case of a tax preparer or accountant. Although these individuals are doing work that affects other individuals, individuals are far removed from the situation, resulting in lower levels of moral intensity as it relates to the *subjective proximity* described by Jones (1991). In these instances, less socially laden aspects of decisions may be more predictive of ethical decision making wherein these ethical decisions may be more rule-based in nature. On the other hand, consider the case of an individual faced with an ethical dilemma completely outside of the work realm. Suppose that this individual is faced with an ethical decision in which they may stand to gain from behaving unethically at the expense of a friend or relative. Although rule-abiding may be important in these contexts as well, it is far more likely that the pro- or anti-social nature of the individual would be more predictive in these situations.

METHOD

Participants

As recommended by Murphy (2002), a power analysis was conducted a priori in ordered to determine an adequate sample size for analysis.

Based on an analysis of the smallest significant correlation coefficient (.24) indicated by Paulhus and Williams (2002), a power analysis indicated that a minimum sample size of 183 would be needed for an alpha level of .05 with a power of .95. A total of 281 participants completed the survey. Participants that took more than two days or less than 15 minutes to complete the study were removed from the data set. This left 229 participants remaining for the analyses. 54 participants were male and 175 were female. Participant ages ranged from 18 to 33 with a median age of 20.

Materials

Six-Factor Personality. The Mini-IPIP6 was used to assess six personality traits, including the five traits from the Big Five model as well as an additional trait of Honesty-Humility from the HEXACO model. Reliability for each trait ranged (Extraversion α = .88; Agreeableness α = .69; Conscientiousness α = .73; Emotional Stability α = .65; Openness α = .75; Honesty-Humility α = .73). Scores for each scale of the personality measure were computed by averaging scores accordingly.

The Dark Triad. Due to previous findings by Maples et al. (2014), the SD3 (Jones & Paulhus, 2014) was used for measuring the dark triad personality traits. An analysis of scale reliability for Machiavellianism, Narcissism, and Psychopathy indicated Cronbach α's of .80, .73, and .72 respectively.

Ethical Decision Making. An ethical measure derived from Brown et al. (2010) was used to measure EDM. This assessment consists of two hypothetical situations that are rated on an 11-point scale whereby each participant will indicate the likelihood of them engaging in an unethical act. Due to the limited nature of this measure, it was decided to develop additional items as well. These items were developed with special care to include a variety of ethical scenarios that are applicable to both college students and those employed elsewhere. Initial analysis of the newly formed measure indicated a Cronbach's alpha of .72.

However, due to the vignette style of each scenario and previous theory by Jones (1991) and Rest (1994), it was decided to investigate the multifaceted nature of the ethical decision scenarios post hoc. Analyses and sorting of items based on wording was conducted by a team of graduate and undergraduate students and indicated five potential context dimensions. These dimensions were not unique to any particular scenario and were found to vary across scenarios. Each scenario was rated on their presence or absence of all five dimensions simultaneously. These dimensions included whether the situation involved (1) other individuals (i.e. organizational versus social); (2) if the scenarios were realistic; (3) if the cost and/or benefits would affect the person making the decision; (4) if the cost and/or benefits would affect the person making the decision someone else; and (5) and the severity of the outcomes. Given the nature of the scenarios it was possible for each to be included in a variety of categories. The most consistent split of items was based on whether the scenario involved other individuals or not whereby eight of the scenarios were social in nature and eight of the scenarios were more organizational in nature. For a complete list of item numbers and their corresponding context dimensions see Table 8.1.

Table 8.1

Item Numbers and Corresponding Context Dimensions

Item	Context	Realistic	Gain	Cost	Outcome	Predictor Variables
11	Organizational	Yes	Personal	Others/Both	Major	C
12	Organizational	Yes	Personal	Others/Both	Minor	—
1	Organizational	Yes	Personal	Others	Minor	C, –M
15	Organizational	Yes	Personal	Others	Major	C, –N
16	Organizational	Yes	Personal	Others	Minor	C, –M
5	Organizational	Yes	Personal	Personal	Major	C
13	Organizational	Yes	None	Personal	Major	(H)
6	Organizational	No	None	Personal	Major	–C, P
8	Social	Yes	Personal	Others	Minor	–O, C, –M
2	Social	Yes	Personal	Others	Minor	(C), A, H, –M
4	Social	Yes	Personal	Others	Minor	—
7	Social	Yes	None	Others	Major	—
14	Social	Yes	None	Others	Major	O
9	Social	No	Personal	Others	Major	(–O, H, –P) –M
10	Social	No	Personal	Others	Major	– (M, P)
3	Social	No	None	Others/Both	Major	H

Note: All predictions based on hierarchical linear regressions in which social desirability and gender were entered in the first step as control variables, Big Five traits were entered in the second step, and Honesty-Humility and Dark Triad traits were entered in the last step. Parentheses indicate marginal significance.

RESULTS

Dimension Consensus

To confirm the five ethical dimensions developed (context, realistic, gain, cost, and outcome) for each question in the ethical decision-making questionnaire, four different graduate and undergraduate research assistants were instructed to indicate which dimension each item fell into. These four raters independently assessed each item in the questionnaire and then submitted their individual ratings. To assess the consistency between raters, two-way random ICCs were used to determine absolute agreement of raters on the dimensions. Overall, raters were consistent at an acceptable level, ICC = 0.81, F (79,316) = 5.20, $p < .001$. Raters agreed on the consistency of each individual dimension, with ICC's ranging from .64 to .90, with four above .78 and all significant at the $\alpha = .05$ level.

Hypothesis Testing

One-tailed bivariate correlations were conducted to test our four initial hypotheses, showing partial support for hypotheses (see Table 8.2 for all relevant statistics). We then investigated the relative predictive validity of the two sets of personality predictors.

Hierarchical linear regression was used to determine the added predictive validity of Honesty-Humility and Dark Triad traits above and beyond that of the Big Five when predicting ethical decision making across decision contexts. Social desirability and gender were entered in the first step

Table 8.2

Item Correlations

	Agreeableness	Honesty-Humility	Narcissism	Machiavellianism	Psychopathy	EDM	Social
Honesty-Humility	.13*						
Narcissism	.10	–.38**					
Machiavellianism	–.22**	–.47**	.22**				
Psychopathy	–.35**	–.21**	.15*	.42**			
EDM	.14*	.30**	–.17**	–.36**	–.27**		
Social	.20**	.30**	–.12*	–.34**	–.27**	.82**	
Organizational	.07	.26**	–.18**	–.30**	–.12*	.88**	.53**

Note. $N = 229$; * $p < .05$; ** $p < .01$

as control variables, all Big Five variables were entered in the second step, and Honesty-Humility and Dark Triad variables were entered in the last step to test model fit across 16 ethical decisions with unique contexts. In support of our fifth hypothesis, results indicated different types of prediction patterns for different decision contexts (see Table 8.3). Specifically, Honesty-Humility positively predicted ethical behavior where individuals will forgo personal gain in order to protect others from bearing the cost of such gain. Overall, conscientiousness and Machiavellianism appeared to be the greatest predictors of ethical decision making in most contexts, but not all. Narcissism was not found to be predictive of ethical decision making in any contexts. Differential effects were found when predicting ethical behavior in social versus organizational contexts, indicating potential domain specificity within the ethical decision-making construct.

DISCUSSION

Results indicated support for our hypotheses in that differential effects were found when predicting ethical behavior based on personality across

Table 8.3

Regression Weights Across Scenarios

Q	O	C	E	A	N	Hum	Narc	Mach	Psycho
1		.18**						–.24**	
2		(.13)		.17*		.20**		–.18**	
3						.16*			
4									
5		.17**							
6		–.16*							.22**
7									
8	–.14*	.24***						–.18*	
9	(–.13)					(.15)		–.19*	(–.14)
10								(–.14)	(–.14)
11		.15*							
12									
13						(.14)			
14	.17*								
15		.28***			–.30**				
16		.15*						–.19*	

Note: * $p < .05$, ** $p < .01$, *** $p < .001$. Parentheses indicate marginal significance.

contexts. Conscientiousness was predictive of those situations that did not involve other individuals directly or were more organizational in nature. This may have been due in part to the rule-abiding nature of individuals with high levels of conscientiousness. However, scenarios that were more social in nature or mentioned other individuals directly were predicted most often by two traits that may represent polar opposites of the prosocial-antisocial spectrum (i.e., Honesty-Humility and Machiavellianism). Thus, it may be particularly useful to investigate individual levels of Honesty-Humility and Machiavellianism when attempting to predict integrity in more social situations or occupations. Given that many personality researchers focus primarily on the Big Five (Salgado, 2002) trait theory of personality, this has serious implications for the future of integrity research as well. While conscientiousness was a predictor in some of the social scenarios as well, it was only a significant predictor in one social situation and a marginally significant predictor in one other. However, the ability for conscientiousness to be predictive across contexts may be indicative of suppositions posited by other researchers that System 2 (i.e., more deliberative) processing may result in more ethical behavior (Sloman, 1996). It is also possible that the vignette style of the scenarios posed required greater concentration from individuals in order to process all aspects of the situations. Therefore, the attention to detail that is characteristic of individuals with high levels of conscientiousness may have played a role in decision outcomes as well. Of particular interest, the current study highlighted an interesting confound to the study of ethical decision making, that of the conscientious Machiavellian.

Our findings indicated that high levels of conscientiousness were predictive of increased integrity in an organizational context, while increased levels of Machiavellianism predicted less integrity in social situations. However, these two personality traits are not mutually exclusive. It is possible for an individual to possess high or low levels of both traits. Although many hypothesize that conscientiousness is always predictive of integrity (Murphy & Lee, 1994), it is possible that previous research is not generalizable to all occupations or situations.

Conscientiousness may be a good predictor in and of itself when attempting to predict ethical behavior for jobs that are primarily paper-based and have little social contact (e.g., accounting), however it may not be as predictive for more social occupations such as those represented by police officers, doctors, or even managers. Therefore, it may be important for individuals focusing on selection to take into consideration applicant levels of Machiavellianism as well.

Previous theorists have often supposed that not all ethical decisions are created equal (e.g., Jones, 1991; Trevino, 1986). To our knowledge, this is the first study that provides quantitative support showing there was a significant difference in ethical decision making between social contexts and those in which individuals were not present. This finding is in-line with previous thought by Jones (1991) in that context appears to be a highly significant factor and that ethical decision making itself may be issue contingent. Indeed, ethical decision making appeared to be more likely in a social context than it was in an organizational context. However, because this study was conducted online with hypothetical situations it is unlikely that the differences in decision making were due to increased behavioral constraints found in organizational settings. It may be that the presence of other individuals may present a constraint due to social desirability or perceived social norms whereas situations without other individuals allow the individual to act more freely.

The strength of personality predictors was found to vary across social and organizational contexts, indicating a potential need to base selection criteria on specific aspects of occupations, such as interpersonal involvement. Although this research is by no means all encompassing, it highlights a specific aspect of ethical decision making not considered in the study of organizations, that individual behavior in social settings may not necessarily reflect their decisions in a business context. Researchers should begin investigating predictors that best predict ethical decision making in an organizational context if they wish to prevent such scandals in the future.

Limitations

Future research should be conducted to evaluate whether this finding holds up in more realistic situations. It may be of benefit to assess these relationships using video cameras and behavioral checklists in real-world settings such as the workplace or to use computer simulations to mimic realistic walk-throughs. It is possible that the nature of the survey elicited more socially desirable responses in the social scenarios than would be present in real-life. Accounting for measurement bias may provide researchers stronger evidence for the relationships between anti-/pro-social traits and ethical decision making in social contexts. This paper assessed only a small portion of ethical decision-making models proposed by previous theorists (e.g., Jones, 1991). This research provides a glimpse into the complexity of ethical decision making but it is important to consider other moderators and personality variables as well, such as ethical decision-making climates. Study 2 was designed to investigate this by looking at the effects of personality variables in a situation in which ethical decision climates were manipulated.

STUDY 2

To accurately predict behavior, one must be aware of both the personality of the individual in question as well as the situation in which the behavior is expected to occur (Funder, 2001). This three-part relationship of person, context, and behavior, was introduced earlier in this chapter. Given the hypothesized immutability of personality in the trait theory model, it is important to examine how changes to the context or situation may affect behavior independent of, or in interaction with personality traits. By illuminating the effects of context manipulations, practitioners may better be able to model environments to encourage desired behavior. This may be especially useful in work environments where employee actions can have drastic consequences and affect an organization's bottom line. However, few researchers have investigated the organizational environment as it relates to predicting cooperative and/or competitive behaviors. In terms of explaining individual or contextual differences in cooperative and competitive behaviors in the workplace, previous work has focused on aspects such as ethnic groups, sex differences, and generational differences in the United States (Becton et al., 2014; Cox et al., 1991; Wahn, 2003). Given the increasingly global work environment, it may be crucial for organizations to know the types of individuals they should hire to ensure cooperative and/or competitive behavior given the goals of the organization. Of course, this may depend on the work context in which the individual is involved.

In order to engage in any given behavior, an individual must feel motivated to do so (cf. Pinder, 2014). According to social identity theory, one motivating factor for engaging in cooperative behavior would be the extent to which an individual identifies themselves as being part of the group on the receiving end of the behavior (Deaux, 1996; Tajfel & Turner, 1979; Tyler & Blader, 2001). Specific to an organizational setting, affective commitment (AC) is the extent to which an employee has a sense of belonging and involvement with an organization (Meyer & Allen, 1991). Individuals with high levels of affective engagement are more likely to be engaged and act in a prosocial manner towards others in the organization (Tyler & Blader, 2001). Thus, it is reasonable to expect that affective commitment would be predictive of cooperative behavior. However, previous research has also indicated that individuals high in Agreeableness are more likely to have higher levels of affective commitment (Matzler et al., 2011). Therefore, because affective commitment may be predicted by personality (especially prosocial personality traits) and is also predictive of cooperative behavior, it is also hypothesized that:

H1: Affective commitment will act as a partial mediator for the relationship between context and cooperative decision making. More specifically, it is believed that individuals in more cooperative contexts are more likely to engage in cooperative behaviors due in part to higher levels of affective commitment.

It has previously been shown that individuals with higher levels of prosocial personality traits (e.g., Agreeableness, Altruism) and lower levels of more antisocial personality types (e.g., Dark Triad traits) are more likely to engage in more communal behavior (Lee et al., 2008; Miller et al., 2011). However, given the Funder Triangle, it is entirely possible that this relationship may depend up whether the work environment in question is cooperative or competitive in nature. Thus, it is hypothesized that:

H2: The relationship between organizational context and cooperative behavior will be moderated by personality. More specifically, it is theorized that individuals with higher levels of more prosocial traits will be more susceptible to social norms and will thus be affected more by context manipulations than those with higher levels of antisocial personality traits.

It is also important to note that organizational factors, such as climate and perceived organizational support, predict individual levels of affective commitment (Rhoades et al., 2001). A large body of research has established linkages between affective commitment and factors such as personal characteristics, work experiences, and job involvement (Meyer et al., 2002). While there appears to be strong relationships between personality facets and affective commitment as well as organizational contexts, there is no current work examining how personality may moderate the relationship between organizational contexts and employees' resulting levels of affective commitment (Matzler & Renzl, 2007; Meyer et al., 2012). Therefore, worker personality may significantly influence the relationship between organizational context and levels of affective commitment, such that:

H3: Personality will serve as a moderator between organizational context and ratings of affective commitment.

A conceptual model of all hypotheses may be found in Figure 8.1.

METHOD

Participants

Our total sample consisted of 361 undergraduate students enrolled in undergraduate classes at a large research university. Students were offered

Figure 8.1

Proposed Conditional Indirect Model

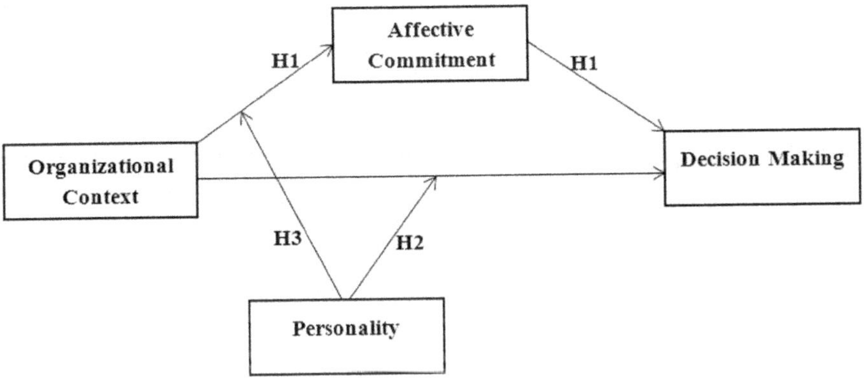

the option of completing the study for extra credit in either their business or psychology courses. The sample for our study was comprised of 95 male and 223 female participants, with 33 participants electing to not disclose their gender. Participant ages ranged from 18 to 41 with a mean age of 20. A randomized, within-groups study was used in which participants engaged in four classic decisions based on game theory that were designed to provide a more comprehensive view of cooperative/competitive decision making.

Cooperative/Competitive Context

Each participant had to make four decisions as if they were working in a competitive sales organization and four decisions from the perspective of working in a more cooperative software development company. Each participant made decisions in both contexts, but these contexts were randomized to ensure that any results are not subject to order effects. See Appendix A for scenario wording.

Cooperative/Competitive Decision Making

Participants had to make four decisions relative to the cooperative and competitive scenarios presented. The wording of the decision prompts were adapted to apply to two different organizational contexts (see Appendix A). As per the recommendation of Halevy & Philips (2015), these decision tasks were designed based on four classic decision-making items in an attempt to measure all aspects of cooperative decision making. The classic decisions on which they were based included the Prisoner's Dilemma, Chicken, Assurance (i.e., Stag Hunt), and Maximizing Difference games.

Affective Commitment

Immediately after reading each scenario and prior to completing the decision tasks, participants completed a 6-item questionnaire indicting their predicted levels of affective organizational commitment (Meyer, Allen, & Smith, 1993; α = .80 (Tech Company), α = .78 (Sales Company)). Since participants were responding to hypothetical scenarios and not actually working in organizations, all questions from this scale were modified to reflect the hypothetical organizations that were being assessed (see Appendix A for wording). For instance, the item previously phrased as [name of organization] "has a great deal of personal meaning for me" was changed to [name of organization] "would have a great deal of personal meaning for me."

Personality

All personality traits were measured using the 100-item HEXACO-PI-R (Lee & Ashton, 2018). Reliability statistics for each personality trait ranged from .76 to .86 (see Table 8.3) with the reliability for the interstitial Altruism scale being .65. Additional information regarding dark triad personality traits was collected using the 27-item SD3 (Jones & Paulhus, 2014). Reliability statistics for this scale ranged from .69 to .80.

RESULTS

An unconditional model in which cooperative decision making (Y) and affective commitment (M) were allowed to vary at both levels of analysis indicated significant variance within and between individuals for both variables. More specifically, the variance of cooperative decision making within individuals, β =.69(.05), and between individuals, β =1.05(.11) was found to be significant at the p = .001 level. Additionally, variance estimates for affective commitment were found to be significant at the p = .001 level within, β =23.72(1.87), and between, β =32.56(3.62) individuals as well. Thus, our data supported the need to conduct analyses using a two-level model.

For our first model, it was hypothesized that the relationship between situation context and decision making would be, in-part, mediated by perceived affective commitment. In order to test our first hypothesis, a conditional model was run in which affective commitment and decision making were allowed to vary within and between individuals. The indirect effects of situational context on decision making via affective commitment were tested at the within-individual level. As indicated by Table 8.4., there was a significant relationship between situational context and decision making such that individuals were more likely to cooperate when faced with the cooperative organization as opposed to the competitive organization. Additionally, and in support of Hypothesis 1, situational context was also found to be a significant predictor of decision making via its relationship with affective commitment.

In order to test the potential moderating effect of personality variables, a random slopes model was used in which affective commitment and decision making as well as the slopes for our a and c' paths were allowed to vary between individuals. Initial analyses indicated that the slopes for the a path ($\beta = 7.17(1.78)$, $p < .001$) and the c' path ($\beta = .09(.04)$, $p < .01$) both had significant variance at the between level of analysis. Thus, there was sufficient evidence to continue with the use of a two-level model for testing our first and third hypotheses, involving moderation. Altruism, honesty-humility, psychopathy, and Machiavellianism were then added as predictors of affective commitment, decision making, and both paths of interest. All

Table 8.4

Personality Trait Scale Reliabilities

	Cronbach's α
Honesty-Humility	.76
Emotionality	.83
Extraversion	.86
Agreeableness	.80
Conscientiousness	.84
Openness to Experience	.79
Altruism	.65
Machiavellianism	.73
Narcissism	.69
Psychopathy	.80

Note: All personality scales derived from the HEXACO-PI-R (Lee & Ashton, 2018) and SD3 (Jones & Paulhus, 2014) personality measures.

relevant statistics related to the outcome of this analysis can be found in Table 8.5. In partial support of our hypotheses, affective commitment was predicted by altruism (β = 2.69(.95), p < .01) and Machiavellianism (β = 2.94(1.19), p = .01). These results indicates that individuals with high levels of altruism and/or Machiavellianism had higher levels of affective commitment when faced with the competitive sales organization. However, affective commitment did not appear to be predicted by either honesty-humility (β = .29(1.14), p = .80) or psychopathy (β = -.86(1.01), p = .40). Affective commitment also remained a significant predictor of cooperative decision making within individuals (β = .04(.01), p = .001). The only personality variable that appeared predictive of cooperative decision making was that of Machiavellianism (β = .43(.20), p = .03). Additionally, no moderating results were found for either path in our analysis, providing no support for Hypothesis 2. Thus, the relationships between personality and affective commitment or cooperative decision making did not appear to be dependent upon the situational context. For reference, Figure 8.2 represents the final conditional indirect model with all significant path coefficients.

DISCUSSION

Our analyses indicated support for our first hypothesis such that context was a significant predictor of cooperative decision making through levels of affective commitment. Researchers have long since noted that organizational climate and culture can have a significant impact on employee behavior (e.g., Sims & Keon, 1999). However, previous research

Table 8.5

Conditional Level 1 Model Unstandardized Variances With Standard Error Estimates

		Estimate	Standard Error
Decision Making			
	Context	–.10*	.04
	Affective Commitment	.42***	.09
Affective Commitment			
	Context	–2.19***	.04
Indirect Path		–.16***	.05

Note: * p <.05; ** p <.01; *** p < .001

Figure 8.2

Final Conditional Indirect Path Model

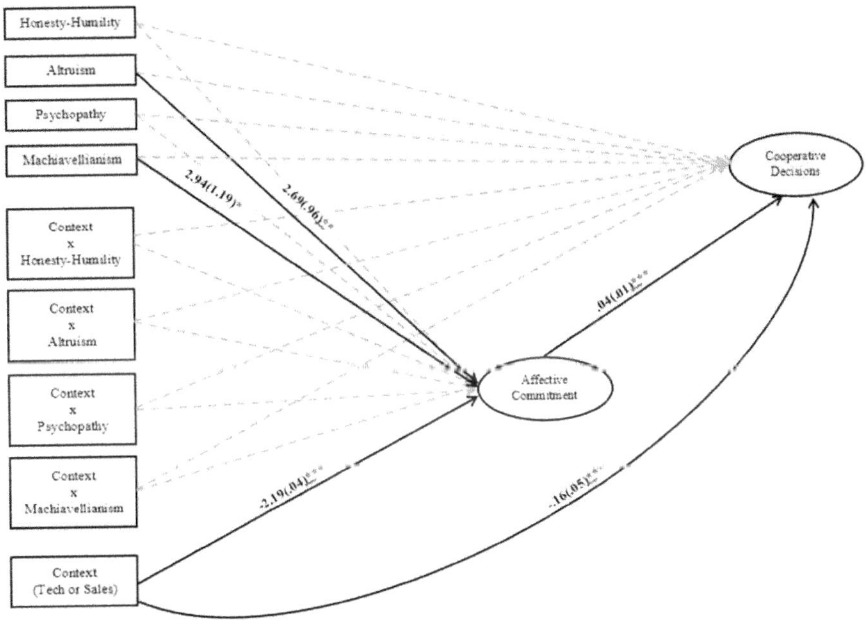

targeted at contextual manipulations has often provided mixed results (Tett & Burnett, 2003). As it relates to cooperative decision making in particular, such research has also been limited by the lack of outcome measures inclusive of all aspects of cooperative decision making (Halevy & Philips, 2015). By providing a more comprehensive measure of the targeted outcome based on context and considering multilevel variance in our analyses, our findings provide more substantive support for prediction of cooperative behavior based on situational context. If organizations wish to encourage more cooperative behaviors between employees, it may be important to emphasize a cooperative environment through aspects of organizational climate such as organizational norms and reward systems (Kaptein, 2008). In turn, companies seeking to encourage competition among employees may wish to emphasize such practices by emphasizing competition in their organizational environments as well. For example, a company seeking to foster a competitive environment may pay bonuses or offer rewards for meeting performance goals above and beyond performance level achieved by the majority of employees within the organization. However, it should be noted that, in the case of our study,

Table 8.6

Conditional Indirect Path Model at Level 2

	Regression Paths	Estimate	Standard Error
Within			
	Decision Making by Affective Commitment	.04***	.01
Between			
	Decision Making by		
	Altruism	.13	.15
	Honesty-Humility	.17	.19
	Machiavellianism	.43*	.20
	Psychopathy	–.05	.20
	Affective Commitment by		
	Altruism	2.69**	.96
	Honesty-Humility	.29	.64
	Machiavellianism	2.94*	1.19
	Psychopathy	-.86	1.01
	Decision Making by		
	Altruism x Context	.16	.09
	Honesty-Humility x Context	–.09	.10
	Machiavellianism x Context	–.17	.12
	Psychopathy x Context	.10	.12
	Affective Commitment by		
	Altruism x Context	–1.01	.59
	Honesty-Humility x Context	.45	.69
	Machiavellianism x Context	–.67	.75
	Psychopathy x Context	.89	.63

Note: * $p < .05$; ** $p < .01$; *** $p < .001$

situational contexts that emphasized more cooperation through teamwork also resulted in greater levels of affective commitment from employees. Increased levels of affective commitment have previously been linked to improved organizational outcomes such as decreased employee turnover (Vandenberghe,et al., 2017) and increased desirable work behaviors (Meyer et al., 1993). Thus, an emphasis on cooperation and teamwork within an organization may be desired even for organizations that function in more competitive environments, such as sales. Although any and all changes to organizational climate should be considered in the context of overall organizational productivity, it may be important to consider the cost of human resources relevant to such changes as well.

In addition to providing an environment in which affective commitment is more likely and cooperative behaviors are more likely to occur, organizations may wish to seek out and employ individuals that are more likely to engage in cooperative behavior regardless of situational context. Previous research has indicated that individuals more likely to engage in cooperative behavior possessed lower levels of antisocial personality traits and higher levels of prosocial personality (Lee et al., 2008; Miller et al., 2011). However, the current study did not support such findings once variance due to context was taken into consideration. These findings may indicate the importance of situational context when investigation work settings. Although Funder (2001) implied that personality and context may play equal roles when predicting behavior, it may be that organizational contexts in and of themselves represent greater levels of situational strength (cf. Mischel, 1977) than other forms of situations. This may be due in part to a higher stakes nature of organizational scenarios such that pay and livelihood are at risk in these contexts. Social situations, on the other hand, are not as likely to affect an individual's livelihood and may thus be less likely to have as strong an impact on behavior. However, more research is needed to compare these contexts in order to make any definitive statements regarding the situational strength or importance of each. It is important to note however, that two personality variables in predictor remained of importance in our final model.

In the present study, Altruism was found to be a significant predictor of affective commitment such that individuals with higher levels of Altruism displayed higher levels of affective commitment. Machiavellians were also found to display higher levels of affective commitment. Due to the opposing nature of these two personality traits, more research is needed to assess why this is the case, especially given that context in this study did not moderate these relationships. More research is clearly needed to substantiate these findings and to highlight potential reasons underlying these relationships such as overcompensation or even oppositional defiance. Regardless of the reasons, our findings make it clear that personality and situational context are both important when considering affective commitment and cooperative behaviors.

Limitations

Like most research studies, the present project was far from perfect in a number of ways. Although participants in our sample were representative of both business and psychology backgrounds, these individuals were still college students. Therefore, future research should be conducted with individuals in organizational settings via sources such as MTurk to ensure generalizability of our results. Additionally, although the current model imposed affective commitment as a mediating variable between situational context and cooperative decisions, all of our data were collected at one time point. Care was taken when designing the study to ensure that individuals were presented with organizational scenarios prior to completing a hypothetical affective commitment measure, which was also presented prior to and on a different page from the cooperative decision tasks. However, without using a time-lagged design, causality regarding variable relationships may be questioned, and further replication of the study is needed to effectively support any and all causal relationships. Additionally, future research could expand upon the current study by utilizing more experimental methods. Because the current study was quasi-experimental in nature and consisted entirely of online surveys, common method bias may have influenced our findings. Given previously mixed results regarding contextual manipulations and behavioral outcomes, it is also unclear whether our results were significant due to the contextual manipulations alone or because the affective commitment measures presented after each scenario caused individuals to reflect upon the scenarios provided. Despite these limitations however, our research contributes to literature in the field by provided support for the interaction between situational context and individual personality when attempting to predict cooperative behavior.

Implications of Study 1 and Study 2 for Organizational Behavior

Our findings indicated support for theories presented by Funder (2001) and others wherein it is thought that personality and context interact to predict behavior. The prediction of ethical behavior within organizations is of particular importance to understand because of the nature of organizations and organizational stakeholders.

It has been proposed that poor performance in organizations may occur because of a lack of person-organization fit (Svyantek et al., 2015). Poor fit is not necessarily a deficit of either the person or the organization. Rather, *misfit* occurs when there is a mismatch between employee value systems and organizational culture. However, for ethical behavior in organizations, organizations may create unethical climates vis-à-vis outsiders and external stakeholders. Here fit will lead to improved career success for organizational members at the expense of these outsiders. This may explain why patterns of unethical behavior may exist among organizations and organizational members when these members do not possess supposed personality traits linked to unethical behaviors. The situation may determine the behavior. These studies show a need to consider contextual differences when developing human resource methods for jobs requiring heightened levels of integrity.

In an increasingly global business environment, it may be important for organizations to encourage cooperative behaviors among employees. In accordance with Funder (2001), our findings indicated that it is important to consider both situational context and personality when attempting to achieve this goal. More specifically, organizations wishing to encourage more cooperative behavior may do so by emphasizing teamwork in organizational policies and reward systems. For example, organizations may also wish to consider applicants' Altruism levels in addition to other job requirements. As an added bonus to practitioners, the Altruism personality trait may be measured using four items as opposed to 16 items for other personality traits on the HEXACO-PI-R (Lee & Ashton, 2018) measure which may provide an abbreviated application process if other personality traits are not of interest. Additionally, companies wishing to encourage continued cooperation among employees may survey employee levels of affective commitment periodically and adjust company policies and climate based on the results as needed.

REFERENCES

Allen, N. J., & Meyer, J. P. (1990). The measurement and antecedents of affective, continuance and normative commitment to the organization. *Journal of Occupational Psychology, 63*(1), 1–18.

Barrick, M. R., & Mount, M. K. (1991). The Big Five personality dimensions and job performance: A meta-analysis. *Personnel Psychology, 44*, 1–26.

Bateman, T. S., & Organ, D. W. (1983). Job satisfaction and the good soldier: The relationship between affect and employee citizenship. *Academy of Management Journal, 26*, 587–595.

Becker, T. E. (1998). Integrity in organizations: Beyond honesty and conscientiousness. *Academy of Management Review, 23*(1), 154–161. https://doi.org/10.5465/AMR.1998.192969

Becker, H., & Fritzsche, D. J. (1987). Business ethics: A cross-cultural comparison of managers' attitudes. *Journal of Business Ethics, 6*(4), 289–295.

Becton, J. B., Walker, H. J., & Jones-Farmer, A. (2014). Generational differences in workplace behavior. *Journal of Applied Social Psychology, 44*(3), 175–189.

Borman, W. C., & Motowidlo, S. J. (1993). Expanding the criterion domain to include elements of contextual performance. In N. Schmitt, W.C. Borman, & Associates (Eds.), *Personnel selection in organizations* (pp. 71–98). Jossey-Bass.

Borman, W. C., Penner, L. A., Allen, T. D., & Motowidlo, S. J. (2001). Personality predictors of citizenship performance. *International Journal of Selection and Assessment, 9,* 52–69.

Brown, T. A., Sautter, J. A., Littvay, L., Sautter, A. C., & Bearnes, B. (2010). Ethics and personality: Empathy and narcissism as moderators of ethical decision making in business students. *Journal of Education for Business, 85*(4), 203–208. https://doi.org/10.1080/08832320903449501

Boudreau, J. W., Boswell, W. R., & Judge, T. A. (2001). Effects of personality on executive career success in the United States and Europe. *Journal of Vocational Behavior, 58*(1), 53–81.

Cox, T. H., Lobel, S. A., & McLeod, P. L. (1991). Effects of ethnic group cultural differences on cooperative and competitive behavior on a group task. *Academy of Management Journal, 34*(4), 827–847.

Craft, J. (2013). A Review of the Empirical Ethical Decision-Making Literature: 2004–2011. *Journal of Business Ethics, 117*(2), 221–259. https://doi.org/10.1007/s10551-012-1518-9

Dalton, D., & Radtke, R. R. (2013). The joint effects of Machiavellianism and ethical environment on whistle-blowing. *Journal of Business Ethics, 117*(1), 153–172. https://doi.org/10.1007/s10551-012-1517-x

Deaux, K. (1996). Social identification. In E. T. Higgins & A. W. Kruglanski (Eds.), *Social psychology: Handbook of basic principles* (pp. 777–798). Guilford Press.

Ethics Resource Center. (2013). National Business Ethics Survey (NBES®) 2013. http://www.ethics.org/research/eci-research/nbes/nbes-reports/nbes-2013

Funder, D. C. (2001). Accuracy in personality judgment: Research and theory concerning an obvious question. In B. W. Roberts & R. Hogan (Eds.), *Personality psychology in the workplace* (pp. 121 – 140). American Psychological Association. http://dx.doi.org/10.1037/10434-005

Halevy, N., & Phillips, T. (2015). Conflict templates in negotiations, disputes, joint decisions, and tournaments. *Social Psychological and Personality Science, 6(1),* 13–22. https://doi.org/10.1177/1948550614542347

Hogan, J., Rybicki, S. L., Motowidlo, S. J., & Borman, W. C. (1998). Relations between contextual performance, personality, and occupational advancement. *Human Performance, 11,* 189–207.

Horn, J., Nelson, C. E., & Brannick, M. T. (2004). Integrity, conscientiousness, and honesty. *Psychological Reports, 95*(1), 27–38.

Hurtz, G. M., & Donovan, J. J. (2000). Personality and job performance: The Big Five revisited. *Journal of Applied Psychology, 85*(6), 869–879.

Ilies, R., Scott, B. A., & Judge, T. A. (2006). The interactive effects of personal traits and experienced states on intraindividual patterns of citizenship behavior. *Academy of Management Journal, 49,* 561–575.

Jones, T. M. (1991). Ethical decision making by individuals in organizations: An issue-contingent model. *Academy of Management Review, 16*(2), 366–395. https://doi.org/10.5465/AMR.1991.4278958

Jones, D. N., & Paulhus, D. L. (2014). Introducing the short dark triad (SD3): A brief measure of dark personality traits. *Assessment, 21*(1), 28–41. https://doi.org/10.1177/1073191113514105

Judge, T. A., & Bono, J. E. (2000). Five-factor model of personality and transformational leadership. *Journal of Applied Psychology, 85*(5), 751–765.

Kaptein, M. (2008). Developing and testing a measure for the ethical culture of organizations: The corporate ethical virtues model. *Journal of Organizational Behavior, 29*(7), 923–947.

Kelley, P. C., & Elm, D. R. (2003). The effect of context on moral intensity of ethical issues: Revising Jones's issue-contingent model. *Journal of Business Ethics,* 48(2), 139–154.

Kristof, A. L. (1996). Person-organization fit: An integrative review of its conceptualization, measurement, and implications. *Personnel Psychology, 49,* 1–49.

Kristof-Brown, A. L., Zimmerman, R. D., & Johnson, E. C. (2005). Consequences of individuals' fit at work: A meta-analysis of person-job, person organization, person-group and person-supervisor fit. *Personnel Psychology, 58,* 281–342.

Lee, K., & Ashton, M. C. (2018). Psychometric Properties of the HEXACO-100. *ASSESSMENT, 25*(5), 543–556. https://doi.org/10.1177/1073191116659134

Lee, K., & Ashton, M. C. (2014). The Dark Triad, the Big Five, and the HEXACO model. *Personality and Individual Differences*, 672–675. https://doi.org/10.1016/j.paid.2014.01.048

Lee, K., Ashton, M. C., & de Vries, R. E. (2005). Predicting workplace delinquency and integrity with the HEXACO and Five-Factor models of personality structure. *Human Performance, 18*(2), 179–197. https://doi.org/:10.1207/s15327043hup1802_4

Lee, K., Ashton, M. C., Morrison, D. L., Cordery, J., & Patrick D. D., (2008). Predicting integrity with the HEXACO personality model: Use of self- and observer reports. *Journal of Occupational & Organizational Psychology, 81*(1), 147–167. https://doi.org/10.1348/096317907X195175

Lehnert, K., Park, Y. H., & Singh, N. (2015). Research note and review of the empirical ethical decision-making literature: Boundary conditions and extensions. *Journal of Business Ethics, 129*(1), 195–219. https://doi.org/10.1007/s10551-014-2147-2.

Maples, J. L., Lamkin, J., & Miller, J. D. (2014). A test of two brief measures of the dark triad: The dirty dozen and short dark triad. *Psychological Assessment, 26*(1), 326–331. http://dx.doi.org/10.1037/a0035084

Matzler, K., & Renzl, B. (2007). Personality traits, employee satisfaction and affective commitment. *Total Quality Management, 18*(5), 589–598.

Matzler, K., Renzl, B., Mooradian, T., von Krogh, G., & Mueller, J. (2011). Personality traits, affective commitment, documentation of knowledge, and knowledge sharing. *The International Journal of Human Resource Management, 22*(02), 296–310.

Meyer, J. P., & Allen, N. J. (1991). A three-component conceptualization of organizational commitment. *Human Resource Management Review, 1*, 61–98.

Meyer, J. P., Allen, N. J., & Smith, C. A. (1993). Commitment to organizations and occupations: Extension and test of a three-component conceptualization. *Journal of Applied Psychology, 78*, 538–551.

Meyer, J. P., Stanley, D. J., Herscovitch, L., & Topolnytsky, L. (2002). Affective, continuance, and normative commitment to the organization: A meta-analysis of antecedents, correlates, and consequences. *Journal of vocational behavior, 61*(1), 20–52.

Meyer, J. P., Stanley, D. J., Jackson, T. A., McInnis, K. J., Maltin, E. R., & Sheppard, L. (2012). Affective, normative, and continuance commitment levels across cultures: A meta-analysis. *Journal of Vocational Behavior, 80*(2), 225–245.

Miller, J. D., Gaughan, E. T., Maples, J., & Price, J. (2011). A comparison of Agreeableness scores from the Big Five Inventory and the NEO PI-R: Consequences for the study of Narcissism and Psychopathy. *Assessment, 18*(3), 335–339. https://doi.org/10.1177/1073191111411671

Mischel, W. (1977). On the future of personality measurement. *American Psychologist, 32*(4), 246–254. https://doi.org/10.1037/0003-066X.32.4.246

Mischel, W., & Shoda, Y. (1998). Reconciling processing dynamics and personality dispositions. *Annual Review of Psychology, 49*, 229–258.

Mischel, W. (2004). Toward an integrative science of the person. *Annual Review of Psychology, 55*, 1–22. https://doi.org/10.1146/annurev.psych.55.042902.130709

Morgan, G. R. (1998). *Organizational theory* (2nd ed.). Addison-Wesley.

Mount, M. K., & Barrick, M. R. (1995). The Big Five personality dimensions: Implications for research and practice in human resource management. In K. M. Rowland & G. Ferris (Eds.) *Research in personnel and human resources management* (Vol. 13, pp. 153–200). JAI Press.

Murphy, K. (2002). Using power analysis to evaluate and improve research. In S. G. Rogelberg, S. G. Rogelberg (Eds.), *Handbook of research methods in industrial and organizational psychology* (pp. 119–137). Blackwell.

Murphy, K. R., & Lee, S. L. (1994). Personality variables related to integrity test scores: The role of conscientiousness. *Journal of Business and Psychology, 8*(4), 413–424.

Namenwirth, J. Z., & Weber, R. P. (1987). *Dynamics of culture*. Allen & Irwin.

O'Fallon, M. J., & Butterfield, K. D. (2013). A review of the empirical ethical decision-making literature: 1996–2003. In A. C. Michalos, D. C. Poff, A. C. Michalos, & D. C. Poff (Eds.), *Citation classics from the Journal of Business Ethics: Celebrating the first thirty years of publication* (pp. 213–263). Springer Science + Business Media. https://doi.org/10.1007/978-94-007-4126-3_11

Organ, D. W., & Ryan, K. (1995). A meta-analytic review of attitudinal and dispositional predictors of organizational citizenship behavior. *Personnel Psychology, 48*, 775–802.

Paulhus, D. L., & Williams, K. M. (2002). The dark triad of personality: Narcissism, machiavellianism, and psychopathy. *Journal of Research in Personality, 36*(6), 556–563. https://doi.org/10.1016/S0092-6566(02)00505-6

Pinder, C. C. (2014). *Work motivation in organizational behavior*. Psychology Press.

Podsakoff, P. M., MacKenzie, S. B., Paine, J. B., & Bachrach, D. G. (2000). Organizational citizenship behaviors: A critical review of the theoretical and empirical literature and suggestions for future research. *Journal of Management, 26*(3), 513–563.

Rest, J. R. (1986). *Moral development: Advances in research and theory*. Praeger.

Rest, J. R. (Ed.). (1994). *Moral development in the professions: Psychology and applied ethics*. Psychology Press.

Rhoades, L., Eisenberger, R., & Armeli, S. (2001). Affective commitment to the organization: The contribution of perceived organizational support. *Journal of Applied Psychology, 86*(5), 825.

Sackett, P. R., & Wanek, J. E. (1996). New developments in the use of measures of honesty integrity, conscientiousness, dependability trustworthiness, and reliability for personnel selection. *Personnel Psychology, 49*(4), 787–829.

Salgado, J. F. (1997). The five-factor model of personality and job performance in the European community. *Journal of Applied Psychology, 82*, 30–43.

Salgado, J. F. (2002). The Big Five personality dimensions and counterproductive behaviors. *International Journal of Selection and Assessment, 10*(1–2), 117–125.

Seibert, S. E., & Kraimer, M. L. (2001). The five-factor model of personality and career success. *Journal of Vocational Behavior, 58*(1), 1–21.

Sims, R. L., & Keon, T. L. (1999). Determinants of ethical decision making: The relationships of the perceived organizational environment. *Journal of Business Ethics, 19*, 393–401.

Smith , C.A., Organ, D.W., & Near, J.P. (1983). Organizational citizenship behavior: Its nature and antecedents. *Journal of Applied Psychology, 68*, 653–663.

Sloman, S. A. (1996). The empirical case for two systems of reasoning. *Psychological Bulletin, 119*(1), 3.

Solomon, R. C. (2004). Aristotle, ethics and business organizations. *Organization Studies, 25*(6), 1021–1043. https://doi.org/10.1177/0170840604042409

Stevens, G. W., Deuling, J. K., & Armenakis, A. A. (2012). Successful psychopaths: Are they unethical decision-makers and why?. *Journal of Business Ethics, 105*(2), 139–149. https://doi.org/10.1007/s10551-011-0963-1

Svyantek, D. J. (1997). Order out of chaos: Non-linear systems and organizational change. *Current Topics in Management, 2*, 167–188.

Svyantek, D. J., & Brown, L. L. (2000). A complex systems approach to organizations. *Current Directions in Psychological Science, 9*(2), 69–74.

Svyantek, D. J., Cullen, K. C., & Doerr, A. (2015). Person-organization fit and its implications for human resource management practices. In W. I . Sauser & R. R. Sims (Eds.), *Legal and regulatory issues in human resource management* (pp. 315–340). Information Age Publishing.

Tyler, T. R., & Blader, S. L. (2001). Identity and cooperative behavior in groups. *Group Processes & Intergroup Relations, 4*(3), 207–226. https://doi.org/10.1177/1368430201004003003

Tett, R. P., & Burnett, D. D. (2003). A personality trait-based interactionist model of job performance. *Journal of Applied Psychology, 88*(3), 500. https://doi.org/10.1037/0021-9010.88.3.500

Trevino, L. K. (1986). Ethical decision making in organizations: A person-situation interactionist model. *Academy of Management Review, 11*(3), 601–617. https://doi.org/10.5465/AMR.1986.4306235

Tajfel, H., & Turner, J. C. (1979). An integrative theory of intergroup conflict. *The Social Psychology of Intergroup Relations, 33*(47), 74.

Vandenberghe, C., Bentein, K., & Panaccio, A. (2017). Affective commitment to organizations and supervisors and turnover: A role theory perspective. *Journal of Management, 43*(7), 2090–2117. https://doi.org/10.1177/0149206314559779

van Vianen, A. M. (2018). Person-environment fit: A review of its basic tenets. *Annual Review of Organizational Psychology and Organizational Behavior, 5,* 75–101.

Wahn, J. (2003). Sex differences in competitive and compliant unethical work behavior. *Journal of Business and Psychology, 18*(1), 121–128.

Zeithaml, A. A., Parasuraman, A., & Berry, L. L. (1990). *Delivering service quality*. The Free Press.

CHAPTER 9

TRAIT EMOTIONAL INTELLIGENCE DIFFERENCES IN PRECAREER AND MIDCAREER UNITED STATES MILITARY LEADERS

Andrew L. Bond
United States Military Academy

Daniel J. Svyantek
Auburn University

Emotional intelligence (EI) has been the subject of extensive practitioner attention and academic research since its emergence. Daniel Goleman's (1995) enormously popular book *Emotional Intelligence* catapulted EI into the international spotlight. Goleman's related article is the most requested publication from the *Harvard Business Review* (Sardo, 2004). The social science and human resource management attraction to this construct is easily understood based on the tremendous scope of possible applications that understanding emotions might yield. In application, the proponents

Organizations Behaving Badly:
Destructive Behavior and Corrective Responses, pp. 181–215

of EI theory anticipated and informed a movement in management and organizational behavior—providing a useful example of the *theoretical prescience* as advocated by Corley and Gioia (2011). Intuitively, we can expect that traits, abilities, and affective self-perceptions associated with EI should differ from person to person and have implications in the workplace (Hochschild, 1983). However, the presence of differences is not enough to make a theory useful—these differences must prove to be useful.

Utility is created when those differences are useful in predicting desired outcomes. The nature of the relationship between EI and workplace outcomes has been hotly debated. The nature of this debate has revolved around concerns that EI lacks discriminant validity from other constructs that are long-established predictors of performance (e.g., general mental ability, personality, emotional stability, and affect related measures). While these arguments have merit on theoretical grounds, consensus is building that EI is an important and useful construct (Joseph et al., 2015b).

The purpose of this study is to investigate differences in trait emotional intelligence between precareer and midcareer military officers. This study seeks to investigate the way in which the context and EI work together for discerning differences between leaders in the military. In doing so, this chapter seeks to identify critical experiences of officers that might contribute to facet-level increases in EI and devise recommendations for training emphasis and leader development.

There are three goals for this chapter: First, we provide a review of empirical evidence, benefits, and applications of the EI construct. Second, readers will find an overview of the Army Leader Attributes and Competencies as described in Army Doctrine Publication (ADP) 6–22 entitled Army Leadership (Army, 2012). These six attributes and competencies are the standard that U.S. Army officers must meet. These attributes will be shown to have clear connections to EI. Third and most importantly, this chapter describes an empirical study that explores the question, "Do individuals at different stages of their career progression differ in Emotional Intelligence?"

EMOTIONAL INTELLIGENCE AND ORGANIZATIONS

There are numerous highly influential works that predate Goleman's that contribute to our understanding of the EI construct—some that date back to the early 20th century. The EI construct has been discussed in social science literature since the early 20th century. The social intelligence construct has a long history. Thorndike (1920) expounded on Dewey's work with his *Harper's Magazine* article "Intelligence and its uses" wherein it is suggested that social intelligence could be conceptualized as the ability to understand people and interact with others wisely (Thorndike, 1920). Interestingly, these conceptualizations are not far removed from current EI theory. However, these precursors to EI were not developed further for more than 60 years. During the 1980s we can see other lines of research beginning that are quite similar to EI. Practical intelligence theory underscores the importance of tacit knowledge in social and professional situations, and has been conceptualized as the capacity to resolve unexpected and difficult situations when existing solutions and theory are insufficient (Langer et al., 2014; Wagner & Sternberg, 1985). The interpersonal implications of this theory overlap with EI facets that pertain to emotion perception and expression.[1]

Our modern conceptualizations of EI find there genesis in Howard Gardner's book *Frames of Mind* (1983) which explored the idea that each person possesses multiple intelligences—including interpersonal and intrapersonal intelligence. Interpersonal intelligence refers to one's interactions with others and empathy, while intrapersonal intelligence refers to one's capacity for accurate introspection. These intelligences translate directly into facets that we find in modern instruments to measure trait emotional intelligence. After Gardner, Salovey and Mayer contributed what has come to be viewed as an important work on EI (1989). Their definition of EI as the "ability to monitory one's own and others' feelings and emotions, to discriminate among them and to use this information to guide one's own thinking and actions" (p. 189) is the foundation for the ability model of EI to be described in the pages to follow.

Prior to describing the two common models for EI it is worth mentioning that EI has not been free of criticism. Murphy (2006) effectively summarizes some of the main points of contention in his important critique by stating that EI has been poorly defined, overlaps with existing constructs, and has been inappropriately propped up by proponents. While some of the concerns above will be discussed in pages to follow, the discussion is intended to inform rather than resolve the ongoing debate. While it is important to acknowledge the arguments against EI, the current study builds on the recommendation by Joseph et al. (2015b) that trait emotional intelligence displays adequate construct validity and can be used with confidence as one of the best predictors of job performance.

Emotional Intelligence Models

EI books, self-help, and professional development seminars, and other materials created a multi-million dollar industry in the last several decades (Grewal & Salovey, 2005). This is further evidenced by the finding that approximately 75% of Fortune 500 companies have incorporated a measure of EI in their personnel selection, development, or promotion systems (Bradberry & Greaves, 2009).

Critiques of EI readers have described a primary problem with the EI construct concerning definitional consensus. There are two predominant models for EI, trait or mixed EI and ability EI. Each model has distinct definitions, measures, and purposes.

Ability Emotional Intelligence (AEI). AEI treats emotional intelligence as the ability to reason about emotions effectively (Mayer et al., 2008). The abilities to accurately perceive emotions, to access and generate emotions so as to assist thought, to understand emotions and emotional knowledge, and to reflectively regulate emotions so as to promote emotional and intellectual growth (Mayer et al., 2004).

The ability EI model is typically divided into four subdimensions: emotion perception, emotion understanding, emotion facilitation, and emotion regulation (Mayer, 1997). This model has been described as an intelligence since measures of AEI have correct answers rather than a series of self-rated perceptions (Daus & Ashkanasy, 2005).Several instruments have been developed to measure ability EI, the most popular of which is the Mayer-Salovey-Caruso Emotional Intelligence Test (MSCEIT). There is building consensus that the MSCEIT and other ability EI measures boast a stronger theoretical foundation when compared to measures of trait or mixed EI (Daus & Ashkanasy, 2005; Matthews et al., 2004; Murphy, 2006). This theoretical foundation is built on findings that measures of ability EI do not correlate with other measures (such as personality or general mental ability) as strongly as mixed or trait EI. Thus it is distinct, but when the predictive utility of ability EI was tested against cognitive ability and Big Five personality traits AEI showed near-zero incremental validity with $\Delta R^2 = 0.002 = 0.2\%$ (Joseph & Newman, 2010) and $\Delta R^2 = 0.004 = 0.4\%$ (O'Boyle et al., 2011). In other words, the construct might be unique, but it fails to add value when predicting job performance.

Trait Emotional Intelligence (TEI). TEI is second model (also described as mixed EI (Bar-On, 1999; Joseph, et al., 2015a; Petrides, 2010). Trait EI is a broad term that has been defined as "a constellation of emotional self-perceptions located at the lower levels of personality hierarchies and measured via the trait emotional intelligence questionnaire" (Petrides et al., 2007). Trait EI is also sometimes referred to as trait emotional self-efficacy (Petrides, 2010). This useful label reflects both the construct's content and the method used to measure it (self-report surveys), but the enormous momentum behind the EI movement has been too much to overcome and so trait emotional self-efficacy is rarely used.

Several meta-analyses have been conducted to explore intercorrelation between AEI and TEI show us that AEI and TEI intercorrelate moderately $\hat{\rho} = .26$ (Joseph & Newman, 2010) and $\hat{\rho} = .14 = .26$ (VanRooy et al., 2005).

Thus, the construct's models appear to be distinct in nature, which adds a great deal of confusion to the EI debate since both AEI and TEI seem to be distinct ways of viewing EI.

TEI instruments have been shown to predict positive outcomes in the workplace and have been adopted by consulting firms and organizations alike (Joseph & Newman, 2010). Further, trait EI is shown to have greater incremental validity when predicting performance above and beyond cognitive ability and Big Five personality when compared to ability EI. In two separate studies, trait EI added considerable value to job performance prediction with $\Delta R^2 = 0.142 = 14.2\%$ (Joseph & Newman, 2010), and $\Delta R^2 = 0.068 = 7\%$ (O'Boyle et al., 2011). This incremental value was explained further in Joseph et al.'s (2015a) meta-analysis which will be discussed in some detail in the correlates of TEI section.

In further studies, TEI has been shown to predict work performance positively in high emotion-demanding jobs and negatively in low emotion-demanding jobs (Joseph & Newman, 2010). This finding is especially pertinent to the present study since military contexts are emotionally demanding and stressful. Beyond work performance, TEI has also been connected to desirable workplace variables such as achievement, motivation, and low impulsiveness (Joseph et al., 2015a; Mayer et al., 2008; Petrides & Furnham, 2001; Zeidner et al., 2004).

Studies have also suggested that TEI has a significant association with relationship satisfaction (Malouff et al., 2014), establishing an inroad for EI to contribute to work-life balance research. From a medical perspective, high levels of emotional intelligence might also have positive health implications (Martins et al., 2010; Schutte et al., 2007). This connection is not surprising when we consider well-established connections between the presence and maintenance of meaningful relationships and improved health. A potential drawback of TEI might be negatively related to learning, especially early in the learning process (Fellner et al., 2012). In a way, this should not be surprising since students who are keenly aware of the emotional events going on around them might attend less diligently to their schoolwork. Having established that TEI is a useful predictor of many valuable outcomes, it is useful to next take a closer look at what existing constructs and theories might be subsumed under the broad TEI umbrella.

Summary. While TEI and AEI are viewed as distinct, the constructs do overlap in some areas as evidenced several findings that reflect $\hat{\rho} = .26$ (Joseph & Newman, 2010) and $\hat{\rho} = .14$ (VanRooy et al., 2005). According to Bern's self perception theory (1972), individuals come to "know their own attitudes, emotions, and internal states partially by inferring them from observations of their own overt behavior and/or the circumstances in which this behavior occurs" (p. 2). Thus, *ability* EI (the aspect of intelligence that relates to emotional abilities) can be expected to correlate with *trait* EI, which measures self-perceptions about one's emotional capacities (Petrides & Furnham, 2001). Our study will deal primarily with TEI. Therefore, we turn to describing the relationship between TEI and other classic predictors of performance, personality, and cognitive ability.

Trait Emotional Intelligence and Known Correlates

Personality. Joseph et al.'s (2015a, 2015b) tried to clarify the structure of the TEI model. Results revealed that TEI is a useful combination of existing domains: Conscientiousness, extraversion, self-related qualities such as self-efficacy and self-rated performance, AEI, emotional stability, and cognitive ability (Joseph et al., 2015a). These correlations constitute the justification behind the criticism that the originators of trait EI may have unknowingly engaged in *domain sampling* (Joseph et al., 2015b). In other words, mixed EI measures draw heavily from other well-established constructs in the field of psychology (Cronbach & Meehl, 1955; Ghiselli et al., 1981; Nunnally, 1978). This is not a concern to Petrides, who considers TEI to be a lower-order construct that should be expected to correlate with cognitive ability and personality traits (Petrides & Furnham, 2006). Thus, it should be accepted that TEI is indeed a combination of well-established constructs, namely personality, cognitive ability, and self-efficacy, the fact remains that in applied settings this is a very *useful* combination.

As mentioned, TEI has been shown in past meta-analytic papers to be related to the Big Five trait conscientiousness, $\hat{\rho}=.38$ in both Joseph and Newman (2010) and O'Boyle et al. (2011). This correlation can be explained by the inclusion of stress management and self-motivation as facets of TEI, which are clearly like the conscientiousness subdomain, dutifulness. The connection between TEI and Conscientiousness describes a propensity to regulate behavior to satisfy established social norms (John & Srivastava, 1999; Joseph et al., 2015a). In the case of Petrides's TEI construct, this theoretical connection can be made with the Sociability factor, which measures self-perceived social awareness and the Emotionality factor which includes measures of self-perceived emotion perception and expression (Petrides & Furnham, 2001). The connection between Conscientiousness and TEI can be theoretically explained because individuals who seek to satisfy social norms will do so through the utilization of their ability to recognize those norms and communicate in an appropriate manner.

Extroversion, a second Big Five trait that correlates with TEI, has been said to contain several pertinent components: social vitality and social dominance (Helson & Kwan, 2000; Joseph et al., 2015a). Social vitality is related to the observation made by Wilson that, for extroverts, happiness is consistently related to "successful involvement with people" (p. 304)

(Hotard et al., 1989; Wilson, 1967). This theoretical connection relates to Petrides's EI facets that measure one's capacity to form and maintain meaningful relationships, and one's capacity to defend their point of view in social contexts (Petrides & Furnham, 2001). Therefore, we can expect that extroverts build meaningful relationships and assert themselves when their views are called into question.

Since TEI is measured through self-report instruments with items that are designed to capture self-perceived social and emotional capacities. This may account for high correlations between TEI and other self-report instruments (self-rated performance and self-efficacy in particular) are considerable (Joseph et al., 2015a; Newman et al., 2010). This connection can be theoretically supported through several different facets in the TEI; most prominently the facet self-esteem which is designed to measure an individual's level of satisfaction with his or her competence when faced with a task.

Lastly, Joseph et al. (2015b) identifies a connection between what she calls mixed EI and emotional stability. This connection can be seen when we understand that emotional stability is a combination of trait-positive affect and the ability to handle the stressors that arise in daily life as well as manage the tendency for stress to have compounding effects (Marco & Suls, 1993; Suls et al., 1998). This clearly relates to the facet of trait EI that is designed to measure one's capacity for managing stress (Petrides & Furnham, 2001). In other words, we can expect that an individual who scores high in measures of TEI will also display higher emotional stability. In a connected finding, we see that EI is a useful predictor for post-traumatic stress disorder when individuals who score high on a measure of EI reported fewer psychological problems related to traumatic events (Hunt & Evans, 2004). There is also some evidence to support a claim that TEI is a useful moderator of the stress-vulnerability-resilience relationship (Armstrong et al., 2011; Davis & Humphrey, 2012; Gohm et al., 2005; Keefer et al., 2013; Martins et al., 2010).

Cognitive Ability. It has been long established that cognitive ability is a strong predictor of job performance and all manner of other useful outcome variables (Hunter, 1986; Schmidt, 2002). While we can imagine that there might be affect-related connections between EI and cognitive ability, the most compelling connection can be found within the concept of adaptability—a consistent component measured in mixed or trait EI instruments (Bar-On, 1999; Petrides, 2010). Adaptability is included as an element of cognitive ability due to the additional cognitive processing requirements that are found in unfamiliar circumstances (Joseph et al., 2015b; LePine et al., 2000). It may be, therefore, there are contextual effects on individuals' use of EI. This would be similar to Murphy's (1989) findings that the relationship between cognitive ability and performance might not be stable over time and across contexts. Cognitive ability is important when an employee is new to a job learning new tasks, but is less useful when attempting to predict performance in the maintenance of learned tasks. This might provide some insight as to why TEI has been shown to predict performance above and beyond cognitive ability. TEI includes a measure of intrinsic motivation, which might help identify workers who are willing to work hard to satisfy an internal desire for competence even after the initial excitement of holding a new job is gone (Petrides & Furnham, 2001).

Having discussed the important correlates of TEI as discovered in recent literature, we can proceed to a detailed review of the construct that will be used in the present study. This review begins in the next section.

Trait Emotional Intelligence Facets

TEI as defined by Petrides (2010) is operationalized into thirteen facets that fit into four factors (well-being, self-control, emotionality, and sociability), and two independent facets. The well-being factor is designed to measure the overall quality of one's emotional life at the time of measurement, and includes three facets: happiness, optimism, and self-esteem. While these facet labels are familiar, it is important to briefly provide the intended definitions for each facet to avoid confusion. Within the well-being factor, happiness is operationalized as the level of contentment with one's present situation and in the TEIQue this facet measures "pleasant emotional states" (Thomas, 2010). Optimism reflects one's disposition toward the future and measures future-oriented feelings. And self-esteem measures one's evaluation of and confidence in abilities and their level of self-respect.

The self-control factor includes facets that measure an individual's level of discipline when it comes to emotions, impulses, and stress. The first facet, emotion regulation, constitutes one's ability to control surges of emotion and remain calm in stressful environments. The second facet in the self-control factor, impulse control, measures one's self perceptions about their propensity to think before they act, succumb to temptation, or make hasty decisions without thinking through second and third-order effects. The third facet, stress management, focuses attention directly on the capacity to operate under pressure.

The emotionality factor describes "your capacity to perceive and express emotions and how you use them to develop and sustain relationships with others" (Thomas, 2010). Emotionality is operationalized into four facets: Empathy, Emotion Perception, Emotion Expression, and Relationships. Empathy is described as the capacity to understand other people's viewpoints and take them into account. Emotion perception is the capacity to understand one's own and other people's emotions. Emotion expression is the capacity to express emotions to other people. Finally, the Relationships facet measures one's capacity to form and sustain fulfilling relationships both at work and in their personal life.

The Sociability factor measures one's capacity for social interaction and interpersonal social influence. Sociability is operationalized into three facets: emotion management, assertiveness, and social awareness. emotion management, which might also be called emotional influence, is one's capacity to influence the emotions of others. In application, this can manifest in efforts to invoke positive feelings such as inspiration, motivation, happiness, or pride; or negative feelings such as shame, guilt, sadness, or disgust. Assertiveness measures one's level of commitment to standing up for their beliefs, views, and conclusions. An individual who rates high on the assertiveness facet is not necessarily an aggressive person, but they may be described as principled and forthright. Lastly, social awareness is described as one's capacity to feel comfortable in social environments and levels of comfort when interacting with strangers. An individual with high social awareness might be thought of as outgoing and extroverted.

The two facets that did not fit nicely into one of the four factors—adaptability and self-motivation—are referred to as independent facets in the TEIQue technical manual (Thomas, 2010). Adaptability measures one's level of comfort with and propensity to seek out change. A person who is low in adaptability prefers a stable work environment with predictable patterns, while high scores in the facet are associated with comfort in dynamic environments and a propensity to seek out change. Self-motivation can also be called intrinsic motivation—as it seeks to measure the degree to which an individual works to satisfy their internal standards for success. Individuals who score low on self-motivation can be externally motivated and are driven by rewards such as positive evaluations, goal achievement, or financial benefits.

These 15 facets constitute the foundational elements investigated in this study. The factors ("well-being," "self-control," "emotionality," and "sociability") are useful tools for categorization, but are not central elements in the present study (in other words, factor-level labels are used to group facets, but the individual facet measures will be used to conduct analysis). Research based on this construct has been shown to have gender-specific implications, especially based on age, that manifest in interesting ways in the workplace (Petrides & Furnham, 2006). In a moderately sized sample of adults ($N_{Female}=87$, $N_{Male}=80$) with higher than average education levels (23% high school, 30.9% bachelor's degree, 43.8% postgraduate degree), Petrides and Furnham found that age was significantly related to mean-level changes in EI in women (zero-order correlation =.389, $p < .001$) but was not significant in males.

The current study looks more deeply at the issue of EI differences between officers from different age groups in the U.S. Army. The next section describes the U.S. Army's leader attributes and competencies that may be connected to TEI.

ARMY LEADER ATTRIBUTES, COMPETENCIES, AND EMOTIONAL INTELLIGENCE

The U.S. Army has a lengthy history of leader development. Efforts to cultivate leadership in enlistees and officers begin at the earliest stages of training and continue throughout a soldier's career. The Army communicates standards and expectations for leaders through doctrine, most recently Army Doctrine Publication (ADP) 6–22 entitled Army Leadership (Army, 2012). In this publication, the Army establishes a list of three Army leader attributes (ALA) and three Army leader competencies (ALC) that describe an optimal mix of traits and abilities. This blend is comprised of the following factors: character, presence, intellect, leads, develops, and achieves (see Figure 9.1). These attributes are not only present in doctrine, they find their way onto the performance evaluation forms for precommission and early-career officers and constitute the yardstick with which officer performance is measured. Army leader attributes/competencies and trait EI enjoy tremendous areas of conceptual overlap that will be explored later in this chapter. Regardless of these striking similarities, it has been noted that there is a severe lack of assessment and training emphasis on the identification and cultivation of EI in the officer corps (Hilmes, 2015). In order to understand the connections between emotional intelligence and the Army leadership model we must take a moment to review these attributes, competencies, and determine why they are important.

Figure 9.1, taken directly from ADP 6-22, depicts the Army leadership requirements model (2012). The abilities and competencies included in the model each include components that contribute to the overall competency or attribute. These components (e.g., empathy, confidence, expertise, etc.) are largely self-explanatory, though several components appeal to an understanding of Army jargon and thus require explanation.

Army Values: listed as a component of the attribute Character, is a list of seven core values taught to every Army service-member in their initial entry training. This list is designed to establish a common foundation for the diverse population of service-members who need to be able to count on each other in the most stressful and dangerous circumstances. The seven Army values are: Loyalty, Duty, Respect, Selfless Service, Honor, Integrity, and Personal Courage.

Figure 9.1

The Army Leadership Requirements Model as Depicted in Army Developmental Reference Publication 6-22 (U.S. Army, 2012)

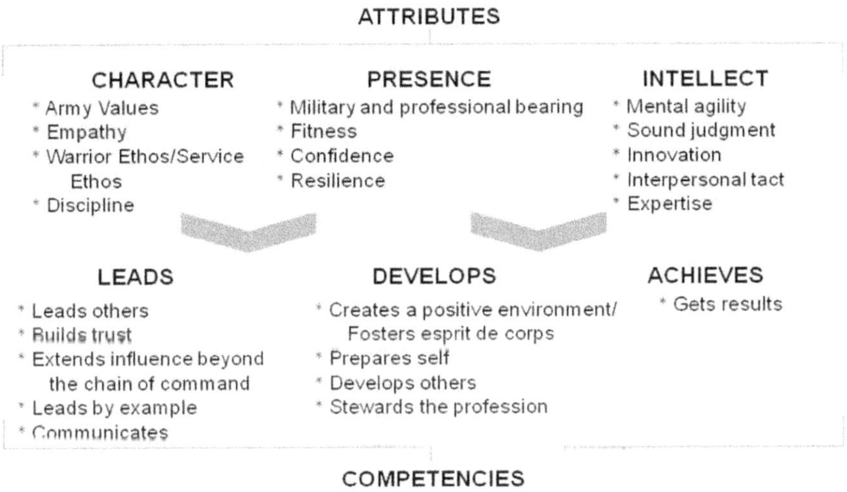

Warrior Ethos: listed as a component of the attribute character, is a small portion of the soldier's creed that is a principle for soldiers to live by. The Warrior Ethos is:

I always place the mission first
I will never accept defeat
I will never quit
I will never leave a fallen comrade

Military and Professional Bearing: listed as a component of the attribute *presence*, could be compared to a combination of composure, professionalism, and self-control. A soldier who loses his or her bearing could be analogous to losing composure, exhibiting poor decorum, or breaching protocol.

Extends Influence Beyond the Chain of Command: listed as a component of the competency leads, can be described as understanding of networks and environments and communicating effectively within those contexts. There is an element of social acumen that is implied in the extension of influence beyond one's own organization. In the military, like many other organizations and vocations, networking is an important element to a leader's duty performance.

These traits and attributes are the criteria that are used to measure officer performance on evaluations. Officers in the first 9 to 10 years of service are evaluated on a form that provides supervisors with blanks for up to five lines of text to describe the rated officer's performance in each attribute and competency (i.e., five lines to describe "Character," five lines to describe "Presence," etc.).

Despite the great importance that is placed on these attributes and competencies, many of them are not incorporated into institutional officer development initiatives. The position taken in this chapter is that the facets of EI overlap considerably with the subcomponents of the leader attributes and competencies outlined in ADRP 6–22, and that efforts spent to identify and develop EI self-awareness in officers during their early career could be tremendously beneficial. This theoretical overlap is illustrated in Table 9.1, which depicts the 15 facets of EI and connects them with ALA or ALC components.

The theoretical connection between subcomponents of the ALA Presence and EI has some existing empirical support. First, TEI has been shown to be positively related to resilience in that high scores in EI facets relate to "lower threat appraisals, more modest declines in positive affect, less negative affect and challenge physiological responses to stress" (p. 909) (Schneider et al., 2013). Confidence, another subcomponent of presence, is clearly related to TEI facet self-esteem as both constructs refer to one's self perceived ability to accomplish tasks successfully. Professional bearing is another subcomponent of presence that can be connected to facets of EI through facets stress management and emotion regulation. A leader able to operate in stressful situations effectively and controls his or her emotions achieves the desired outcome of having professional bearing. Bearing also has connections to social awareness, as leaders who are high in that facet of TEI might be more able to identify appropriate behaviors in social contexts.

The theoretical connection between Army leader attribute character and EI begins with the ALA subcomponent discipline and TEI facet impulse control. Discipline refers to one's ability to persevere and resist temptation, which is more easily accomplished when an individual is deliberate about their actions and lacks impulsivity. Character and EI are also clearly connected through identically named subcomponent and TEI facet empathy. In addition to this connection, it might also be supposed that EI facet emotion perception might enhance a leader's ability to show empathy.

Lastly for ALA, we can see connections between ALA intellect and TEI. Subcomponent interpersonal tact can be theoretically connected to social awareness, emotion management, and emotion expression. Leaders who understand social dynamics, can influence the emotional states of others, and who are able to communicate their emotions effectively will be seen

Table 9.1

Theoretical Connections Between Trait EI and Army Leader Requirements

Trait Emotional Intelligence		Army Leader Requirements	
EI Factor	EI Facet	Attribute or Competency	Subcomponent(s)
Well-Being	Happiness	Attribute Presence	Resilience
	Optimism	Attribute Presence	Resilience
	Self-Esteem	Attribute Presence	Confidence
Self-Control	Emotion Regulation	Attribute Presence	Professional Bearing
	Impulse Control	Attribute Character	Discipline
	Stress Management	Attribute Presence	Professional Bearing
Emotionality	Empathy	Attribute Character	Empathy
	Emotion Perception	Attribute Character	Empathy
		Competency Develops	Prepares Self
	Emotion Expression	Competency Leads	Communicates
	Relationships	Competency Leads	Builds Trust
		Competency Develops	Develops Others
Sociability	Emotion Management	Competency Develops	Creates a positive environment
		Attribute Intellect	Interpersonal Tact
	Assertiveness	Competency Leads	Leads Others
	Social Awareness	Attribute Intellect	Interpersonal Tact
		Competency Leads	Extends influence beyond the chain of command
Independent Facets	Adaptability	Attribute Intellect	Mental Agility
		Attribute Intellect	Innovation
	Self-Motivation	Attribute Character	Warrior Ethos (Never Quit)

Note: Table contents derived from Petrides (2010) and the Trait Emotional Intelligence Questionnaire Sample Report.

as having interpersonal tact. Further, we can see that intellect subcomponents mental agility and innovation are theoretically related to TEI facet adaptability. A mentally agile leader adjusts to unique challenges and create innovative solutions. Interestingly, another conceptual connection can be made between TEI impulse control and ALA Intellect Subcomponents

Mental Agility and Innovation since low scores in impulse control are also associated with being creative and adventurous, thus creating a theoretical inverse relationship.

While the theoretical connections depicted in Table 9.1 cannot be verified in the present study due to the fact that there is no empirical measure for the ALA and ALC, one of the benefits of this study is to show that existing trait emotional intelligence measures overlap with ALA/ALC so considerably that they could be used within military contexts for officer development. Additionally, the present study is designed to shed light on the experiences and influences that might produce facet, factor, and general score-level differences in trait emotional intelligence between populations of military officers.

Hypothesis 1: Midcareer officers have higher general scores on the TEIQue than precommission cadets. As mentioned above, longitudinal research on TEI in adults is extremely limited. One longitudinal examination of TEI was conducted on subjects during late-childhood and adolescence (Keefer et al., 2013), while others have been limited in duration (typically one to two years) and focus (primarily on predictive utility) (Jellesma et al., 2011). Thus, it is useful to investigate the extent to which the combined value of experience and added maturity will lead to a mean-level difference between the precareer and midcareer sample.

Hypothesis 2: Midcareer officers often are rated higher on the Self-Control Factor of the TEIQue than precommission cadets (*H2a* Emotion Regulation, *H2b* Impulse Control, and *H2c* Stress Management). This constitutes one of the most important aspects of the expected findings, since the facets that are contained within the Self-Control factor are extremely valuable in military contexts. Given the high-stress nature of military duty both in garrison and in deployed environments, there is a strong expectation that officers who excel in this factor will uniquely prepared for the professional rigors of military duty.

Hypothesis 3: Midcareer officers are rated higher on the Sociability factor of the TEIQue than precommission cadets (*H3a* Emotion Management, *H3b* Assertiveness, and *H3c* Social Awareness). These expectations are based on the perspective that the first years of military service include experiences that typically improve an officer's confidence and discipline. For example, every Infantry officer (and some Armor officers) attends Ranger school, which is an elite tactical training leadership training program. Officers are also exposed to various and varied professional environments that likely improve their social awareness. For example, military culture is filled with official social events that range from casual to extremely formal. These social events provide young leaders with unique insights into the professional social domain wherein participants must interact comfortably yet be mindful of underlying rank structures and social norms. This hypothesis has enormous implications for training and personnel management initiatives and will indicate whether the typical young officer develops refined sociability during the first years of service.

Hypothesis 4: Midcareer officers are rated higher than cadets on the Adaptability facet. Military service exposes leaders with dynamic situations and complex problems that may be more effectively managed by experienced officers (an adaptable leader is a savvy leader). The other independent facet (self-motivation) will note be investigated due to the expectation that students at military academies are typically quite self-motivated.

After investigating differences between early and midcareer officers, it will be important to closely examine the midcareer population to discover how much of the variance in EI can be explained by certain experiences, training, and demographic variables. While this investigation will not be sufficient to prove causal relationships, it could provide useful insight into the most beneficial aspects of an officer's first years of service. These findings could influence future training initiatives to accelerate the acquisition of critical EI skills, increase self-awareness, and improve leader performance.

First, young infantry and armor officers experience direct leadership responsibility to a degree that they have never experienced before. As a platoon leader, an officer is responsible for 20–40 soldiers, and is financially accountable for millions of dollars in military equipment. This massive amount or responsibility is overwhelming at first, but over time most platoon leaders grow in maturity and confidence.

Second, combat training center experience is defined as a rotation at either the National Training Center at Fort Irwin, California; The Joint Readiness Training Center at Fort Polk, Louisiana; or the Joint Multinational Readiness Center at Hohenfels, Germany. These centers receive military units from all over the world and guide them through an intense scenario-based training environment that is designed to prepare them for deployment. Young officers are challenged with important decisions and are pushed physically and mentally in the fast-paced scenario. Combat training centers place great emphasis on learning and leader development. After action reviews are conducted and leaders are encouraged to introspect at every stage of the training rotation. These "pressure cooker" environments are optimal for the development of EI in a short period of time.

Third, completion of a challenging military training course, such as Ranger School; Special Forces Assessment and Selection (SFAS); Sapper; and resident Survival, Evasion, Resistance, and Escape (SERE) courses indicate the presence of mental ability, self-control, persistence, discipline and mental agility. We can expect that individuals who successfully complete these courses will reflect higher TEIQue scores in the Self-Control factor, Sociability factor, and the Adaptability and Self-Motivation facets. This study also includes an item to measure completion of 40 or more hours of comprehensive soldier and family fitness (CSF2). This training stems from positive psychology principles and focuses on positivity, resilience, and mindfulness.

There are several experiences that could be considered as critical and formative in the early career of an infantry or armor officer. The effects of these experiences are critical to understanding TEI over a career. Therefore, the fifth hypothesis of this study was developed.

Hypothesis 5: Variance in midcareer officer EI scores is explained by a combination of deployment experience, Combat training center experience, and training experience (Ranger, SFAS, Sapper, SERE, and CSF2). The current study expects to find that deployment experience adds to the model in several ways. First, the challenges that are often faced during deployment lead to changes in the Self-Control factor (emotion regulation, impulse control, and stress management) and the Sociability factor (emotion management, assertiveness, and social awareness). This study also expects to find some negative relationships with regard to deployment based on the emotional numbing that can occur during exposure to combat operations (Campbell & Renshaw, 2013; Kashdan et al., 2006; Keenan et al., 2014; Shu et al., 2014).

A related experience, deployment, provides a context which impacts ratings of military officers. Therefore, the sixth hypothesis of this study was developed.

Hypothesis 6: Midcareer officers with deployment experience rate lower on the Empathy (*H6a*), Emotion Perception (*H6b*) and Emotion Expression (*H6c*) subfactor of Emotionality than midcareer officers with no deployment experience. It should be noted that "deployment experience" is too broad a term if the intent is to accurately measure a leader's exposure to highly stressful conditions during deployment. Thus, items in the demographic portion of the survey were designed to assess the number, location (Iraq, Afghanistan, both, or other). This was designed to filter out any deployments to locations that may be technically considered a combat zone but might not meet the intent of the present study.

METHOD

To test the hypotheses listed above, a TEI measure, the Trait Emotional Intelligence Questionnaire or TEIQue, was administered to a population of midcareer officers at a large military installation and compared to an existing dataset from a population of precareer cadets from a large military academy. Demographic items to identify pertinent military service and training experience were added to the TEIQue survey to facilitate the analysis of Hypotheses 5 and 6.

Participants

Sample 1, the precareer sample, consists of 175 military academy students who were selected to serve in the U.S. Army as infantry or armor officers. All students at the military academy were required to complete the TEIQue as part of their development as a leader. Only those branched armor and infantry are used in this study to avoid competing hypotheses when comparing samples 1 and 2. Sample 1 is 100% male, mean age 21.68 years old (SD=.96). Ethnically, sample 1 is comprised of 77% White (not Hispanic), 6% Asian descent, 6% Hispanic, 3% African American, 1% Native American and 6% elected not to indicate their ethnicity. All individuals in sample 1 were United States citizens. Students had some knowledge of the EI construct, based on a course they received more than two months before taking the measure.

Sample 2, the midcareer sample, consists of 211 midcareer Armor and infantry officers attending a mandatory career progression course at a major military installation in the United States. The sample consists of the student population from four separate classes in the same professional military education course. In other words, all students in four classes were offered the opportunity to participate, but participation was not required. Participation rates for sample 2 was 64.22%. Sample 2 is 100% male, mean age 29.22 years old (SD = 3.61 years). Ethnically, sample 2 is comprised of 83% White (not-Hispanic), 4% Asian descent, 4% Hispanic, 3% African American, 1% Native American and 5% elected not to indicate their ethnicity. While sample 2 originally included international officers, these officers were filtered out to ensure that the midcareer sample consists entirely of U.S. citizens.

Sample 1. Sample 1 (precareer sample) answered the TEIQue via a web link contained in an e-mail, and participants completed the measure on their own. Though completion of the measure was not a part of the student's curriculum, it was a mandatory assignment in the interest of professional development.

Sample 2. Participants received a 15-minute introduction to the study prior to signing consent forms. This was done to provide similar exposure to emotional intelligence theory. The lead researcher obtained informed consent at the introduction brief. A link for the study was provided to all participants via email no more than 24 hours after the introduction brief. Sample 2 completed the measure on their own. Participants then had between 7 and 14 days to complete the study (length varied for each class due to scheduling constraints). Each class then received a 55-minute collective feedback briefing wherein the researcher discussed general trends in the results. In addition, self-awareness strategies for leaders was discussed. Five students requested and received one-on-one feedback sessions to discuss their results.

Participants in Samples 1 and 2 were not offered any monetary incentive. They were informed that the value associated with the feedback and counseling that was offered in association with this study exceeds $250. Collective feedback sessions led by graduate students who received training on TEIQue feedback from Thomas International were conducted within one week after participants took the TEIQue. All analysis was conducted at the aggregate level, with the identities of each participant completely unknown to the researcher. The measure took an average of 22.6 minutes (*SD* =17.15) to complete (average and *SD* calculated after removing four outliers who likely left their computer on without finishing the measure and thus took more than 200 minutes to complete the measure).

Measures

The TEIQue is a 155-item self-report trait emotional intelligence measure distributed by Thomas International Ltd. The measure asks participants to respond to statements on a 1 to 7 Likert-type scale (1 for "Disagree Completely and 7 for "Agree Completely"). The instrument was developed by Petrides (2001), and is available on his website (psychometriclab.com), but the version offered by Thomas International was used in order to provide participants with individual professional development feedback on their EI profile (participants received a report via email and were given the opportunity to review the report with a TEIQue-certified I/O Psychology graduate student). The test-retest reliability of the TEIQue has been shown to be quite robust in a sample of 907 females (.89) and 759 males (.92), showing that measures remained generally stable one year after the original instrument was completed (Thomas International, 2011).

Criterion-related validity evidence for the TEIQue has been supported through concurrent validation based Pearson product-moment correlations with pro-social and antisocial behavior such as coping styles (Rational coping, r =.50; Rational, r =.67; Detached, r =.47; Emotion, r = –.62; and Avoidance, r = –40) and depressive affect (Dysfunctional attitudes, r = – .38; and Depression, r = –.56). In work domains, the TEIQue has been shown to correlate with Achievement (r = .49), higher levels of Perceived Job Control (r = .28), and Job Commitment (r = .24). All reported correlations satisfy $p < .05$ threshold for significance and are listed in the TEIQue Technical Summary (Thomas International, 2011).

Analytic Strategies

Hypotheses 1 was examined using several techniques. First, independent sample t tests compared composite score (for general EI, factor-level composites, and facet-level score) means between the precareer and midcareer sample. In order to gain a more refined understanding of what is going on at the facet level, Multivariate Analysis of Variance (MANOVA) was used to identify differences in each of the 15 facets of EI between precareer and midcareer military leaders. This method explored the differences between groups of scores across groups. The MANOVA combined mean scores for all TEI facets in precareer sample and compared them in one step against the same group of facet-level means for the midcareer sample.

Hypotheses 2 through 4 proposed differences in facet-level scores between precareer and midcareer military leaders. Hypotheses 2 through 4 will be evaluated using independent sample pairwise *t*-tests.

Hypothesis 5, investigating the nature of EI variance in midcareer officers, will be answered using multiple regression analysis to discover which experiences and demographic variables are most useful in predicting variance in EI facets. This model used all study participants in Samples 1 and 2. The experiences for Sample 1 zeros in all predictor variables

Lastly, Hypothesis 6 will be analyzed through *t*-tests comparing midcareer officers who have deployed versus midcareer officers who have not deployed (all within Sample 2, midcareer military leaders). Considerations are made in this analysis for location of deployment (Iraq, Afghanistan, or both), and duration of deployment time (total time spent in a combat zone). These considerations are important to evaluate competing hypotheses related to the nature of deployment in each geographic location.

Outliers

Prior to conducting any tests, outlier analysis was conducted on the precareer and midcareer samples. SPSS box plots for each facet were used to identify outlier, cases that satisfied a combination of two criteria were removed: first, the case had to be identified as an outlier in two or more facets of EI. And second, start times and end times were analyzed to determine the likelihood that the outlier was caused by careless responding. Thus, cases that were outliers in two or more facets and who had survey completion times of less than 10 minutes were excluded from the analysis.

As a result of this procedure, the midcareer sample was reduced from 211 to 206, and the precareer sample was reduced from 175 to 173. All seven of the outliers were low-end outliers.

RESULTS

Hypothesis Testing

Hypothesis 1. Hypothesis 1 proposed that the midcareer officer sample would have a higher global TEIQue score than the precareer sample (see Table 9.2). A comparison of means using independent sample *t*-test (equal variance assumed based on Levene's test) did not provide support for Hypothesis 1: midcareer (M = 5.29), and precareer (M = 5.28); t (377) = – .174, p =.862. This null result may be interpreted in several ways. First, it is entirely possible that precareer and midcareer military leaders do not differ in overall metrics of EI. Proponents for the stability of TEI over time would see this cross-sectional result as support for their assertion that changes are minimal over time. A second possibility is that the age and experience difference between the two samples was not wide enough to identify the hypothesized difference. Ideally, the midcareer sample would have measured officers who already completed what are called "key and developmental" positions in their current rank as captains. However, the midcareer sample in this study was comprised of relatively new promotees to the rank of captain and thus differences might not be as stark as they would be otherwise. It is also necessary to consider that the selective nature of the military academy that produced the precareer sample. The selection process for these individuals could skew results since the midcareer sample was comprised of 34% academy graduates. There was a total of 72 academy graduates in the midcareer sample, which was adequate to test all hypotheses using precareer academy Cadets, and midcareer academy graduates. In the case of general EI scores (Hypothesis 1), there was no significant difference between precareer cadets and midcareer academy graduates: midcareer (M = 5.19), and precareer (M = 5.28); t (245) = .926, p =.355.

Hypothesis 2. Hypothesis 2 proposed that the midcareer sample would exhibit higher scores on the Self-Control factor with Hypothesis 2a comparing emotion regulation, Hypothesis 2b comparing impulse control, and Hypothesis 2c comparing stress management between the precareer and midcareer samples (see Table 9.3). At the factor level, the comparison of means between midcareer (M = 5.23), and precareer (M = 5.10) was not significant; t (377) = 1.673, p = .095. However, there is evidence of differences between the samples when facet-level analysis is conducted.

Table 9.2: Hypothesis 1

Results of T-Tests and Descriptive Statistics GTE for Precareer and Midcareer Military Leaders

Outcome	Group						95% CI for Mean Difference		
	Precareer			Midcareer					
	M	*SD*	*n*	*M*	*SD*	*n*		*t*	*df*
Global Score	5.26	.5667	175	5.26	.5636	211	−.1211, .1060	−.131	384
Global Score (outliers del.)	5.28	.5312	174	5.29	.5117	206	−.0899, .1216	.296	377

* $p < .05$, †$p < .01$

Equal variance assumed based on Levene's Test for Equality of Variance, outliers calculated using SPSS box-plots.

Comparison of means provided some support for Hypothesis 2a (emotion regulation): midcareer (M = 5.23), precareer (M = 5.08); t (377) = 2.004, p = .046. This result is tempered by power analysis which produced a small effect size (.21), 1 −β =.52. This modest finding indicates that it is possible that midcareer military leaders are indeed more able to control their emotional states than precareer military leaders. The mean raw score difference translates into a difference of four percentile points (precareer mean scores are in the 69th percentile, while the midcareer sample mean score is the 74th percentile). Thus we can say that all military personnel in the study appear to have higher than average scores in Emotion Control when compared to the United States Norm that is used to score the TEIQue, and there is evidence to suggest that this difference may increase during the first four to six years of military experience.

Comparison of means provided strong support for Hypothesis 2b (impulse control): midcareer (M = 5.1), precareer (M = 4.81); t (377) = 3.003, p = .003. This result is reinforced by power analysis that produced $1-\beta$ = .85, though small effect size remained small (.31). This finding indicates that midcareer military leaders are less likely to be influenced by their impulses than precareer military leaders. The mean raw score difference translates into a difference of 13 percentile points (precareer mean scores are in the 52nd percentile, while the midcareer sample mean score is the 65th percentile. The military personnel in the study appear to have scores above the 50th percentile in impulse control, and there is evidence

Table 9.3: Hypothesis 2

Results of T-Tests and Descriptive Statistics Self-Control Factor for Precareer and Midcareer Military Leaders

Outcome	Group								
	Precareer			Midcareer			95% CI for Mean Difference		
	M	*SD*	*N*	*M*	*SD*	*n*		*t*	*df*
Self-Control	5.09	.6206	173	5.20	.6275	206	−.2343, .0189	1.67	377
EmReg	5.08	.7072	173	5.23	.7463	206	−.2983, −.0028	2.00*	377
ImpCon	4.80	.8335	173	5.10	.7829	206	−.4132, −.0862	3.00†	377
StressMgmt	5.37	.8004	173	5.27	.8280	206	−.2624, .0655	−1.18	377

* $p < .05$, †$p < .01$

Equal variance assumed based on Levene's Test for Equality of Variance. EmReg = Emotion Regulation, ImpCon = Impulse Control, StressMgmt = Stress Management.

to suggest that this difference may increase during the first four to six years of military experience.

Comparison of means did not provide support for Hypothesis 2c (stress management): midcareer ($M = 5.32$), precareer ($M = 5.40$); $t\ (377) = .992$, $p = .322$. Thus, there does not appear to be a difference between precareer and midcareer leaders in their ability to operate in stressful situations. The rigor of academy training could partially explain this result since the precareer sample is comprised of cadets who are in their fourth year of training and might have already benefited from an increase in this facet in their first four years.

The significant differences in emotion regulation and impulse control may underscore findings related to the neurological development of the prefrontal cortex (PFC)—the area of the brain that is associated with decision making and self-control. Imaging studies indicate that the PFC continues to develop between the ages of 20 and 30 (Diamond, 2002; Sowell et al., 1999). While it is possible that military experience (such as training and deployment) could account for development in this factor, the findings of this study do not support that explanation (see discussion on Hypothesis 5). Thus, we are pointed toward a biological explanation. In summary, differences between precareer and midcareer military leaders in the areas of emotion regulation and impulse control indicate that leaders with more experience are more able to control their emotional states, and less prone to impulsiveness.

Hypothesis 3. Hypothesis 3 proposed that the midcareer sample would exhibit higher scores on the Sociability factor with Hypothesis 3a comparing Emotion Management, Hypothesis 3b comparing Assertiveness, and Hypothesis 3c comparing Social Awareness between the precareer and midcareer samples (see Table 9.4). The tests comparing means did not produce any significant results at the factor or facet levels, thus Hypothesis 3 is not supported.

As with Hypothesis 1, it is possible that this null result reflects stability of the Sociability factor across samples at different points in a leader's career. It is also possible that the highly structured environment and leadership cultivation emphasis at the military academy in the precareer sample positively influenced the precareer sample in terms of Social Awareness, Assertiveness, and Emotion Management. Future analysis could compare military samples to a civilian norm group to ascertain whether or not military training appears to have an effect on Sociability in military leaders.

Table 9.4: Hypothesis 3

Results of T-Tests and Descriptive Statistics Sociability Factor for Precareer and Midcareer Military Leaders

Outcome	Group								
	Precareer			Midcareer			95% CI for Mean		
	M	*SD*	*n*	*M*	*SD*	*n*	Difference	*t*	*df*
Sociability	5.33	.6454	173	5.26	.6027	206	–.0616, .1909	1.007	377
EmotMan	5.35	.7055	173	5.25	.6655	206	–.0373, .2401	1.44	377
Assertive	5.29	.7903	173	5.31	.7022	206	–.1729, .1287	–.288	377
SocAware	5.35	.7715	173	5.24	.8165	206	–.0478, .2751	1.384	377

$^*p < .05$, $^\dagger p < .01$. Equal variance assumed based on Levene's Test for Equality of Variance. "EmotMan" = Emotion Management, "Assertive" = Assertiveness, "SocAware" = Social Awareness.

Hypothesis 4. Hypothesis 4 proposed that the midcareer sample would exhibit higher scores on the Adaptability facet of TEI between the precareer and midcareer samples (see Table 9.5). The test comparing means did not produce significant results, thus we can say that Hypothesis 4 is not supported: midcareer military leaders do not appear to be more able to adapt to new circumstances when compared to precareer military leaders.

Table 9.5: Hypothesis 4

Results of T-Tests and Descriptive Statistics Adaptability Facet for Precareer and Midcareer Military Leaders

Outcome	Group								
	Precareer			Midcareer			95% CI for Mean Difference		
	M	*SD*	*n*	*M*	*SD*	*n*		*t*	*df*
Adaptability	4.76	.7015	173	4.8014	.6950	206	–.1800, .1031	–.534	377

$^*p < .05$, $^{\dagger}p < .01$. Equal variance assumed based on Levene's Test for Equality of Variance.

Adding to the possible explanations listed above for the null results in Hypotheses 1 and 3, it is possible that scores on the adaptability facet reflect preference more than trait-level differences. For example, midcareer military leaders might prefer well-established systems that have proven to be effective to new methods. This theoretical preference would not preclude the possibility that midcareer leaders might respond more favorably when the environment requires adaptability. Future studies could compare military samples to civilian samples to see if interesting differences emerge.

Hypothesis 5. Hypothesis 5 proposed that variation in midcareer EI scores can be explained through a combination of deployment and training experience. The block regression analysis did not produce significant results (see Table 9.6). Additional analysis was conducted to see if the model would accurately predict variation in the facets of Impulse Control and Emotion Regulation based on the significant differences between precareer and midcareer leaders listed above. This additional analysis resulted in significant prediction of Impulse Control, ($R^2 = .013$, $p = .024$), but did not predict Emotion Regulation. For Impulse Control, it was important to consider ΔR^2 in order to more precisely describe the relationship between predictors (deployment in months, and training) and the dependent variable. Results clearly indicate that deployment in months is the strongest predictor since training-related predictors were not significant when deployment months were in the model (see Table 9.8). Subsequent analysis using age as a predictor for Impulse Control was completed in order to identify whether increases in Impulse Control might be interpreted as a result of aging, regardless of deployment experience. Age was a significant predictor of Impulse Control ($R^2 = .012$, $p = .033$), and deployment in months did not add to the model when age was added first (see Table 9.6).

These findings suggest that the proposed model does not predict variation in Trait Emotional Intelligence or Emotion Regulation but does

Table 9.6: Hypothesis 5

Summary of Regression Results Using Deployment Months and Training Experience to Predict Trait Emotional Intelligence

	β			
Variable	**Model 1**	**Model 2**	**R^2**	**ΔR^2**
1. Deployment Months	.027	.048	.001	.001
2. Training Experience			.009	.008
CTC		–.069		
Ranger		.051		
SFAS		.037		
SERE		.016		
CSF2		–.053		
Sapper		.009		

$^*p < .05$, $^\dagger p < .01$

"CTC" = Combat Training Center; "SFAS" = Special Forces Assessment and Selection; "SERE" = Survival, Evasion, Resistance, and Escape; "CSF2" = Comprehensive Soldier and Family Fitness.

predict Impulse Control through deployment experience (in months). Additionally, it appears that variations in Impulse Control as predicted through deployment time is more strongly related to the natural aging process than the unique experiences in deployed environments.

There are several possible explanations for this result. First, it is possible that the coding system proposed in this study does not accurately capture training experience or combat training center experience. Developments in TEI are likely due to increased self-awareness obtained through experience. Accordingly, it is possible that merely experiencing the training might not be enough; the training would need to have had an impact on self-awareness. In future studies, it would be wise to incorporate items that measure self-report impact of training, rather than dichotomous items.

Deployment coded in months was not a significant predictor of variation in TEI, which can be viewed as a positive result in application since deployment frequency and intensity are currently much lower than they were during the height of the wars in Iraq and Afghanistan. The increases that we find when we compare precareer and midcareer leaders in Impulse Control and Emotion Regulation indicate important developments in the first years of military service. If those developments were explained by deployment to combat, then it would follow that midcareer leaders who do not deploy would remain at their precareer levels of Impulse Control and Emotion Regulation. As it is, it appears that another variable—perhaps time in service—might explain this development. Unfortunately, time in service was not a useful variable in the data set. This probably because the midcareer leaders in the sample attend the course at the same phase of their career.

Hypothesis 6. Hypothesis 6 proposed that the midcareer leaders with combat deployment experience exhibit lower scores than midcareer leaders with no combat deployment experience on several facets within the Emotionality factor with Hypothesis 6a comparing Empathy, Hypothesis 6b comparing Emotion Perception, and Hypothesis 6c comparing Emotion Expression (see Table 9.7). The tests comparing means did not produce any significant results at the factor or facet levels, thus we can say that Hypothesis 6 is not supported.

Table 9.7: Hypothesis 6

Summary of Regression Results Using Deployment Months and Training Experience to predict Impulse Control

	β			
Variable	**Model 1**	**Model 2**	**R2**	**ΔR2**
1. Deployment Months	.116	.051	.013	.013*
2. Training Experience			.021	.008
CTC		.070		
Ranger		.047		
SFAS		0.00		
SERE		–.008		
CSF2		.014		
Sapper		.003		

*$p < .05$, †$p < .01$

"CTC" = Combat Training Center; "SFAS" = Special Forces Assessment and Selection; "SERE" = Survival, Evasion, Resistance, and Escape; "CSF2" = Comprehensive Soldier and Family Fitness.

There are several possible reasons why we might not find significant differences between deployed and nondeployed military leaders. First, it is possible that the sample size for the nondeployers (n = 47) was not large enough to accurately identify differences. Second, the survey was not designed to measure the intensity of the leader's combat experience. The survey item only allowed the leader to indicate whether they were deployed to Iraq, Afghanistan, or both. Since most of the midcareer leaders in the study entered active service after 2010, it is quite possible that the roles they filled during their rotations—especially in Iraq—were advisory-oriented rather than combat oriented. Future research should seek to quantify combat experience with greater specificity.

Finally, a MANOVA was used to compare the 15 facets of emotional intelligence between the precareer and midcareer samples. This is related to Hypothesis 1 but does not use the "Global EI Score" as provided by the TEIQue instrument, and instead examines all facets against each other simultaneously. This multivariate procedure generated a significant outcome based on a Wilks' Lambda value of .889 ($F = 3.026$, $p < .001$), indicating the presence of a linear combination of the 15 facets between precareer and midcareer military leaders that are significantly different. In order to understand this difference more precisely, it was necessary to perform a discriminant analysis to determine which facets contributed to the significant MANOVA. The results of the discriminant analysis identify the top 10 (in order of importance) contributing facets as Impulse Control, Emotion Regulation, Emotion Perception, Emotion Management, Social Awareness, Emotional Expression, Self-Motivation, Empathy, and Stress Management. Further detail was acquired by performing the Roy-Bargman stepdown process as proposed in Tabachnick and Fidell (2007), and Stevens (1996).

The Roy-Bargman process evaluated contributing facets that were identified in the discriminant analysis as they were entered one-at-a-time. This stepdown process revealed that Impulse Control continued to be the greatest contributor to the model $F(1, 377) = 9.02$, $p < .01$, and Emotion Regulation (which was previously the second most important predictor) was no longer significant. This indicates that Impulse Control accounted for most of the variance that contributed to the significant pairwise t test in Hypothesis 2. The other significant contributors to MANOVA as identified through the Roy-Bargman procedure are Emotion Perception, $F(1, 375) = 7.91$, $p < .01$; Emotion Expression $F(1, 372) = 11.29$, $p < .001$; and Stress Management $F(1, 369) = 9.09$, $p < .01$. The significance of Stress Management offers some reinforcement for Hypothesis 2, building on the position that there appear to be important differences between precareer and midcareer officers on the Self-Control factor.

DISCUSSION

The results of this study indicate that there do not appear to be systemic differences in EI between precareer and midcareer military leaders in 13 of the 15 facets measured in the TEIQue. However, differences do seem to exist within the Self-Control Factor. These differences manifest most clearly in the facets of Emotion Regulation (ER), and Impulse Control (IC). Mackay et al. (2012) noted that ER and IC are important facets for effective leaders. As mentioned, it appears that in the first formative years of a military career, infantry and armor officers improve their ability to regulate their emotions and control their impulses, but the present study does not adequately explain what variables in the midcareer sample might explain this development. Two explanations are proposed: First, it might be that military culture cultivates leaders who have stronger abilities to regulate their emotions and control their impulses. Second, it is quite likely that these changes are due to the neural development in the prefrontal cortex. The second explanation is supported through regression analysis that showed age as the most significant predictor of Impulse Control. However, it might be the case that age is only a predictor of Impulse Control within military samples.

Practical Implications

For the military, the results of this study reinforce the building body of evidence in the private sector, and indicate that TEI could be a useful construct to identify successful leaders (Mackay et al., 2012). Should military leaders seek to utilize the Petrides model as used in this study, items designed to measure Adaptability should be adjusted to reflect Mental Agility as described in ADP 6-22 more accurately. Mental Agility implies an ability to effectively adapt to a dynamic or changing environment, not necessarily the propensity to seek out change—which is more consistent with the Army Leader Attribute "Intellect" subcomponent "Innovation." Additionally, "Self-Motivation" items might be modified for military use to accommodate the positive aspects of goal-orientation. In military contexts, self-motivation might be described as being driven or goal-oriented. Interestingly, someone who is goal-oriented might score low on the Self-Motivation facet as measured in the TEIQue since being driven by goals could be construed as being externally motivated.

The similarities between the TEI model and Army Leader Attributes and Competencies as outlined in ADRP 6-22 and evaluated on Officer Evaluation Reports demand attention (Hilmes, 2015). The Army invests tremendous effort in leader development and talent management, but many of the efforts vary greatly from branch to branch (e.g., infantry to signal corps) and from unit to unit. EI has been shown to be a useful predictor of performance in the civilian sector, but its predictive ability has not been assessed in military contexts. Future studies should evaluate the extent to which TEI measures can predict success in key and developmental military positions. If TEI can be shown to predict performance in these duty assignments, it may be time for the military to consider the incorporation of a TEI measure into officer recruitment and development efforts.

It is important to point out that leaders should choose between two goals—recruitment or development—based on the competitive connotation that will emerge if an instrument is used for high-stakes decisions (such as selection or promotion). For this reason, we advocate the use of Trait Emotional Intelligence instruments as a self-awareness tool to be used in concert with (and nested in) other leader feedback instruments.

Limitations

The first limitation of this research is generalizability concerns revolving around the unique nature of the study participants that were used. Not only are all study participants in the military, they constitute two branches within the military (infantry and armor), and are exclusively male. It is unclear if the findings in this study would be consistent across all branches and genders because of the nature of the samples used led to all males in both samples. There are also several missed opportunities in the present study. First, the demographic items used to build the regression model to predict TEI could be greatly improved. Deployment was measured in months, but there might be other useful ways to measure combat experience (such as total number of patrols, patrols per day, or other similar items). Additionally, time spend in direct leadership positions was not included in the survey. Junior military leaders are afforded varying amounts of leadership time in their platoons and as company executive officers. Additionally, some junior leaders are exposed to the challenges of combat deployment during their leadership time, while others lead in garrison. The rich variety in these experiences, if measured, might have provided valuable insight into the development of midcareer leaders.

In addition to deployment experience, the theory proposed in this study placed special emphasis on combat training center (CTC) experience. These training facilities are designed to expose rotational units to a wide array of challenges that mirror combat or other real-world mission sets as closely as possible. Coding of CTC rotations in this study did not adequately parse out the varying levels of learning that might occur as a result of CTC experiences, and could only be used in the model as a simple dichotomous variable. There is no way to know if more accurate measurement might have made a difference in the model, but it is clear that CTCs play a unique role in leader development in high-stress team learning contexts. Should the military seek to incorporate EI familiarization and training, the CTCs would be a useful venue for such an initiative. One way this could occur is through EI-trained instructors at CTCs who could provide leader feedback during after-action reviews utilizing "EI language." For example, "let's talk about your efforts to inspire and motivate your exhausted subordinates during that protracted engagement." Such feedback would provide useful self-awareness information related to EI facets emotion management, emotion perception, and emotion expression.

Variation in EI was not explained by the combination of deployment experience and training in this study. However, future studies should continue to investigate what factors might influence facet, factor, and global TEI scores in military leaders. Several shortfalls of this study, some elaborated upon in the limitations section below, might be addressed in future studies to improve results. First, items should be generated to better measure the leadership experience in the midcareer sample. For example, number of months spent as a platoon leader would provide interesting (and quantifiable) insight into a formative period in a leader's professional development. It should also be noted that the training experiences in this study were a combination of dichotomous responses and did not reflect any efficacy-related training results. In other words, it might be that training experience will only influence EI in leaders who see that training as valuable or formative in their career. Other important variables to measure might include more specific measurement of combat exposure, performance history, cognitive ability, and time spent in direct leadership positions (platoon leader and executive officer) versus staff positions (e.g., assistant operations officer). We might find that length of time in these formative leadership positions might explain some variation in EI facets.

Lastly, it is necessary to address several considerations when evaluating Hypothesis 6. The primary concern when evaluating Hypothesis 6 (combat deployment effects on Emotionality factor) was the relatively small sample size that was present in the nondeployed group. Only 47 individuals did not have deployment experience to either Iraq or Afghanistan, which was not a large enough sample to accurately reflect group-level differences. Additionally, it could be that military culture might have a negative impact on Emotionality factor scores. Subsequent studies could compare military personnel to a similar aged civilian sample to investigate these possible explanations.

Future Research Directions

Given these results, there is more work to be done in the use of EI in a military context. The military has rich legacy of innovation in talent management and contributions to the social sciences. EI research could be the next important direction for military psychologists to direct their focus and could lead to important insights into the art and science of leadership.

First, the importance of the military context on these results should be investigated. Researchers who are interested to know if differences in the Self-Control factor are due to age or military culture could conduct a follow-on study to compare the precareer sample to a civilian sample that matches the midcareer sample in as many aspects as possible (age-range should be matched at a minimum). If there is no difference between a precareer and civilian sample, it might be surmised that military culture influences individual scores in emotion regulation and impulse control. Second, it might be the prefrontal cortex development position would be strengthened if we find that the civilian sample of relatively older individuals does reflect higher levels of ER and IC when compared to the precareer sample.

The present cross-sectional study could be expanded in future studies through a larger sample of military leaders with varying levels of experience. Such a study could identify the possible impact that time in service might have on facet-level increases in impulse control and emotion regulation. Such a study could essentially map out EI over the course of military careers and could produce useful insights into the most important experiences, jobs, and training experiences that might contribute to development. Most importantly, researchers should seek to obtain samples of leaders who are currently or recently served in key and developmental positions, such as command or high-profile staff positions (to include operations officers and executive officers). These are the professional gates that successful officers must navigate through in order to be viable candidates for promotions and selective assignments.

REFERENCES

Armstrong, A. R., Galligan, R. F., & Critchley, C. R. (2011). Emotional intelligence and psychological resilience to negative life events. *Personality and Individual Differences, 51*(3), 331–336.

Army, U. S. (2012). Army Doctrine Publication 6–22: Army Leadership .

Bar-On, R. (1999). *BarOn emotional quotient inventory: Technical manual.* Multi-Health Systems

Bern, D. J. (1972). Self-perception theory. In L. Berkowitz (Ed.), *Administration and technical manual* (Vol. 6, p. 2). Academic Press.

Bradberry, T., & Greaves, J. (2009). *Emotional Intelligence 2.0.* TalentSmart.

Campbell, S. B., & Renshaw, K. D. (2013). PTSD symptoms, disclosure, and relationship distress: Explorations of mediation and associations over time. *Journal of Anxiety Disorders, 27*(5), 494–502. https://doi.org/10.1016/j.janxdis.2013.06.007

Corley, K. G., & Gioia, D. A. (2011). Building theory about theory building: what constitutes a theoretical contribution? *Academy of Management Review, 36*(1), 12–32.

Cronbach, L. J., & Meehl, P. E. (1955). Construct validity in psychological tests. *Psychological Bulletin, 52*(4), 281.

Daus, C. S., & Ashkanasy, N. M. (2005). The case for the ability-based model of emotional intelligence in organizational behavior. *Journal of Organizational Behavior, 26*(4), 453–466.

Davis, S. K., & Humphrey, N. (2012). Emotional intelligence as a moderator of stressor–mental health relations in adolescence: Evidence for specificity. *Personality and Individual Differences, 52*(1), 100–105.

Diamond, A. (2002). Normal development of prefrontal cortex from birth to young adulthood: Cognitive functions, anatomy, and biochemistry. *Principles of frontal lobe function*, 466–503.

Farr, J. L., & Tippins, N. T. (2010). Handbook of employee selection: An introduction and overview. In J. L. Farr & N. T. Tippins (Eds.), *Handbook of employee selection* (pp. 1–6). Routledge/Taylor & Francis Group.

Fellner, A. N., Matthews, G., Shockley, K. D., Warm, J. S., Zeidner, M., Karlov, L., & Roberts, R. D. (2012). Using emotional cues in a discrimination learning task: Effects of trait emotional intelligence and affective state. *Journal of Research in Personality, 46*(3), 239–247.

Ghiselli, E. E., Campbell, J. P., & Zedeck, S. (1981). *Measurement theory for the behavioral sciences: Origin & Evolution*. WH Freeman & Company.

Gohm, C. L., Corser, G. C., & Dalsky, D. J. (2005). Emotional intelligence under stress: Useful, unnecessary, or irrelevant? *Personality and Individual Differences, 39*(6), 1017–1028.

Goleman, D. (1995). *Emotional intelligence*: Bantam.

Grewal, D., & Salovey, P. (2005). Feeling Smart: The science of emotional intelligence A new idea in psychology has matured and shows promise of explaining how attending to emotions can help us in everyday life. *American Scientist, 93*, 330–339.

Helson, R., & Kwan, V. S. (2000). Personality development in adulthood: The broad picture and processes in one longitudinal sample. *Advances in Personality Psychology, 1*, 77–106.

Hilmes, A. C. (2015). *Emotional intelligence*. Air War College Thesis.

Hochschild, A. R. (1983). *The managed heart: Commercialization of human feelings*. University of California Press.

Hotard, S. R., McFatter, R. M., McWhirter, R. M., & Stegall, M. E. (1989). Interactive effects of extraversion, neuroticism, and social relationships on subjective well-being. *Journal of Personality and Social Psychology, 57*(2), 321.

Howard, G. (1983). *Frames of mind: The theory of multiple intelligences*. Basics Books.

Hunt, N., & Evans, D. (2004). Predicting traumatic stress using emotional intelligence. *Behaviour Research and Therapy, 42*(7), 791–798.

Hunter, J. E. (1986). Cognitive ability, cognitive aptitudes, job knowledge, and job performance. *Journal* of *Vocational Behavior, 29*(3), 340–362.

Jellesma, F. C., Rieffe, C., Terwogt, M. M., & Westenberg, P. M. (2011). Children's sense of coherence and trait emotional intelligence: A longitudinal study exploring the development of somatic complaints. *Psychology & Health, 26*(3), 307–320. https://doi.org/10.1080/08870440903411021

John, O. P., & Srivastava, S. (1999). The Big Five trait taxonomy: History, measurement, and theoretical perspectives. *Handbook of Personality: Theory and Research, 2*(1999), 102–138.

Joseph, D. L., Jin, J., Newman, D. A., & O'Boyle, E. H. (2015a). Why does self-reported emotional intelligence predict job performance? A meta-analytic investigation of mixed EI. *Journal of Applied Psychology, 100*(2), 298–342.

Joseph, D. L., Jin, J., Newman, D. A., & O'Boyle, E. H. (2015b). Why does self-reported emotional intelligence predict job performance? A meta-analytic investigation of mixed EI. *Journal of Applied Psychology, 100*(2), 298–342. https://doi.org/10.1037/a0037681

Joseph, D. L., & Newman, D. A. (2010). Emotional intelligence: An integrative meta-analysis and cascading model. *Journal of Applied Psychology, 95*(1), 54–78. https://doi.org/10.1037/a0017286

Kashdan, T. B., Elhai, J. D., & Frueh, B. C. (2006). Anhedonia and emotional numbing in combat veterans with PTSD. *Behaviour Research and Therapy, 44*(3), 457–467. https://doi.org/10.1016/j.brat.2005.03.001

Keefer, K. V., Holden, R. R., & Parker, J. D. A. (2013). Longitudinal Assessment of Trait Emotional Intelligence: Measurement Invariance and Construct Continuity From Late Childhood to Adolescence. *Psychological assessment, 25*(4), 1255–1272. https://doi.org/10.1037/a0033903

Keenan, M. J., Lumley, V. A., & Schneider, R. B. (2014). A group therapy approach to treating combat posttraumatic stress disorder: Interpersonal reconnection through letter writing. *Psychotherapy, 51*(4), 546–554. https://doi.org/10.1037/a0036025

Langer, N., Slaughter, S. A., & Mukhopadhyay, T. (2014). Project managers' practical intelligence and project performance in software offshore outsourcing: A field study. Information *Systems Research, 25*(2), 364–384. https://doi.org/10.1287/isre.2014.0523

LePine, J. A., Colquitt, J. A., & Erez, A. (2000). Adaptability to changing task contexts: Effects of general cognitive ability, conscientiousness, and openness to experience. *Personnel Psychology, 53*(3), 563–593.

Lievens, F., & Chan, D. (2010). Practical intelligence, emotional intelligence, and social intelligence. In J. L. Farr, N. T. Tippins, J. L. Farr, & N. T. Tippins (Eds.), *Handbook of employee selection.* (pp. 339–359). Routledge/Taylor & Francis Group.

Mackay, S., Hogg, P., Cooke, G., Baker, R., & Dawkes, T. (2012). A UK-wide analysis of trait emotional intelligence within the radiography profession. *Radiography, 18*(3), 166–171.

Malouff, J. M., Schutte, N. S., & Thorsteinsson, E. B. (2014). Trait emotional intelligence and romantic relationship satisfaction: A meta-analysis. *The American Journal of Family Therapy, 42*(1), 53–66.

Marco, C. A., & Suls, J. (1993). Daily stress and the trajectory of mood: spillover, response assimilation, contrast, and chronic negative affectivity. *Journal of personality and Social Psychology, 64*(6), 1053.

Martins, A., Ramalho, N., & Morin, E. (2010). A comprehensive meta-analysis of the relationship between emotional intelligence and health. *Personality and Individual Differences, 49*(6), 554–564.

Matthews, G., Roberts, R. D., & Zeidner, M. (2004). Seven myths about emotional intelligence. *Psychological Inquiry*, 179–196.

Mayer, J. (1997). What is emotional intelligence? In P. Salovey & D. J. Sluyter (Eds.), *Emotional development and emotional intelligence*. Basic Books.

Mayer, J. D., Roberts, R. D., & Barsade, S. G. (2008). Human abilities: Emotional intelligence. *Annual Review of Psychology, 59*, 507–536.

Murphy, K. R. (1989). Is the relationship between cognitive ability and job performance stable over time? *Human Performance, 2*(3), 183–200.

Murphy, K. R. (2006). *A critique of emotional intelligence: What are the problems and how can they be fixed?* Routledge.

Newman, D. A., Joseph, D. L., & MacCann, C. (2010). Emotional intelligence and job performance: The importance of emotion regulation and emotional labor context. *Industrial and Organizational Psychology, 3*(2), 159–164.

Nunnally, J. (1978). C.(1978). *Psychometric theory*. McGraw-Hill.

O'Boyle, E. H., Humphrey, R. H., Pollack, J. M., Hawver, T. H., & Story, P. A. (2011). The relation between emotional intelligence and job performance: A meta-analysis. *Journal of Organizational Behavior, 32*(5), 788–818.

Petrides, K. (2010). Trait emotional intelligence theory. *Industrial and Organizational Psychology, 3*(2), 136–139.

Petrides, K., & Furnham, A. (2001). Trait emotional intelligence: Psychometric investigation with reference to established trait taxonomies. *European Journal of Personality, 15*(6), 425–448. https://doi.org/10.1002/per.416

Petrides, K., & Furnham, A. (2006). The role of trait emotional intelligence in a gender-specific model of organizational variables 1. *Journal of Applied Social Psychology, 36*(2), 552–569.

Petrides, K., Pita, R., & Kokkinaki, F. (2007). The location of trait emotional intelligence in personality factor space. *British Journal of Psychology, 98*(2), 273–289.

Salovey, P., & Mayer, J. D. (1989). Emotional intelligence. *Imagination, Cognition and Personality, 9*(3), 185–211. https://doi.org/10.2190/DUGG-P24E-52WK-6CDG

Sardo, S. (2004). Learning to display emotional intelligence. *Business Strategy Review, 15*(1), 14–17.

Schmidt, F. L. (2002). The role of general cognitive ability and job performance: Why there cannot be a debate. *Human Performance, 15*(1–2), 187–210.

Schneider, T. R., Lyons, J. B., & Khazon, S. (2013). Emotional intelligence and resilience. *Personality and Individual Differences, 55*(8), 909–914.

Schutte, N. S., Malouff, J. M., Thorsteinsson, E. B., Bhullar, N., & Rooke, S. E. (2007). A meta-analytic investigation of the relationship between emotional intelligence and health. *Personality and Individual Differences, 42*(6), 921–933.

Shu, I. W., Onton, J. A., Prabhakar, N., O'Connell, R. M., Simmons, A. N., & Matthews, S. C. (2014). Combat veterans with PTSD after mild TBI exhibit greater ERPs from posterior–medial cortical areas while appraising facial features. *Journal of Affective Disorders, 155*, 234–240. https://doi.org/10.1016/j.jad.2013.06.057

Sowell, E. R., Thompson, P. M., Holmes, C. J., Jernigan, T. L., & Toga, A. W. (1999). In vivo evidence for post-adolescent brain maturation in frontal and striatal regions. *Nature Neuroscience, 2*(10), 859–861.

Stevens, J. (1996). *Applied multivariate statistics for the social sciences.* Pearson.

Suls, J., Green, P., & Hillis, S. (1998). Emotional reactivity to everyday problems, affective inertia, and neuroticism. *Personality and Social Psychology Bulletin, 24*(2), 127–136.

Tabachnick, B. G., & Fidell, L. S. (2007). *Using multivariate statistics.* Pearson.

Thomas, L. I. (2010). *Trait Emotional Intelligence Questionnaire Technical Manual.* Thomas International Ltd?

Thorndike, E. L. (1920). Intelligence and its uses. *Harper's Magazine, 140,* 227–235.

VanRooy, D. L., Viswesvaran, C., & Pluta, P. (2005). An evaluation of construct validity: What is this thing called emotional intelligence? *Human Performance, 18*(4), 445–462.

Wagner, R. K., & Sternberg, R. J. (1985). Practical intelligence in real-world pursuits: The role of tacit knowledge. *Journal of Personality and Social Psychology, 49*(2), 436.

Wilson, W. R. (1967). Correlates of avowed happiness. *Psychological Bulletin, 67*(4), 294.

Zeidner, M., Matthews, G., & Roberts, R. D. (2004). Emotional intelligence in the workplace: A critical review. *Applied Psychology: An International Review, 53*(3), 371–399. https://doi.org/10.1111/j.1464-0597.2004.00176.x

NOTE

1. For further information, Lievens and Chan (2010) provide an informative review of commonalities and differences between Practical, Social, and Emotional Intelligence and how these constructs in their chapter in the *Handbook of Employee Selection* (Farr & Tippins, 2010).

ABOUT THE AUTHORS

Andrew L. Bond, received a Master's of Science Degree in Industrial and Organizational Psychology from Auburn University in 2016 and a Master's degree in National Security and Public Safety Leadership from George Washington University in 2014. From 2016 to 2019 he served as an Instructor of Military Leadership and Psychology in the United States Military Academy's Department of Behavioral Sciences and Leadership. His current position is Chief of the Office of Institutional Research at the United States Military Academy. His research interests include personnel select, training, character development, and data visualization.

Erin L. Borry is Associate Professor and Director of the Masters of Public Administration Program in the Department of Political Science and Public Administration at the University of Alabama at Birmingham. Her research interests include organizational ethics, equity, rules, and red tape and she has published in *Public Administration Review, Public Administration, International Public Management Journal,* and *American Review of Public Administration* among others. She is a fellow of the Center for Organization Research and Design (CORD) and the Local Government Workplace Initiative (LGWI).

Stephanie E. V. Brown is a PhD student in Industrial and Organizational Psychology at Texas A&M University. Her primary research interests center on workplace sexual harassment and military spouse employment. Stephanie also studies the intersections of race, gender, and sexual orientation in organizations; barriers facing women in traditionally male-dominated areas (particularly in the military and STEM fields); ally behavior and bystander intervention; and the relationship between sound psychological research and the formation of public policy. She has conducted research at the Haas Center for Economic Research and Development at the University of West Florida and the Public Policy Research Institute at Texas A&M University.

Alexa Doerr, PhD, is an assistant professor at Towson University. Dr. Doerr received her PhD in Industrial/Organizational Psychology from Auburn University in 2016. Her research interests include safety culture, person-environment fit personnel selection, and employment testing. Additionally, Dr. Doerr is interested in implicit influences on important organizational processes including employee selection and organizational socialization. Dr. Doerr has applied experience in test development and validation at the Society for Human Resource Management, as well as consulting experience at the American Institutes for Research.

Regan E. Gaskin graduated from the University of Alabama at Birmingham with a bachelor's in psychology in 2017 and Masters in public administration in 2019. She seeks to continue to conduct research on workplace bullying/abuse in the public sector, focusing on the role of leaders in preventing negative workplace behaviors

Samantha C. January is a PhD student in Industrial and Organizational Psychology at Texas A&M University in College Station, Texas. During her graduate career, she has published several articles in *Industrial and Organizational Psychology: Perspectives on Science and Practice* and has presented several papers as part of symposiums at the Society for Industrial and Organizational Psychology (SIOP), Work-Family Researchers Network (WFRN), Conference on Commitment, Academy of Management (AOM), and Work, Stress, and Health annual conferences. She has consulted with several organizations, helping them develop, collect, analyze, and evaluate data on their organizational climate and culture. She is particularly interested in how, why, and when job attitudes (such as organizational commitment) fluctuate over time. In addition, her research interests include turnover, job attitudes, person-organization fit, workplace mistreatment, and organizational culture and climate.

Elizabeth A. Ritterbush, PhD, received her PhD degree in Industrial and Organizational Psychology from Auburn University. She has an extensive background in performance management, project management, statistics, personality assessment, and decision making. She is currently a consultant at DDI where she partners with global organizations to develop, design, and implement leadership selection, succession, and acceleration programs. She has authored and coauthored research nationally and abroad on a variety of topics including performance management, personality, organizational commitment, employee cooperation, and ethical decision making. She continues to publish and present thought leadership in the areas of cross-cultural leadership, personality, and ethical decision making in addition to her work as a consultant.

Adam M. Smith, PhD, received his PhD degree in Industrial/Organizational Psychology from Auburn University. He currently works as an associate consultant with Kincentric, a talent services and advisory consulting firm. In his consulting work, he specializes in the areas of employee assessment, leadership selection and development, and talent strategy, working with clients to identify, select, and develop leaders at all levels of the organization. He also supports the development of the employee assessment technology, portfolio, and strategy for Kincentric. In addition to his consulting work, he serves as an adjunct faculty member at Wentworth Institute of Technology and an Instructor at Harvard University in Boston, MA, teaching courses on the topics of Industrial/Organizational Psychology and statistics. His research interests include leadership and follower dynamics, workplace personality, and statistical methods. He has presented his research at numerous international conferences, including *The Society for Industrial and Organizational Psychology, The Association for Psychological Science,* and *The International Convention for Psychological Science*. He is also the coauthor of a book on the application and use of the statistics software *SPSS*.

Daniel J. Svyantek, PhD, received his degree from the University of Houston in 1987. He was a faculty member in the Industrial/Organizational Psychology PhD program at The University of Akron from 1987 to 2003. He is currently a Full Professor in the Psychology Department of Auburn University. He has served as the Program Director of the Industrial/Organizational Psychology Ph.D. program from 2003 to 2008 and as Chair of the Auburn University Psychology Department from 2008 to 2014. He has published in journals such as the *Journal of Applied Psychology, Journal of Vocational Behavior, Journal of Applied Behavioral Sciences,* and *Human Relations*. He has served as associate editor of *Management Decision,* editor of the journal, *Organizational Analysis* and is currently Series Editor for the annual series, *Research in Organizational Sciences*. He has consulted with several organizations on organizational change projects in the areas of problem solving, compensation systems and implementing work teams. He is particularly interested in the development of new evaluation methods for assessing the practical value of applied research within applied contexts. In addition, his research interest areas include person-organization fit issues and the role of organizational culture and climate as the context for the expression of individual behavior in organizations.

Rachel Whitman, MS is a PhD candidate studying Industrial-Organizational Psychology at Auburn University under the supervision of Dr. Daniel Svyantek. She received her Master's in Science from Auburn University in 2019 and is currently working on requirements for her doctorate. Her research interests include psychological factors impacting organizational and personal resilience, the role of the psychological contract during organizational change, and advanced analytic methods.

Thomas Wilmore, received his Bachelor of Science degree in Psychology from the University of Louisiana at Lafayette in 2018. He is currently a second-year doctoral student in Auburn University's Industrial and Organizational Psychology program working in Dr. Svyantek's lab. Some of his current research interests include the impact of organizational culture and climate on decision making, deviant behavior in organizations, and personality antecedents of job performance.

www.ingramcontent.com/pod-product-compliance
Lightning Source LLC
Chambersburg PA
CBHW051151180926
51611CB00001B/21
9781648023545